# Praise for *Conscio*

"The stories in *Conscious Change* provide powerful and honest looks at people coping with differences and conflict and acknowledge the hard work that comes with personal change and reflection."
—ABBY BAKER, Senior Vice President and
Chief Human Resources Officer, Rinchem

"A book of this sort is rarely a page-turner, but *Conscious Change* is that! The transparency exhibited by the storytellers, the scientific under-pinnings, and the applicability of the 'tools' to both personal and work relationships make the book extremely useful."
—ROBERTA BURROUGHS, FAICP, President and CEO,
Roberta F. Burroughs & Associates

"*Conscious Change* is a must-read guide for personal and professional growth, for navigating diverse and complex workplaces, and for embark-ing on a life-changing journey in our everyday relationships."
—MENAH PRATT, JD, PhD, Vice President for Strategic Affairs
and Diversity, Virginia Tech University, and author of *Blackwildgirl*
and *From Cotton Picking to College Professor*

"*Conscious Change* outperforms any other book about navigating difference and fostering inclusion."
—SUNITA SEHMI, organizational development consultant;
executive leadership coach; diversity, inclusion, and belonging
advisor; and author of *The Power of Belonging: How to Develop Safety,
Inclusion, and Belonging for Leaders and Organizations*

"This is an absolute gem of a book! Using an engaging writing style, the authors offer a clear framework for change at the personal, interpersonal, and systemic levels."
—SUSAN P. ROBBINS, PhD, LCSW, Cele S. and
Samuel D. Keeper Endowed Professor in Social Justice,
University of Houston Graduate College of Social Work

"The authors take us on a heart-opening journey through the challenges and opportunities of creating healthy, diverse work environments."
—BETTY SANDERS, past President of the National Human
Factors and Ergonomics Society, Humanomics, Inc.

"This book is so incredibly useful and timely! The authors share robust yet digestible information and tools that can help anyone who is looking to show up to the conflict in their lives in a clearer manner."
—DANIELLE MURPHY, LCSW, SEP, therapist at
Somatic Freedom Psychotherapy

"Readers may pick this book up and simply begin reading—at the beginning, in the middle, wherever the book happens to fall open—and will naturally be drawn into a narrative in which a leader worked within a given system to create change, moved the needle on a hard issue, and grew themselves as a person and change agent in the process."
—JILL CARROLL, PhD, former Executive Director,
Boniuk Center for Religious Tolerance, Rice University,
and author of *World Religions: A Beginner's Guide*

"*Conscious Change* draws on compelling stories from nineteen individuals who successfully navigated difficult professional and personal challenges."
—DR. ROCHELLE PARKS-YANCY, Professor of Management, Texas
Southern University, and coauthor of *Be Your Best Career Architect*

"The book offers practical guidance on nurturing inclusive relationships by emphasizing the demanding yet transformative practice of staying consciously present."
—AMANDA POLICH, leader, Executive Relationships at
Ultimate Kronos Group, Certified Dare to Lead™ Facilitator,
and board chair for Houston Council on Recovery

"The book is filled with rich stories that made me mutter, 'I've been there. I've been in that difficult situation . . .' This is one of those books you can open just about anywhere and find something that hits home."
—RICK MAURER, speaker, advisor/coach, and author of *Seizing Moments of Possibility*, *Beyond the Wall of Resistance*, and *Feedback Toolkit*

"As a leader in talent development, I found *Conscious Change* to be a transformative read. It brilliantly intertwines real-life examples with practical strategies, providing invaluable insights for fostering positive change and enhancing workplace dynamics."

—NATHALIE SALLES, former VP of Talent Development, Bloom Energy, and former director of Coaching, Team, and Organizational Development, Meta

"In addition to the application of Conscious Change principles, the book is filled with wisdom nuggets such as the three ingredients of an effective apology; the direction to distinguish intent from impact; the encouragement to 'Give grace by not assuming others' intentions'; and to 'Call others in rather than calling them out.'"

—DR. BARBARA LOVE, professor emeritus,
Social Justice Education, University of Massachusetts, and
author of *Developing Liberatory Consciousness*

"The digestible format makes *Conscious Change* an ideal workplace or social book club selection."

—TRACY RATHE, Senior Vice President of Organizational
Performance and Development, Nebraska Health Care Association

"This book is a must read for anyone who wants to learn how to manage their emotions, think clearly and rationally, navigate challenging situations, and have better interpersonal relationships."

—CAROL STEWART, executive coach and author of *Quietly Visible*

"Our prosperity and well-being depend on our ability to work together in harmony, and this book has vital answers for how we can avoid negative and self-defeating reactions while experiencing the pleasure of being at our best."

—PETER MICHAELSON, psychotherapist, founder of
WhyWeSuffer.com, and author of *Our Deadly Flaw*

"Latting and Ramsey again deliver knowledge, principles, and skills powerful enough to change the world, one person at a time."

—LAURA EASTON, LMSW, OD Consultant and
Executive Coach, Easton Consulting, LLC, and
advisory board member, Houston Council on Recovery

# CONSCIOUS CHANGE

Published 2024
Printed in the United States of America
Print ISBN: 978-1-64742-708-5
E-ISBN: 978-1-64742-709-2
Library of Congress Control Number: 2023924187

For information, address:
She Writes Press
1569 Solano Ave #546
Berkeley, CA 94707

Interior Design by Tabitha Lahr

She Writes Press is a division of SparkPoint Studio, LLC.

# CONSCIOUS CHANGE

## How to Navigate Differences
## and Foster Inclusion
## in Everyday Relationships

Jean Kantambu Latting and V. Jean Ramsey

with Stephanie Foy and Amy Foy Hageman
Forewords by Brené Brown and Myrtle P. Bell

SHE WRITES PRESS

# For Educational and Informational Purposes Only

This book contains stories of how people resolved problems. The information in the book is for educational and informational purposes only. Nothing should be construed as a substitute for advice from a mental health or other professional who is aware of the facts and circumstances of your individual situation.

Applying the principles and skills described in this book is no guarantee that you or any other person will be able to obtain similar results. Your ultimate success or failure will be the result of your own efforts, your individual situation, and innumerable other circumstances beyond the control and/or knowledge of the authors of this book.

Neither the authors, Leading Consciously, nor any of its employees or owners shall be held liable or responsible for any damage you may suffer as a result of taking action based on your understanding of the material, for failing to seek advice from a professional familiar with your situation, or for any errors or omissions in the book.

To Maconda Brown O'Connor,

- whose legacy as a philanthropist and social worker will live forever in our hearts and the hearts of many;
- who was a role model for the value and promise of changing systems so individuals can flourish;
- whose steadfast support made this work possible.

# Contents

## Chapter 10. I Need to Understand Where She's Coming From *by Ashley Ochoa*

## Chapter 11. De-escalate Tense and Dangerous Situations *by Larry Hill (with Eli Davis)*

## Chapter 12. Change in a Bureaucratic Organization Can Be a Slog *by Chamara Harris*

# Foreword

## S( )R

This symbol represents the secret to the universe. Okay, maybe it's not the secret to the entire universe, but it's a critical reminder to me about how to navigate the universe—how to show up in an often beautiful and always challenging world and stay aligned with my values.

The symbol is my shortcut reminder of this quote: "Between stimulus and response there is a space. In that space is our power to choose our response. In our response lies our growth and our freedom."

The attribution of this quote is unknown. It's been credited to Stephen Covey, but he said he came across it on a vacation in Hawaii and it's not his. I confirmed this with his son Stephen M. R. Covey. It's also been attributed to Viktor Frankl, but scholars who study Frankl agree that it's not in any of his writing. Both thinkers capture the essence of the quote in their work, but neither of them captured the words as we often see them expressed.

I don't need to know who wrote them to know it's true—and to know that transforming this knowledge into a daily practice will absolutely change your life.

If I look back at all of the major waypoints in my life, each one has redirected me toward a practice of creating more space between stimulus and response so that I can make choices that are intentional, disciplined, and values-aligned.

I grew up in a culture and family where there was no space between something happening and responding. *Don't think. Act.* In fact, you might even say I was raised to believe in negative space—to anticipate something happening and swing first. Beat hurt, vulnerability, and uncertainty to the punch.

Transformative waypoints along my journey have included my studies, my sobriety, and the personal work and leadership coaching that remain an essential part of my practice. Another eye-opening waypoint was the time I spent as Jean Latting's student and mentee at the University of Houston Graduate College of Social Work. Jean shaped how I see the world and how I see myself moving through it. She challenged me in ways that were equal parts enlightening and infuriating. I hated how still she forced me to be, and I loved what emerged from the stillness. This has not changed.

What's funny is that I could not articulate what she taught me until I read *Conscious Change*. I wouldn't go so far as to say that I thought it was magic, but I did think it was a weird and probably unnameable thing rather than a teachable skill. I was wrong. As I read this book, I kept thinking, *This is that thing she taught me—the thing that I love and hate and need to do and don't want to do.*

*Conscious Change* is the playbook for prying open the space between stimulus and response.

What's made so clear in the examples in the book is the skill it takes to cognitively understand the stimulus rather than emotionally react to it, the commitment required to be intentional and values-aligned in our responses, and the level of discipline it takes to make this a practice.

I'll confess that I often found myself wanting the protagonist in each of the following stories to forget about the space between stimulus and response and just defend, attack, or blame. I've reread a couple of the stories and I'm still conflicted about the missed opportunities to be right, righteous, and completely justified in shutting down. What I'm not conflicted about is how impeccably the book takes us through the process of creating the space to be who we want to be even when we're hijacked by emotion and 100 percent right.

This is not easy work, but it's essential. The way the authors are able to slow down time and take us behind the scenes of our brains and hearts is teaching at its finest.

I would say more about what I've learned, but I'm letting myself linger in the space between reading this book and understanding it, the space between pretending I don't know how to do it and holding myself accountable for doing it. The space between stimulus and response is not a comfortable space, but one thing I know for certain is that being brave and living into our values is not supposed to be comfortable.

—Brené Brown, PhD

# Foreword

At the time of this writing, I'm the Thomas McMahon Professor in Business Ethics and the associate dean for Diversity, Racial Equity, and Inclusion at the University of Texas at Arlington, a large urban university. The latter position was formed after the murder of George Floyd, when many organizations were trying to do something in the face of an abject anti-Blackness that could no longer be denied. I've been trying to "do something" about anti-Blackness, racism, sexism, ableism, and other isms for all my life, and formally for over thirty years. I've served in numerous academic professional diversity-related roles and am the author of *Diversity in Organizations*, a research-based textbook used for teaching diversity at many universities. Its fifth edition (with Dr. Joy Leopold) is forthcoming in 2024.

I met Dr. Jean Ramsey, one of the authors of *Conscious Change*, when I was a doctoral student at my first academic conference to present my first academic paper. Along with teaching, disseminating one's research is an important part of the professorial role. The day of the conference, I got up early to rehearse. Sensing my unease, my husband asked if any Black people would be there. Having noticed "Dr. V. Jean Ramsey, Texas Southern University," an HBCU, on the program as a participant in my session, I responded happily that there would be at least one.

When I got to the room, Jean, a White woman, walked in and stretched out her hand. "Hi. I'm Jean Ramsey." She burst out laughing when I stammered, "You're supposed to be Black!" and replied, "Many people think it, but few people say it!" We both warmed to each other, laughing, and sat together. I was struck that this White woman with a

PhD from Michigan, who could be anywhere, chose to be at an HBCU, where she could have the greatest impact. Jean's commitment to doing work that mattered, where and as she wanted to do it, helped me do likewise. Teaching diversity remains my most important work—work that helps bring about change in individuals, organizations, and society, as is the goal of *Conscious Change*.

*Conscious Change: How to Navigate Differences and Foster Inclusion in Everyday Relationships* is aptly named. With actionable principles applied to navigation of real-life examples of interactions at work, *Conscious Change* can be used in many university courses—change management, diversity, ethics, leadership, and organizational behavior, among others. The real examples—like cases used in many courses—provide students with actual situations, dilemmas, and authors' conscious decisions, coupled with a summary of the Conscious Change principles used at the end. I see *Conscious Change* as a blueprint to help us learn to work with others, with inclusivity as the goal, regardless of field of study or occupation, and as (or with) clients, customers, executives, leaders, managers, peers, or subordinates.

People carry with them different expectations and experiences that are often based on their identities, such as their race, sex, social class, occupation, or status. These identities shape our and others' ways of viewing and participating in interactions and situations. *Conscious Change* can help with learning to work with others, consciously aware that our and others' identities influence interactions and, with that knowledge, to approach those interactions with the goal of fostering inclusion instead of exclusion, rejection, and intolerance. The authors, trained behavioral scientists with decades of teaching, research, and consulting experience, used their knowledge to develop ways we can learn to engage in conscious change in myriad situations, increasing the likelihood of positive outcomes. We can apply these principles when someone interrupts us when we are up against a hard deadline and want to scream at them, as was described in one chapter. In DEI practitioner work or teaching in particular, we can use these resources with those who may doubt the need for DEI efforts or deny the veracity of someone's experiences with discrimination, or in any of myriad frustrating situations.

In teaching diversity, I intentionally use research and data to help open eyes that are sometimes tightly squeezed shut, and thus I was drawn to the use of research in developing *Conscious Change*. The science is engaging and practical, and I wrote affirmations in the margins as I read: "wow," "this is so good," "THIS!," "YES!," and "research supports this!" The principles spoke to me as a person and as a professor, sending students into the complex and diverse world of work, needing strong skills in interpersonal interactions. These principles are useful for both dominant- and nondominant-group members in an array of occupations and roles; we can all stand to learn to behave consciously.

- "Move from the answer to the question." Is there a possibility that our perceptual filters have led us to an erroneous perception? Are they late turning in this document because someone was late getting required materials to them, rather than because people like them are always late? Did they not tell me in advance because of cultural differences in speaking up to management? Am I using my own view of time as the standard to judge others' behavior?[1]
- "Assume all people, including you, can grow and learn." The "including you" part is one we likely all need to remember.
- "Identify with your values, not your emotions" is a critical skill in today's organizations, for everyone, at all levels. When those values include fostering inclusion, as many of us claim, purposefully identifying with those values can shape inclusive behaviors.
- "Give grace by not assuming others' intentions," and "Call others in rather than calling them out." Both can be immensely helpful in fostering inclusion in our classrooms, organizations, lives, and society.

These and other research-based principles, ideas, and examples in *Conscious Change* can help *anyone, anywhere,* who interacts with others who have different backgrounds, beliefs, experiences, expectations, and values—which we all do, daily. I, Dr. Diversity, as my students call me, and the author of a diversity textbook, have the principles of Conscious Change on display in my office. We can *all* practice and strengthen our ability to make conscious decisions—at home, at work, in school board meetings, on crowded planes, and elsewhere. In return, we can expect better outcomes and responses from others as we control what only *we* can control and what we only *can* control—our own behaviors and reactions to others.

—Myrtle P. Bell, PhD

*\* The above opinions expressed are my own.*

## CHAPTER 1.

# Real-Life Change Meets
# Behavioral Science Research

Not many leaders could have kept their cool like Charles. Under the gun to deliver a high-stakes project to thousands of customers, Charles began to dread the daily meetings with his team. Not only was the team under-resourced, understaffed, and confronted with new challenges almost daily, but Charles also felt some team members were challenging his authority by nitpicking him at every turn.

Tense and exhausted, he knew he had to do something. He was a Black man leading a team of White women who had no clue how often their subtly demeaning demands and pointed comments struck him as microaggressions.

A particular meeting nearly sent Charles over the edge emotionally. Amid a hectic day, one of his team members grilled him for failing to send her a status report on an earlier meeting. Her interrogation was the last straw. He knew if he lost his cool, it would send his group into a downward spiral of recriminations, so instead of scolding the team member, Charles decided to draw on several Conscious Change principles and skills he had learned through our consulting work.

By the following day, Charles had resolved months of tension and began turning previously exhausting meetings into productive, positive sessions. His staff finally believed he understood their pressures and limitations. And they grasped how their sometimes-combative tones and pushy demands came across as racially charged challenges to Charles's leadership. A few weeks later, despite their many limitations on staffing and resources, Charles's team delivered a highly successful product receiving rave reviews.

How did Charles so rapidly turn around such an emotionally charged, potentially explosive situation where opportunities for failure and misunderstanding abounded? That is what we're going to talk about in this book. You will find more of Charles's story from his perspective in a later chapter. You will also read a diverse collection of stories showing how intentionally incorporating the skills of Conscious Change, like those used by Charles, can deliver incredible results.

Knowing how well Conscious Change strategies worked for Charles and our other chapter authors fueled our appetite to share their stories in this book. We are convinced the skills can also work for you. Our research and consulting experience with multimillion-dollar companies, small businesses, and nonprofit and government organizations of all sizes have demonstrated that these skills most certainly can benefit you.

Yet before we relate the stories demonstrating these principles and skills and flesh them out with our analysis, we want to briefly describe how we developed them.

## Simple Practices Based on Research

Every day, people face challenging situations that can spark strong emotions, fracture relationships, and provoke stress. In our work as researchers, our goal was to translate sound behavioral science theory into practices anyone could use.

Our teaching, consulting, and research experience helped us understand people's struggles as they handled vital trouble spots in their personal and professional lives. Questions and statements like these arose in our classes and training sessions:

*What do I do if my manager seems to be undermining me?*

*I cry easily. Is something wrong with me? How do I get better control of myself?*

*Suddenly my coworker is avoiding me. What do I do?*

*I'm afraid they will call me racist if I criticize their performance even slightly. What should I do?*

*My manager has asked me to do something I think is not right. How can I say no and keep my job?*

*Our work culture is the pits. I don't want to have to quit. I don't know what to do.*

Each person felt unique in their suffering and was unaware of existing principles and skills—well-researched and tested—for dealing with these issues. Our goal was to bring these to students in a usable way.

We began by developing a set of research- and theory-based guidelines for powerful self-reflection, bridging cultural divides, and spearheading change.[1] Through our classes and coaching, we witnessed immediate results with our students and clients.

This prompted us to promote our ideas more widely in our book, *Reframing Change*.[2] Once we had codified the concepts and principles in *Reframing Change*, we continued teaching the related skills in our classrooms and training programs across a decade.

In the consulting and training organization we formed, Leading Consciously, Jean Latting, Stephanie Foy, and a now-deceased colleague, Mary Harlan, began conducting training programs and teaching the skills at organizations.[3] In training session after training session, participants reported how they had been confronted with a difficult situation, stopped, reflected, and then chose to utilize one or more of the skills they were learning.

Relationships were prevented from being broken, while broken relationships were often repaired. Those who had felt shunned suddenly found themselves being noticed, even having a positive influence. People on dysfunctional teams were able to initiate more positive working relationships. Those who felt estranged from coworkers found a way to gain acceptance and feel they belonged. Leaders with disengaged direct reports were able to motivate them and inspire accountability. Racial divides gave way to amicable relationships.

*Reframing Change* proved as valuable as we had hoped. We continued searching out empirical research to fine-tune the skills and principles and improve our ability to describe and illustrate them. Students and training participants told us how they used the tools to reduce conflict, resolve problems, and improve interactions with their coworkers, managers, friends, and family members. Their stories wowed us and awed us.

Hearing these stories both pleased and amazed us. We knew we had something worth sharing more widely.

The next step became obvious. We sought out powerful stories from readers of *Reframing Change*, stories providing vivid illustrations of our methods and strategies. In this, our second book, we share a few of these to make it easier for you to put the Conscious Change skills into practice in your workplaces and homes.

## Practical Benefits of Behavioral Science Research

If we were to ask a group of people whether they would like to learn about "behavioral science research," we are pretty sure there would be crickets in the room. However, if we asked these same people if they would like to learn how to manage their emotions better, improve their relationships, or resolve conflicts more effectively, we are confident there would be plenty of takers.

That's what *Reframing Change* does: it describes principles and skills based on behavioral science research to increase your personal sense of effectiveness, the strength of your interactions with others—especially those different from you in some way—and your ability to influence your work environment. Readers of *Reframing Change* tell us they continue to refer back to the Conscious Change principles as they learn how to act more intentionally and consciously make choices in multicultural environments.

This book, *Conscious Change*, is your chance to witness sound research applied to everyday situations and relationships—many with uniquely high stakes. The individuals who wrote the stories in this book have learned Conscious Change principles and skills and put them to practical use. These stories, and the analyses accompanying them, will help you better understand the skills and the principles behind them.

We emphasize that these principles did not just come out of our heads willy-nilly. Instead, we based them on solid behavioral science theories, empirical research, and our own hard-earned practical experience. Our goal is to provide actionable yet research-based information about how to draw on your own resources—thoughts, emotions, and behaviors—as you influence others and bring them together to initiate positive change.

## How to Apply Conscious Change Principles with Confidence and Success

The Conscious Change principles are at the core of our work. In the next chapter, we will cover each of the six principles and their thirty-six associated skills. Once you learn how to use them, the skills can help you navigate some of the most challenging dilemmas in human relationships with greater confidence and likelihood of success. These transformational tools will lead to a stronger sense of your personal capacity as a leader, to better interpersonal relationships, and to the beginnings of greater equity and inclusion.

As you read, please be aware that contributors have condensed tense situations into only a few pages and described how they resolved them. Do not assume it was as simple as it might seem. As you will learn, in the thick of the dilemmas they faced, the author of each story experienced consternation.

The authors describe situations in which they first had to reflect and then decide to apply the principles and skills of Conscious Change. Doing so was not second nature. Yet stopping to think, then changing course to implement these skills, made all the difference. Thus we call the framework *Conscious* Change. Doing what you have always done will get you what you have always gotten. Changing the outcome of problematic situations requires making conscious decisions to try something different. Using these skills seldom comes naturally.

Several of the skills were revolutionary when we first conceptualized them. Jean Latting was literally heckled in a graduate class she was teaching when she first described the tools of emotional clearing. Now, we regularly encounter emotional-clearing processes (such as mindfulness and meditation) in self-help journals as well as in more mainstream ones like *Harvard Business Review*.[4] As you read the stories and the reflections accompanying them, expect some of the skills to be familiar to you and others to be new.

Whether you have heard of most, some, or none of the principles, remember there is a chasm between knowing about or describing a skill (such as hitting a home run or winning a spelling bee) and performing the act competently. The skills require practice, particularly when using two or more simultaneously. If you are willing to practice the skills until they feel comfortable, the time investment will yield benefits beyond what you might imagine possible.

Personal change requires time and effort. You may feel awkward and unsure as you try out the new skills. Persistence will pay off, however. Conscious choices will become easier to make, and the skills will become easier to practice.

We will stop short of saying this book is the end-all and be-all for healthy relationships. Yet we easily declare that none of the authors can imagine going back to a life when they did not have the principles and skills to deal with all the uncertainty and disappointments life serves up. In those days, all we knew to do in response was to ruminate in pain, get angry, or drop people from our lives.

We are delighted that these nineteen contributors were willing to share their stories about how they applied the skills, so that you may learn and grow from them. As you will see, the setting really does not matter. The skills are effective in all industries, jobs, demographics, and situations—because they are rooted in well-researched behavioral science principles.

One of Jean Latting's clients once said her coaching had been invaluable to him because she "understands human nature." After reading the stories in this book, we hope you will gain greater insight into human nature and your options for what to do when you find yourself in situations where someone else's "human nature" is at odds with your own. One by one, skill after skill, you can impact lives and make the difference you are seeking.

Our own lives have improved immeasurably from learning the principles and skills, and we know we have made a difference to the people with whom we have lived and worked. We also have reason to believe the ripple effect of this work has extended far beyond us as authors . . . "us" being the book authors, the nineteen chapter authors, and the many others who have applied the skills of Conscious Change. As each of us improves our presence and makes a positive contribution to the world, all of us will be better off.

We encourage you to study the principles and practice the skills, and to seek opportunities to implement them in your life. In the final chapter, we suggest how you might develop a plan for yourself to practice the skills. You would not have read this far if you did not want to make a positive difference in your life and the world. This book can provide you with the tools to do this.

If the stories here resonate with you, we hope you will let us know. We would love to receive your feedback and hear about your successes, attempts, and questions. If you want to learn and study more, we tell you how you can do so at the end of the book—where you can also learn how to reach us.

# What to Expect as You Read

There are several things to keep in mind as you read the book.

### ■ *Depth, Not Superficiality*

As you read, we encourage you to be patient with yourself. Not every principle or skill may make sense on first reading. There is a *lot* packed into the thirty-six skills of Conscious Change. We would not expect you to absorb all of them in an initial, quick reading, especially since we have abbreviated the explanation of each skill.

Some of the skills may sound simple or familiar. Yet as you read the stories and see more and more examples of how the authors used the skills in different settings and diverse ways, you will begin to understand the nuances of each skill. You will also see ways in which the skills can be helpful in your everyday life, not just in work situations.

### ■ *Capitalization of Black and White When Referencing People*

Publishers have moved toward capitalizing Black, Indigenous, and other identifiers when referencing people of color but most still use lower case "white."[5] Some claim that very few people view "White" as their ethnic identity, while people of African descent have a shared sense of history, identity, and community. Another argument is that capitalizing "White" elevates its status to the same level as other racial or ethnic identities and could also promote a sense of White supremacy.

We are among those who think otherwise. We believe that not capitalizing White ignores the realities of how Whiteness functions in this and other societies; it implicitly sets Whiteness as the standard or the norm. We also note that most White people do, indeed, have a racial identity. Some may also have an ethnic identity (e.g., Italian), yet may also say they are White, not Black or Brown.

### ■ *Use of the Term Latiné, Not Latinx or Hispanic*

We were persuaded to use the term "Latiné" by Dr. Melissa Ochoa, a guest on the Leading Consciously podcast.[6] Latiné is more easily understood by Spanish speakers and is the preferred term in Spanish-speaking countries.

According to Dr. Ochoa, fewer than 4 percent of people of Hispanic or Latin descent identify with the term "Latinx." Argentina and Spain have banned the term. "Hispanic" is also problematic since it masks the great diversity within the Latiné population, e.g., many citizens of Brazil, Argentina, and Uruguay are descended from countries other than Spain.

## CHAPTER 2.

# Conscious Change Described

Conscious Change means focusing less on getting others to change. It is about the power of self-change: the potential to initiate change by focusing on yourself and the effects of your actions on others.

As illustrated on the next page, Conscious Change consists of six principles. Each principle contains its own set of skills for a total of thirty-six skills in all. Each of the principles and skills is described briefly in this chapter, then illustrated in-depth with real-life examples in subsequent chapters.

## Test Negative Assumptions

Assumptions are not facts. They are only hypotheses about what we believe to be true. Yet real or not, assumptions, especially those we make about others and the meaning of their words and behaviors, can create a great deal of havoc in our interpersonal relationships and interactions. Conscious leaders test negative assumptions as a regular habit. The first four skills provide ways to do so.

### ■ *Move from the Answer into the Question*

Being in the question entails wondering what things mean or what people intend instead of assuming you already know. It involves treating your

# SIX PRINCIPLES OF CONSCIOUS CHANGE

### TEST NEGATIVE ASSUMPTIONS

1. Move from the answer into the question
2. Look for multiple points of view
3. Consciously test your negative assumptions
4. Check to see if you are making cultural assumptions

### CLEAR EMOTIONS

5. Identify with your values, not your emotions
6. Avoid emotional suppression
7. Clear your negative emotions
8. Build your positive emotions

### BUILD EFFECTIVE RELATIONSHIPS

9. Engage in powerful listening
10. Develop skills in inquiry and openness
11. Learn how to give, receive, and seek feedback
12. Distinguish intent from impact
13. Apologize effectively

### BRIDGE DIFFERENCES

14. Address underlying systemic biases
15. Learn to recognize dominant/nondominant dynamics
16. Check for stereotyping tendencies, unconscious bias, and lack of awareness in your behavior, especially as a dominant-group member
17. Sustain chronic unease toward exclusionary behaviors
18. As a dominant-group member, provide support to nondominant-group members
19. As a nondominant, resist any tendency toward internalized oppression or viewing dominants as beyond your ability to influence
20. As a nondominant, recognize dominants' potential unawareness about the impact of their behavior
21. Call others in rather than calling them out

### CONSCIOUS USE OF SELF

22. Accept responsibility for your own contributions
23. Maintain integrity
24. Seek to understand others' perspectives
25. Focus on others' strengths
26. Adopt a growth mindset
27. Recognize your power and use it responsibly
28. Build resilience through self-affirmation

### INITIATE CHANGE

29. Commit to personal change
30. Emphasize changing systems, not just individuals
31. Surface undiscussables
32. Gain support one person (or small group) at a time
33. Set direction, not fixed outcomes
34. Learn from resistance
35. Cultivate radical patience through the time lag of change
36. Acknowledge small wins

SIX PRINCIPLES OF CONSCIOUS CHANGE

first thought as a hypothesis rather than a statement of truth. When you recognize there might be a question, you're willing to learn something new about a situation. This takes more work—and humility—than being in the answer. It requires searching for alternative explanations for others' behavior.[1]

To move from the answer into the question, consider the possibility that you may be making up stories about what happened during an interaction or exchange—stories that may or may not be accurate.[2] We all have perceptual filters limiting what we see, think, or feel.[3] Be willing to explore whether your first thought about what is going on might simply be incorrect. In the following chapters, you'll find many examples of moving from the answer into the question.

### ■ *Look for Multiple Points of View*

Too often, situations are viewed through the lens of either/or: either it's your fault or it's my fault, but it can't be both.[4] Either/or thinking often inappropriately reduces a complex situation to a dichotomy. While quite common, this simplistic thinking narrows the range of possibilities we consider. We often use it to justify assigning blame without having the necessary information.

Inevitably, situations are more complex than they appear at first glance. Taking time to look beneath the surface and search for alternative explanations can often avoid unnecessary misunderstandings.[5]

### ■ *Consciously Test Your Negative Assumptions*

You don't have to test assumptions with every single person in every situation.[6] Use this tool when you have formed a negative belief about someone and the situation is sensitive, or you believe it is too risky to ask directly about the negative sentiment. Testing assumptions—obviously in a respectful manner—is a way to surface your negative beliefs while minimizing the risks of offending.

### ■ *Check to See If You Are Making Cultural Assumptions*

Considering possible cultural factors is another way of testing your initial assumptions. Researchers have identified several cultural assumptions as sources of frequent conflict among individuals from different social groups.[7] They include differences in how people view individual vs. collective responsibility, competitive vs. cooperative behavior, hierarchical vs. flat organizational structures, and more.[8]

Cultural differences go beyond national or ethnic origin. All social groups have unique cultural norms influencing their members' assumptions, views, and beliefs. Consider the impact of your ethnicity, biology (e.g., gender, age, sexual orientation, or identity), hierarchical status (socioeconomic class, occupation, positional authority), geographic location (nation, region, urban vs. rural), and other factors on how your view of the world may differ from that of another.

## Clear Emotions

Emotions are complex physiological responses. They are automatic, unconscious reactions, rather than products of conscious thought. Because we feel our emotions before we form conscious thoughts, our emotions influence our thinking.

When you are upset, the fight-or-flight response of your brain's amygdala (the seat of emotional processing in your brain) and related areas of your brain and body are activated. As a result, your prefrontal cortex (where perception, interpretation, analysis, and decision-making occur) must work harder to gain your attention. In short, if your emotions are on fire, it may be hard to focus or concentrate.[9]

If you are thrown into a "high alert" situation—by something as serious as mortal danger or by something as familiar as feeling insulted—you may find yourself emotionally hijacked. Your thinking is short-circuited. You are emotionally flooded, propelled into a "fight, flight, or freeze" reaction. Learning to recognize when you are emotionally hijacked, even in hindsight, is a critical skill.

If you can learn how to transition out of a state of stress and into a neutral or even positive emotional state, you will be better able to think clearly, develop creative solutions to problems, and work effectively with others. The more skilled you are at regulating your emotions, the more resilient you become when stressors arise.[10]

## ▪ *Identify with Your Values, Not Your Emotions*

You may say, "I am furious," rather than "I feel furious." There's a world of difference between these two statements. The first connotes permanent identification with your emotions; the second describes a temporary state that may change over time.

People who identify with their emotions tend to see themselves through that lens, making it harder for them to manage their emotions effectively or adapt to challenging situations. They can become solidified in their feelings. The upset felt may become a self-fulfilling prophecy, lingering well past its cause.

You are not your emotions or feelings. You are having an experience with your emotions—one that will go away at some point. You won't always feel this way. Your values are more enduring qualities that help define who you are.[11] Consider uncovering the values conflicts that give rise to your negative emotions. What important values do you believe are being undermined and causing you consternation?[12] These are the values you stand for. Choose to identify with those values (the cause) rather than the emotion (the effect).

## ▪ *Avoid Emotional Suppression*

Even if you try to ignore them, your emotions make themselves known internally. Emotions are unconscious and automatic physiological responses to stimuli. You may not want to believe you feel depressed, enraged, or even victimized and isolated. Yet when you suppress those unconscious feelings, they are likely to bubble up later in the form of uncontrollable emotions and reactions.[13]

Both your thinking and your behavior are affected. You may find yourself being distracted, ruminating, blaming, or scapegoating. You may say or do something you will later regret. These behaviors are unhelpful in moving toward a positive solution and may even be self-sabotaging.[14]

## ▪ *Clear Your Negative Emotions*

When you suppress your emotions, they remain buried inside, ready to erupt at the slightest trigger. When you clear your emotions, they quietly dissipate, and you get a palpable sense of relief. After clearing your emotions, you are no longer triggered in that moment.[15]

Many methods are available for clearing negative emotions.[16] Journaling is one example.[17] Emotional clearing techniques require you to focus on and label what you feel. For some people, simply naming and monitoring their negative emotions reduces activation of the amygdala and increases activation of the prefrontal cortex.[18] This is likely to decrease the intensity of their negative emotions and improve their ability to think more clearly. Other people may require more advanced and longer-term techniques to calm the amygdala. Such techniques may involve bringing repressed feelings or memories to the light, so we may discover our truer selves. There is significant difference between distraction or suppression (where you temporarily put aside the negative emotion) and honest-to-goodness clearing (where a greater sense of calm, clarity, and authenticity replaces the emotional churning).

### ■ *Build Your Positive Emotions*

Welcoming and amplifying positive emotions is as important as learning to clear negative emotions. Many of us know how to sink into misery yet find it strange to allow ourselves to feel proud, happy, delighted, glad, elated, contented, grateful, encouraged, joyful, satisfied, or exhilarated.[19]

Yet both negative and positive emotions are vital for our physical and mental health and help develop our resilience.[20] Negative emotions alert us to challenges in life that need our attention—physical threats or relationship issues, for example. Positive emotions are significant contributors to our ability to flourish—to experience a sense of positive psychological and social well-being most of the time.[21] Research shows that people who flourish are more confident, optimistic, energetic, easier to live and work with, and more resilient.[22] They are also better prepared to deal with life's adversities and to pursue and achieve their goals, and are more likely to live healthier and longer lives.

Even if it feels unfamiliar at first, learn to savor good feelings as they come.[23] Welcome and share your positive feelings and whatever gifts they bring.[24]

# Build Effective Relationships

Little gets accomplished within organizations by individuals operating solo. It is in and through relationships that work gets done. Effective relationships are characterized by regularly occurring open and honest communications. It takes more than good intentions, however, to have such relationships. It requires skill and practice.

## ▪ *Engage in Powerful Listening*

Powerful listening is active rather than passive and can have positive outcomes.[25] It involves doing whatever you can do, nonverbally, to demonstrate genuine interest in what someone is saying through your body posture, eye contact, head nodding, and facial expressions. For example, you put down your phone or look up from your computer. When you listen powerfully, the other person recognizes your engagement and is more likely to work with you on shared goals.[26]

## ▪ *Develop Skills in Inquiry and Openness*

Inquiry goes beyond simply asking questions. Generally, you ask questions to ascertain facts. However, you engage in inquiry to uncover the other person's underlying assumptions and meaning. Through skillful use of inquiry, you learn more about the other person's intent—and then are able to test your understanding of it. Skillful inquiry is rigorous, requiring genuine curiosity and remaining in the question.[27] The payoff is when your questions encourage the other person to surface what might otherwise have remained hidden or even undiscussable.

Openness is about what you are willing to tell—how transparent you choose to be to others.[28] If you want others to think of you as an open leader, you must go beyond giving facts and orders (the what) to explaining your intent, reasons, and expectations (the why).[29] By providing clarity, you set the context for effective performance. Openness may require a change in mindset. It is better to discard the belief that your assumptions are common sense and should be apparent and reasonable to others. In fact, like everyone else, you probably operate on assumptions others may not share. By practicing openness, you make your assumptions and thinking processes visible.

## ■ *Learn How to Give, Receive, and Seek Feedback*

Feedback is a core ingredient of all open, honest, and effective relationships. It is important to learn to give both supportive and corrective feedback *to* others, and equally important to seek and receive feedback *from* others.

*Give supportive feedback.* By learning to give strength-focused feedback, you make it easier for others to listen to sometimes-painful truths.[30] Supportive feedback is a meaningful way to let people know you appreciate them or something they have done. Most people crave more recognition and supportive feedback than they get. You are more willing to follow leaders who give regular, heartfelt, and supportive feedback than those who are more miserly in their verbal support.

*Give corrective feedback.* Do your best to clear your negative emotions before providing corrective feedback. Move into an emotional state that feels open. And make a conscious effort to adopt a growth mindset, one that views the other person as capable of change rather than stuck and limited.[31]

*Receive corrective feedback.* When others provide you with feedback, look for the grain of truth regardless of the source.[32] Your task is often one of converting poorly delivered feedback into information you can use. You may not like the messenger (who says it) or the medium (how they say it), but the message (what they are trying to communicate) may be valid. If the feedback pushes some emotional buttons for you, ask for time to think about it and do some emotional clearing. Demonstrate a willingness to change.[33]

*Seek feedback.* Many people won't voluntarily tell you when you do something that annoys them. You must seek it out, sometimes with a thumping heart. Still, victory goes to people who can push past their anxiety and ask others to tell them how they are effective and how they might improve.[34] The more specific your request, the more valuable the information you are likely to receive. Further, if you have a leadership role, openly sharing the feedback you receive with your team demonstrates your commitment to acting on it, increases their sense of psychological safety, and increases the probability of their reciprocation.[35]

## ■ *Distinguish Intent from Impact*

You want the impact of your words to match your intent. The only way to ascertain whether others understand what you are saying is to ask. Both openness and inquiry help here. You may choose to be open about your concerns and to inquire about the other person's perceptions and meanings.

People's words may also land inaccurately or even poorly on you. Give them grace by not assuming their intentions. Instead, ask if the individual really intended the impact their words or behavior had.[36] We do not mean to imply that people's words do not negatively impact you—if it hurts, it hurts. The point is the outcome will be better if you do not automatically assume the other person is being intentionally hurtful.[37]

### ▪ *Apologize Effectively*

An effective apology has three ingredients: authentic expression of regret, genuine reflection of the harm or inconvenience caused, and an offer to make restitution.[38] When you know your actions have caused damage, asking the simple question "How can I make it up to you" can diffuse animosity and reduce your own self-blame.[39] Restitution doesn't always have to be this direct. Instead, it can be, "We will revise our policies (or I will change what I do) so this doesn't happen again to anyone else."[40]

## Bridge Differences

Learning how to live and work with people who differ from you has become imperative.[41] Study after study has shown diverse groups to be more creative and innovative and to produce better decisions.[42] At the same time, diverse groups experience more conflict and tension than homogeneous groups. To be effective in culturally diverse settings, we must become more sophisticated about cultural differences, master skills to bridge differences, and foster inclusive and equitable work environments.

### ▪ *Address Underlying Systemic Biases*

Because patterns of behavior that routinely advantage Whites (or the dominant group in a particular setting) have been normalized and justified, systemic biases are often unnoticed.[43] Yet they produce adverse outcomes for people of color or other marginalized groups. At the organizational level, policies and regulations may grant legitimacy to one group while denying it to another.[44] Unwritten rules or norms of behavior can have the same effect.[45] For example, in some organizations, proper leadership is defined as an aggressive, "winner-take-all" style of taking charge. In these settings, women and members of cultures who value respect and collegiality may not be viewed as ready for "real" leadership.

Systemic biases can be difficult for dominant-group members to see, so they must ask nondominant-group members about this specifically and give credence to what they have to say.

### ■ Learn to Recognize Dominant/Nondominant Dynamics

Systemic biases can result in dominant/nondominant dynamics at the interpersonal level.[46] Dominance dynamics (a shorthand term we sometimes use for dominant/nondominant group dynamics) occur when people are tacitly or overtly assigned unequal power or status based on groups to which they belong.[47] There are many bases for this assignment to dominant- vs. nondominant-group status: organizational position, physical attractiveness, religious beliefs, age, race, sexuality—the list goes on.[48] The resulting inequality plays out both in work and in personal relationships. Because members of dominant and nondominant groups often have different assumptions and expectations about what is acceptable behavior, they may end up feeling uncomfortable, awkward, or even threatened during their interactions. People often interpret conflicts caused by these dynamics as interpersonal without recognizing the underlying social forces setting the stage for unease.

Since we all belong to multiple social groups, we may simultaneously experience nondominant and dominant statuses—a phenomenon known as intersectionality.[49] For example, a person can be a senior leader (dominant) and physically disabled (nondominant) at the same time. Intersectionality adds to the complexity of interactions.

### ■ Check for Stereotyping Tendencies, Unconscious Bias, and Lack of Awareness in Your Behavior, Especially as a Dominant-Group Member

Stereotyping is generalizing about a person because of their group membership or generalizing about a group after contact with only one of its members. Stereotypes are frequently based on kernels of truth but generalized without discerning whether they apply to a specific individual or group.

Unconscious bias functions as an unintentional, ingrained habit, beyond your immediate awareness.[50] As a dominant-group member, acknowledging the existence of unconscious bias and its distorting effect on your judgment and decisions is the first necessary step.[51] You can learn to recognize and label the results of unconscious bias. Pay special attention to situations in which you feel threatened. When you feel threatened, it's easy to justify your unconscious stereotypes as being based on the other person's actions.[52] ("I'm not prejudiced; he's just taking advantage.")

Unawareness means not noticing what others notice about you. If you are a dominant-group member in an interaction, it is all too easy to think the system is working just fine for everyone—because it *is* working for you and your group members. Seeing your advantages can be very, very difficult. It is easy to be oblivious to how your verbal and nonverbal reactions and responses may have different meanings for members of other social groups.

### ■ *Sustain Chronic Unease toward Exclusionary Behaviors*

Inclusion occurs when organizational or group members feel valued for themselves and can freely contribute their ideas and talents. Examples of exclusionary behaviors include leaving people out of the information loop, ignoring their input, not "hearing" them when they make contributions, and overlooking them during informal interactions or activities.

Chronic unease means *not* assuming your group or organization automatically includes everyone.[53] Instead, watch for signs indicating that a situation could or does lead people to feel excluded, and act before the threat is realized—by taking proactive steps to include them, so they have a sense of belonging.[54]

### ■ *As a Dominant-Group Member, Provide Support to Nondominant-Group Members*

Look for ways in which contributions of nondominant-group members are being overlooked. Increase your awareness of other microaggressions experienced by them, intended or not—as well as the historical foundations and stereotypes that give rise to them.[55] Learn to recognize four common types of microaggressions: gaslighting (causing the nondominant person to doubt their perceptions), 'splaining (speaking for them without allowing them to speak for themselves), victim blaming (implying they are at fault), and abandonment (failure to address the microaggression at all).[56] If you maintain chronic unease, you will increase your ability to notice these and intervene.

Dominant-group members should also acknowledge the reality of nondominants if they describe their exclusion—and act to remedy it.[57] Staying silent when nondominants speak of their exclusion is not a response. You can intervene by verbally and publicly supporting those excluded and by privately and gently alerting those engaging in the exclusion (again, whether intentional or not).[58]

When speaking up, be careful, though, not to appear self-serving by taking over rather than supporting.[59] You will be more effective if you operate from a position of behavioral humility and power-sharing.[60] Assuming your decision to speak up stems from moral courage rather than image concerns, positive outcomes are predicted for three groups: the nondominants you stand up for, the individuals you confront, and the bystanders observing the interactions. The nondominants you speak up for will think more highly of you and will feel validated—which will increase their own self-esteem.[61] The persons you confront will be less likely to use prejudicial statements in the future—about that group or any group.[62] Bystanders will be more likely to confront similar others in the future.[63] Additionally, if your statement is endorsed by others in the group, you signal to the nondominant-group member that they are safe in that setting.[64]

## ■ *As a Nondominant, Resist Any Tendency toward Internalized Oppression or Viewing Dominants as beyond Your Ability to Influence*

As a nondominant, stay alert to signs of internalized oppression, i.e., unconscious acceptance of society's discriminatory messages.[65] Internalized oppression is rooted in assumptions of inherent powerlessness or less-than status—it results in an emotional tax, leaving you constantly on guard and depleted.[66] Instead, consciously choose to consider yourself capable of influencing dominance dynamics—and then take steps to do so, however large or small.

### ■ *As a Nondominant, Recognize Dominants' Potential Unawareness about the Impact of Their Behavior*

Dominant-group members often do not know what they do not know. As a nondominant, find the strength to try new ways of explaining the impact of dominance dynamics to dominants, again and again.[67] It has become popular to say that it is not up to nondominants to educate dominants—or, more specifically, that it is not up to people of color to educate Whites.

That's the ideal world. In that world, nondominants become irritated by dominants for not knowing what they obviously do not know. In the world in which we (the authors) live, we know how challenging it is for people to educate themselves about behaviors they don't know they're engaging in. People in dominant groups may read the right books but still not know what to do in any given situation. There is a world of difference between knowing a concept and being able to act on it. To the extent you, as a nondominant, are able and willing, consider extending yourself to inform dominant-group members who do want to learn and grow.

If nondominants do not speak up, well-meaning dominants may never know what is wrong or how to make it right. Nondominants may miss out on the surge of self-efficacy and enhanced productivity that comes from standing up for themselves and their group in ways that cause dominants to rethink old habits.[68]

### ■ *Call Others In Rather than Calling Them Out*

There is a distinct difference between calling people out (finger-pointing and blaming) and calling them into the community (explaining what has been uncomfortable or off-putting and appealing to the person's better angels). Calling out excludes and focuses on the person; calling in includes and focuses on the behavior.[69]

The research is clear and consistent: shaming may promote short-term changes in behavior but will not lead to long-term attitudinal change.[70] Threats and warnings do not work in changing people; compassion and a belief in their inherent goodness do.

# Conscious Use of Self

The essence of conscious use of self is being aware of and intentional in your interactions with others—mindful of your assumptions and feelings and how others perceive you.[71] It is the deliberate use of your mind, body, and emotions to facilitate positive interactions and influence others. This requires being aware of and taking responsibility for how you show up in your interactions with others and your attempts to impact them while staying in integrity according to your values.

### ■ *Accept Responsibility for Your Own Contributions*

When interactions go wrong, a common and immediate reaction is to figure out who to blame. A universal human experience is to believe that whoever the villain is, it is not you. But insisting on placing all the blame for conflictual situations on the other person can put you in the role of victim and promote feelings of shame. This mindset reduces your ability to affect others or change conditions constructively.[72]

If you believe you had nothing to do with the failure of the interaction, you may also feel that you have no power to make it better. Accepting both your own and others' contributions to a troubling interaction or relationship gives you greater control because you may then begin to influence what happens next, in a conscious way.[73]

### ■ *Maintain Integrity*

People will believe you have integrity if they see you acting consistently with your values and they can count on you to do what you say.[74] Your words, values, and actions must all match.[75] You honor your word. If people believe you have integrity, they are more likely to trust you and to follow your lead.[76] By honoring your word—and being accountable when you cannot—you maintain (or restore) your integrity, motivation, sense of self, and potential for high performance.

### ■ *Seek to Understand Others' Perspectives*

Going into inquiry about another's perspective and being genuinely curious about it are effective ways of learning more. Don't confuse understanding another's perspective (putting yourself in their shoes) with agreeing with them. Just because you understand another's viewpoint does not mean you share it.

Without this ability to understand another's perspective, it is challenging to build a team, induce others to follow your lead willingly, or overcome your own lack of awareness.[77] Understanding others' perspectives can also increase your effectiveness in identifying and successfully managing dominance dynamics.[78]

### ▪ *Focus on Others' Strengths*

Change can be threatening, especially when individuals do not feel accepted as they are. A strength-focused approach toward others' misconduct or errors provides them with the emotional reservoir required for change. It helps them become more willing to risk change and strengthens their belief in their ability to do so if they choose.[79]

### ▪ *Adopt a Growth Mindset*

People with a growth mindset view others as capable of change. If you think someone will never change, you are right, and they never will—at least in your eyes. If you do not truly feel that others are capable of change, you sabotage your own efforts to influence them, and you sap any energy they might have to keep trying to demonstrate improvement in your eyes. It is much more effective to assume that all people, including you, can grow and learn.[80] When you embrace the possibility of learning and growth, then the nature of your interactions, the questions you ask, and the options you consider may expand beyond what you initially thought possible.[81]

### ▪ *Recognize Your Power and Use It Responsibly*

Most people think of power as formal, authorized, or bestowed as part of their official responsibility. Although sometimes harder to recognize, power—as the ability to influence others—can also be informal or personal. Individuals who know how to use themselves consciously, especially in charged situations, can exert a strong influence even when the deck seems stacked against them.[82]

■ *Build Resilience through Self-Affirmation*

Self-affirmation is a tool for building your emotional health and resilience and is one of the actions you can take to increase your sense of your own mental, physical, and spiritual well-being.[83] If you want to make a difference in the world, begin by taking care of your own emotional well-being. This will give you the emotional wherewithal to positively influence others and infuse the climate, wherever you are, with respect and inclusivity.

Too often, we do not take time to replenish ourselves or are discouraged from acting as if we value ourselves. Some people grew up learning that *any* focus on themselves was selfish or self-indulgent. To be clear, we are talking about *self*-affirmation—too much bragging about accomplishments to others can indeed be obnoxious. Affirming yourself *to yourself* or to your trusted friends and colleagues is quite different, because the goal is different.

The more you neglect yourself or discourage yourself from feeling good, the fewer emotional reserves you will have to invest in others—especially those who trouble you. In contrast, self-affirmation will repay itself in your increased courage and resilience.[84]

# Initiate Change

Trying to force change is rarely effective. Instead, encourage change or the willingness to change by operating from an understanding that people do not resist change, they resist *imposed* change.[85]

Change is a process, not an event. The trajectory of change is a series of ups and downs. Conscious Change agents learn how to bide their time and wait for the right moment to plant the right seed in just the right spot. Then they cultivate the soil and wait patiently for the seed to germinate. Whether you seek personal change (e.g., to get more organized) or systemic organizational change (e.g., to broaden the pool of job applicants to bring about greater diversity), it will not happen overnight.

■ *Commit to Personal Change*

Effective change begins by assessing whether *you* are willing to commit to changing yourself as you work to bring about broader change.[86] If the answer is yes, start by monitoring your assumptions, emotions, and relationships, particularly those with people different from you. In particular, consider getting trained or training yourself to view being a change agent or ally as part of your identity—a foundational part of who you are rather than an action you take from time to time.[87]

Changing your attitudes and behaviors can elicit different responses from others. As you change, others may well change in return.[88] Your long-term goal is to see your personal change reflected in what is happening around you and in organizational values and commitment. If you stick with it for the long haul, you can have an enduring impact.

## ▪ *Emphasize Changing Systems, Not Just Individuals*

When we try to change only the attitudes and behaviors of individuals, we leave the underlying conditions or unspoken ground rules intact.[89] This sets the stage for different versions of the same problems to recur, no matter how often you attempt to resolve them. Alternatively, by focusing on organizational systems—established channels for getting things done—you have a greater chance of uncovering more fundamental issues that keep the problem in place. Lasting change requires changing systems.[90]

When you focus on systemic change, you also increase the likelihood of others supporting your change efforts.[91] Individuals may resist efforts pushing them to change but may be willing to help alter systems they find constraining.

## ▪ *Surface Undiscussables*

Any threatening issue people in groups and organizations avoid talking about is an undiscussable.[92] This includes taboo topics, hidden assumptions, unspoken rules, or any socially sensitive issue.[93] If even one person in an interaction is uncomfortable and avoids talking about an issue, it becomes an undiscussable. Often, people do not even talk about the fact that they are avoiding a subject, making it undiscussable even to say there is an undiscussable.

Undiscussables impede change. It is hard to change anything you're unwilling to talk about. For change to occur, the elephant in the room must be named, no matter how uncomfortable the conversation. Learning to surface undiscussables is a skill you can acquire if you choose.[94]

You can name the elephant directly or indirectly. A direct reference would mention the issue in a way that implied disapproval. A less risky approach would simply point out the discrepant behavior without giving your opinion about it. For example, if a team member inappropriately references another team member's gender as a reason to exclude them from some activity, you might say, "It's interesting that you think gender is relevant."[95]

### ■ *Gain Support One Person (or Small Group) at a Time*

Begin the change process by talking with one person at a time.[96] As you speak with others, one of your goals is to help them form an image of what might be possible if change were to occur.[97]

If someone has a negative response, it may simply be a knee-jerk reaction to the unfamiliar. In the early stages of a change effort, your task is to make the unfamiliar familiar.[98] For many people, their first "no" is a reaction, not a position. Given more information or time, some may change their position.[99]

### ■ *Set Direction, Not Fixed Outcomes*

Creating a vision or goal and then trying to sell it often triggers adverse reactions and resistance. In contrast, a shared vision for change is more likely to surface from the involvement and commitment of those affected.[100] For an authentic shared vision to emerge, consider involving others in creating it. Make room for others to influence the outcome.

Setting a goal and then sticking to it no matter what new circumstances arise can undermine your efforts. It is not hard to remember how many goals set before the pandemic shutdown of 2020 became obsolete within a few weeks.

You may also benefit from others' involvement when setting goals, especially if these individuals are closer to the ground and to emerging trends than you are. Setting a direction that others may influence increases the probability that the goals will stay current, relevant, and implementable.

### ■ *Learn from Resistance*

People's resistance to change can be an invaluable source of learning. Although counterintuitive, embracing resistance, exploring it, and even welcoming it can uncover new considerations. By doing so, you gain information to improve the change effort and increase the odds of its success.

When you encounter resistance, instead of explaining the benefits of the change, move into inquiry. With an open heart and mind, listen deeply to uncover what resisters are really concerned about—what they are trying to protect by holding on to the status quo.[101] If you discover what they are trying to defend and adjust for it, you may end up with a more satisfying result.

### ■ *Cultivate Radical Patience through the Time Lag of Change*

Not everyone accepts change at the same rate.[102] People need time to adjust to change. One of your most demanding jobs as a change agent will be maintaining a patient, accepting attitude toward those slower to join the change. Change does not occur rapidly or in a linear way. Instead, it occurs at an excruciatingly slow pace with exhilarating highs and heart-stopping lows. Be prepared for a time lag between when you attempt to initiate the change and when you can see tiny signs that change may be emerging. The time lag of change is part of the process and why radical patience is needed.

Persevere through the inevitable ups and downs of change.[103] If your initial change efforts fail, do not beat yourself up. Instead, keep going. If you embrace failure as part of the process and learn from it, then when you begin to worry that all is lost, you can cut yourself some slack and figure out another way to make it work.

### ■ *Acknowledge Small Wins*

Don't wait for the big win to congratulate yourself. Instead, seek out small steps in the right direction—incremental changes—and commend yourself and others for them. This will help you maintain the required patience and staying power.

Successful change efforts require a mindset of continuous improvement: expect small steps toward a goal with intermittent setbacks. The "winner" is the person who perseveres, no matter what. Since change takes a long time, there will be many peaks and valleys. You would be wise to anticipate and plan for regression.

# Real-Life Examples of Conscious Change

In the following chapters, you will read stories from multiple contributors illustrating these Conscious Change principles and skills. Each author describes a situation in which they used some of the skills—with most experiencing satisfactory outcomes. The authors tell their stories in their own unique ways. They have a variety of backgrounds yet have applied the skills successfully in a wide range of circumstances. Some work in offices with high-level leadership responsibilities. Others work in gritty street settings in a part of America many people never see. Their language use ranges from highly professional to raw. The chapter authors and stories are real. With only a few exceptions, the identities themselves are real. In most chapters, authors changed the names of specific individuals or omitted the name and nature of the organizations to protect their privacy and public image. For the same reason, in a few chapters, descriptions of events were based on facts but altered in some way to prevent identification.

After each story, we identify the specific Conscious Change principles and skills used by the author and how their actions made the situation better. As the stories proceed, they become increasingly complex; more skills are used and discussed.

As you read the stories, you may find it helpful to occasionally return to this chapter to refresh your memory of how some skills are defined. After seeing examples of the skills in real-life settings, you will likely understand our discussion in new ways. This deeper understanding will increase your ability to practice the skills yourself, which is what we wish for you.

## CHAPTER 3.

# Hijacked!

## *By Emily Schwartz Kemper*

Photo © Alex Kemper

I had a report due by the end of the day and was feeling really pressed for time. I'd been working on it all afternoon and had come to an especially important section requiring my full concentration.

I heard "knock, knock" as my coworker, Keisha [fictitious name] entered my office. "Where's that list of clients? You promised you'd get it to me so I can get ready for tomorrow's meeting."

"I don't have time for that right now!" I burst out angrily. "Can't you see I'm busy?"

"Well, excuse me!" came her reply. "You were supposed to email it to me. Where is it? I can't proceed without it."

My pulse was racing; I wanted to cry in frustration. The exchange quickly deteriorated into a shouting match. Through gritted teeth, and with a great deal of resentment, I gave her what she needed, practically throwing it at her.

# Stress Leads to Blame and Resentment

Keisha slammed my office door on her way out, a clue that she, too, was emotionally charged. We were both under a great deal of stress. The pressure each of us felt led to mutual emotional flooding and we ended up blaming one another.

Keisha was in her midfifties, with health problems. She had missed quite a few workdays in the last month or so and was worried about her job status. I knew she felt pressure to demonstrate her capabilities to the rest of the staff. I also knew the client list was an essential part of what she needed to cover in the next day's staff meeting . . . and I had failed to fulfill my promise to get her the list she needed.

But I didn't take any of that into account in the emotionally flooded moment. I was enmeshed in my own anxiety, with a report due by the end of the day. If I was going to get it done, I had to stay focused. The information I had was important to Keisha and of course I'd promised to deliver, but that was before I fell behind on my own work. I resented Keisha for asking me to do something I felt I didn't have time for.

Prior to this episode, Keisha and I hadn't had any conflicts. In this interaction, however, we became almost enemies, neither interested in the needs of the other.

When she interrupted me, my fight-or-flight emotional state kicked in and I did what she wanted, then blamed her for my inability to stand up for myself and my own priorities. I recognized the emotion I was feeling in my chest as fear. I felt afraid—a position I'd been in many times. Rather than admitting my vulnerability and processing my fear in some way, I tried to stuff it back down inside of me and got stuck in it. This "stuckness" then manifested as feelings of anger and resentment.

Sadly, Keisha was let go soon after the incident, but by then our relationship had returned to normal, for the most part. We were cordial but didn't really engage in any meaningful way. At one point, she asked my boss to tell me to stop being friends with a member of her staff, even though he had been my former intern. In response, I simply stopped talking with my former intern—again, acquiescing to someone else and not standing up for myself.

## Dealing with a Flood of Emotions

In reading *Reframing Change*, I learned that many of my immediate responses were really about flight from past emotional experiences. I tend to freeze when a current event triggers negative emotions from the past. I feel as if I'm in danger, my emotions become flooded, and I shut down communications for fear of being hurt again.

Since that interaction with Keisha, I have found several methods effective in dealing with the emotional flooding. The first is to focus on my breathing whenever I feel my heart starting to race or my jaw clenching. I inhale slowly, as deeply as I can, then exhale as far as I can. I find this relaxes my emotional state enough to be able to pay attention to what is being said.

It also helps to take a break, a walk if I can. This allows me time to center myself, especially important when I am highly invested in the outcome of an interaction. The most effective way of clearing negative emotions learned from *Reframing Change* was to use the visual image of a balloon. I imagine I'm blowing all the negative emotions I feel into a balloon, then envision it floating away into the sky. I am a visual person, so this works well for me.

Had I used one of these emotional clearing techniques at the time of my unfortunate encounter with Keisha, I could have responded to her request in a more effective way. Instead, I immediately assumed she was being rude by interrupting me—surely, she'd seen how busy I was. That was the "answer" I provided to myself in the moment. What if I had moved to being in the question instead? I knew her worry and fear about her job security had heightened her emotions. I could have taken that into account in my response to her.

## What Could Have Been

Now that more time has passed and I've reread *Reframing Change*, here is my idealized version of what could have happened if I had used the principles and skills of Conscious Change:

Keisha knocks on the door and asks, "Where's that list of clients? You promised you'd get it to me so I can get ready for tomorrow's meeting."

I push my chair back and take a couple of deep breaths and exhalations before responding, "I'm sorry, would you mind waiting about twenty minutes so I can finish the report I'm working on? My stress level is high, and it's difficult for me to stop when I'm in the middle of something. I know I promised to send it to you, and I will . . . as soon as I'm done with this report."

She agrees and returns to my office a half hour later. Upon entering, she gives a deep sigh and sits down. The report is taking longer than I anticipated, so I minimize my computer screen and print out four copies of the client list.

"I really appreciate you taking the time to do this," she says when I hand the copies to her. "I noticed you took a couple of deep breaths before responding to me earlier. You seemed to be having a lot of anxiety. That can be really hard."

"Yes. Sometimes I really struggle to get control over it. And I find it hard to talk about."

"It looks like you're really working at it, though," she says in what I recognize is an attempt to be supportive.

I nod, and then she says, "Thanks again. I'll leave now so you can get back to your work." She smiles as she walks away. I smile too, because we both seem to recognize how heated a situation can become when our emotions flood our minds and bodies.

## A More Conscious Approach

After reflecting on this, I came away with several insights:

1.  Recognizing signs of emotional flooding will help me find ways to postpone responses or interactions until I have an opportunity to clear my emotions.
2.  When I feel signs of emotional flooding, I should ask for a five-minute break to practice my emotional clearing techniques.
3.  Lowering my voice and taking deep breaths during emotionally stressful situations may help me de-escalate them.
4.  I need to consider the viewpoints of coworkers in situations different from mine. Putting myself in the other person's shoes

may help me empathize with them, and hopefully lower my stress level.

5. Staying in the question does not automatically make me a doormat. I can maintain my boundaries while being in the question.

6. Becoming emotionally flooded on a regular basis may be a signal that I need to better manage the stress I'm experiencing. There are few reasons for me to continuously operate at such a high-stress level.

## Recognize Emotional Flooding before It Washes Out Reason (Reflections on Emily's Story)

• • •

Haven't we all been there? The interaction between Emily and Keisha is more common than most of us like to admit, especially under high-stress working conditions. Too often both parties to interactions are under extreme stress and take it out on one another.

Emily and Keisha were both emotionally flooded, their intense emotions overriding any hope of a rational and positive outcome of their interaction. Not only was Emily emotionally hijacked, but her outburst led to Keisha becoming hijacked as well.

Unaddressed emotions commonly result in unaddressed relationship issues. The workplace interactions of Emily and Keisha could have been much more positive if they had tried to clear up their blowup afterward. Instead, they went from having a single explosive but short-lived conflict to having a more passive, ongoing conflict.

The ongoing conflict was illustrated by Keisha's complaint to the supervisor about Emily's relationship with the intern. By simply ceasing communication with the intern, Emily missed an opportunity to go into inquiry with Keisha—seeking to understand what was driving her request, what impact Emily's continuing friendship with this former intern was having on Keisha. Neither the incident nor their relationship was discussed or examined.

Only later did Emily learn and practice some techniques for clearing her negative emotions: she talks about having learned to take breaks, to inhale deeply, and to utilize visualization.

Becoming aware of the impact of emotional flooding is the first important step. It may be unrealistic, however, to believe that she could quickly develop the ability to clear her emotions in the moment, while the person who triggered the emotional hijack was still in the room.

Asking for a five-minute break may be the better choice in the short term. With practice, it is possible to shorten the time between recognition of the onset of emotional flooding and the ability to engage in necessary emotional release, i.e., to override the amygdala. If it is not possible to use an emotional clearing technique in the moment, it is important to do so as soon as possible following the triggering event to avoid a festering resentment.

Emily also now recognizes that taking time to clear her negative emotions allows her to step back from situations and question her conclusions about what's going on. She sees that being in the question does not make her a doormat; instead, it gives her more choices.

Emily belatedly recognized her own contribution to the conflict—she'd failed to provide Keisha the information she needed, which Emily had promised to provide. She also came to understand the importance of putting herself in others' shoes, of being more empathetic.

It is, of course, too late to remedy her relationship with Keisha, but hopefully her more recent understanding will keep her from experiencing relationship breakdowns with others.

• • •

## Conscious Change Principles and Skills in This Chapter

■ *Test Negative Assumptions*
- Move from the answer into the question

■ *Clear Emotions*
- Avoid emotional suppression
- Clear your negative emotions

■ *Build Effective Relationships*
- Develop skills in inquiry and openness

■ *Conscious Use of Self*
- Accept responsibility for your own contributions
- Seek to understand others' perspectives

# About Emily

Emily Schwartz Kemper received her LCSW from the University of Houston Graduate College of Social Work. She studied Conscious Change skills in a leadership class taught by Dr. Jean Latting. She has enjoyed working in the nonprofit sector with homeless women struggling with mental health issues and substance abuse. Emily enjoys gardening, swimming, playing the piano, and spending time with her family—Gunther, Alex, and Fronia.

## CHAPTER 4.

# Choosing a Career Can Be Emotional Work!

*By Shanquela Williams*
*(with Amy Foy Hageman)*

Photo © Tonya Williams

As a freshman in college, I felt confident about my life's path. I majored in nursing, consistent with my history of service to others. A bonus was the great group of friends I had in the nursing program.

## Vanishing Confidence

By my sophomore year, however, I was feeling completely lost. I was bored with the nursing program but extremely stressed out by the idea of trying to find another major. What else could I do that would serve others but also guarantee a decent income? My friends didn't seem to understand what I was going through. But how could they? I was too embarrassed to even tell them I wasn't enjoying the classes the way they were. And though I had a close and supportive family, the idea of telling them what I was feeling was anxiety-producing. The confident path I had been on vanished. I was left spinning.

When I found my way to the guidance counselor at my university, she asked me all sorts of questions about my life and interests. I remember talking a lot about my history as a volunteer with the Salvation Army and local nursing home.

After hearing all this, she asked, "Have you considered social work as a career?"

I laughed out loud. "Isn't the whole point of college to get a degree that prepares me to support myself? Social workers work really hard, put in long hours at all times of day and night, and often place themselves in possibly dangerous situations—separating kids from their parents, for example. And all that for little to no money. No way do I want to get into that profession!"

"I hear your doubts, but social work seems like such a natural fit with your past history and values," she responded. "How about at least exploring it as an option? What if you enrolled in just one course, Introduction to Social Work, next semester? Just to see what all the field entails. Even if you don't end up majoring in social work, the course would count as an elective."

## Finding My Own Way

I did enroll in the course the guidance counselor recommended but also decided to do some in-depth research on my own on the field of social work. I figured if I didn't find anything I was interested in, maybe I could get out of the social work class and find something else. But the more I researched, the more surprised I became at the vastness of the field. I found jobs I never would have guessed fell under social work education. And many of those answered my felt calling of helping others, as much if not more than nursing would.

I started seriously considering changing my major from nursing to social work. But if I felt lost before, now I was panicked. With the nursing major it seemed simple—my family and friends were all on board and I would easily get a job with steady pay. Changing my major to social work would totally uproot that plan. I couldn't see a direct path to success. And I knew that my friends and family would think the same things I had thought—that social work would be all work and little pay.

I decided to separate myself from my friends during this time of indecisiveness. I felt a need to focus on myself and my well-being. I was afraid spending time with loved ones right then would only inflame my anxieties. I would only hear more doubts about a career path and financial security.

## Emotional Clearing and Affirmations Reveal My Path

I started journaling. I wrote everything I could think of—how scared I was to change majors, the opinions of my friends, the judgments I'd probably receive, the possibility that I would invest so much in my education only to gain a low-paying job, the agony of not having as clear a career path as nursing provided, the fear of being an outcast among my friends. The list went on.

After several days of writing down predominantly negative emotions, I thought of Jeremiah 29:11. ("For I know the plans I have for you," declares the Lord. "Plans to prosper you and not to harm you, plans to give you hope and a future.") This prompted me to write down affirmations:

*This is my path and there will be a way.*

*This is MY journey, and I WILL prosper.*

*I WILL find a job that allows me to serve while blessing me with abundance.*

After days of these affirmations, I felt able to believe in myself and in my decision to change my major to social work. I also felt prepared to talk to my friends and family about it. When I did so, I also told them of all the research I had done and my discovery that social work was a giant field offering a vast variety of job roles and opportunities. Some of my friends were surprised and, as I expected, quite skeptical. But many of them were happy for me. They didn't seem to have the intensity of judgment I expected.

I had found my path.

## Want Decision-Making Clarity? Try Emotional Clearing (Reflections on Shanquela's Story)

• • •

Shanquela was emotionally hijacked—a state of intense emotion that blocked her ability to think clearly. Her story describes the steps she took to clear those emotions. It is also a story of how making assumptions can cause unnecessary pain.

Shanquela had a mistaken set of assumptions about the field of social work. While social work as a career choice might be aligned with her values of service to others, she believed it would not satisfy her goal of financial stability. She tested that assumption through her conversations with the guidance counselor, by gathering more information about social work as a profession, and by stepping up to take the introductory course. As she gained new information, she moved from the answer (certainty about what she knew) into the question (openness to new viewpoints) and felt better about possibilities available to her.

Yet new information also brought a new set of dilemmas. She became even more anxious when she imagined telling her friends and family members about her contemplated change of academic major. She believed they shared her views of the field of social work and would disapprove such a change. She was afraid they would think less of her if she switched career paths.

With this new set of worries, she became immobilized and fearful. Recognizing that her intense emotion about the decision was clouding her ability to think clearly, she withdrew temporarily from interactions with friends and family: "I felt a need to focus on myself and my well-being."

Once something happens that triggers us emotionally, we have three options: (1) pretend we don't feel what we feel by suppressing the underlying emotions, (2) find a temporary distraction to take our mind off our constricting, swirling emotions (which leaves the emotion suppressed), or (3) resolve the unacknowledged emotions by facing the emotional upset. Shanquela wisely chose the last, rather than leaving the suppressed emotions to fester, or to reveal themselves later in unanticipated ways.

Although she didn't have a name for it at the time, Shanquela used what is called uncensored journaling, an effective tool for clearing emotions. She describes writing "everything I could think of"—her fears and uncertainty, her concern about the reactions of her friends and family, even her fear "of being an outcast among my friends." This last seems improbable, but when the amygdala (the seat of emotional processing in our brain) has control and is reacting faster than the prefrontal cortex (where perception, interpretation, analysis, and decision-making occur), it skews perceptions.

Shanquela was not explicit in her story about when she reached the release point (an important stage in the uncensored journaling process). She does explain that writing about her negative emotions for a significant amount of time freed her up to identify positive emotions to replace the negative ones. Welcoming and amplifying positive emotions is another important way to clear negative emotions and build resilience.

Her use of uncensored journaling was intuitive, preceding her formal introduction to the principles for Conscious Change. With a fuller understanding of the process by which emotions influence thoughts and behaviors, she can now intentionally utilize uncensored journaling, or perhaps other techniques, to clear negative emotions. Gratitude journaling is also helpful in building positive emotions.

Shanquela had great instincts for how to manage her emotional hijack. In the future, she will likely recognize her hijacks sooner and be more prepared to alleviate the emotional buildup. Practice makes perfect. The more you practice clearing emotions, the better you become at it.

• • •

# Conscious Change Principles
# and Skills in This Chapter

- ■ *Test Negative Assumptions*
  - • Move from the answer into the question
  - • Look for multiple points of view
  - • Consciously test your negative assumptions

- ■ *Clear Emotions*
  - • Avoid emotional suppression
  - • Clear your negative emotions
  - • Build your positive emotions

- ■ *Conscious Use of Self*
  - • Build resilience through self-affirmation

# About Shanquela

Shanquela Williams received a Master of Social Work from the University of Houston Graduate College of Social Work (GCSW), where she was introduced to the field of health behavior. She is currently a candidate for a Doctor of Philosophy in Public Health. Shanquela also worked as a financial coach for two years and is passionate about the influence of financial health on young adults.

Shanquela enjoys spending time with her family, traveling the world, and volunteering at a foster care facility. She is committed to using her experiences to bridge gaps and enhance communities, local and global. She first encountered the Conscious Change skills in a course entitled Dynamics of Leadership at GSCW, taught by the late Mary Harlan.

## CHAPTER 5.

# Learning to Test Negative Assumptions

## By Eli Davis

Photo © Eden Torres with Pride Portraits

My first real job after college was in human resources for an established but still humble retail company. I was drawn to the culture more than the job itself. The organization had a team-based environment championing employee excellence, self-determination, and leadership over management. Having started as a local mom-and-pop business, it had a history of anti-corporate sentiment. The problem was the company was now *becoming* one of those large corporations the founders detested.

## Growing Pains

This growth did not mean managers had to abandon our values, but it did require us to reevaluate many of our systems. Over almost a decade, my job functions and the overall structure of my department morphed dramatically. The bigger we got, the more liability we had, and the more I was expected to protect the corporation and reduce risks. I was still accountable to my direct boss on site, but I also now reported to and was expected to comply with directives from Regional Human Resources (HR). This shift was particularly daunting as my direct boss was of the lingering anti-corporate mindset.

To reduce corporate liability, Regional HR dictated new protocols and standards for managing personnel. For example, my boss and I no longer had the authority to hire or terminate employees without HR approval.

About a week after this policy was handed down, my boss, whom I'll call Eric, walked into my office and declared, "We've got to let Michael [fictitious name] go."

Knowing this lackluster employee was still in his probationary period but had no documentable major infractions, I told my boss, "I'll be happy to present your concerns to Regional HR, but I don't expect them to approve termination. There just isn't enough on paper to justify it."

Later that day, Eric called me into his office to say, "I'm going to terminate Michael. Would you get the paperwork ready?"

Somewhat in shock and still processing, I asked, "Have you spoken to Regional about this?"

"No, this was my call."

Figuring we were already in hot water, I attempted to salvage the situation. "They're going to see it on my reports, plus they'll be notified if there's an unemployment claim, and I'm sure there will be. Should I alert them now?"

"Don't worry about it. I'll deal with it."

Eric's body language indicated he was done with this discussion, so, internal warning bells ringing loudly, I returned to my office. But I found myself distracted as I prepared the requested documentation. This went against our directive. My inner voice continued to nag at me as I contemplated my potential next move.

*Should I email Regional anyway?* my internal conversation went. *Would that be considered insubordination in the eyes of my direct boss? Will he retaliate by denying me future promotions or salary increases if I go above his head? If I stay out of it, will Regional reprimand or fire me when they find out? What will happen if the company gets sued over this and I didn't alert the appropriate people when they still had the potential to intervene?*

My internal inquisition was interrupted only by my occasional attempts to explain Eric's behavior to myself: *He's just doing what he wants and doesn't care about repercussions to the company or anyone else. He doesn't respect my opinion or judgment.*

In the end, I did as I was told without contacting Regional, following Eric's instructions to let him shoulder any blame. Shortly afterward, I transferred to a different department. I cited professional opportunity as the reason, but the truth was that I felt burned out. In hindsight, much of my frustration and exhaustion was from the energy I spent navigating the evolving corporate structure and expectations. It was not the changes per se causing the stress but how I chose to respond to them. I never confronted Eric about the situation with Michael and will likely never know the truth behind his decision. Nor did I ever hear anything about Regional's reaction to his disobedience.

Six years later, having learned of the importance of testing negative assumptions, I reflect on the turmoil I felt and wonder how I might have handled it differently. Looking back, I realize I had only negative assumptions about Eric, feeling caught in a damned-if-I-do, damned-if-I-don't situation.

Fortunately, I knew better than to march into his office and say that to his face. Still, I was stuck. His actions triggered my emotions, and in that state, I could only imagine the worst. My range of imagined choices was limited. I couldn't see a way out.

## Exploring Assumptions and Testing Hypotheses

Suppose I had known to test my negative assumptions by using the Generating Three Hypotheses Method, as described in *Reframing Change*. What might I have done? Well, I'll put myself back in that time and pretend I knew then what I know now . . .

## Applying the Three Hypotheses Method

### Step 1. Define the negative hypothesis.
My underlying negative hypothesis in this instance was that Eric deliberately violated protocol to get *what* he wanted *when* he wanted it, without considering consequences for the company, his career, or my career.

### Step 2. Define possible situational and good-intent hypotheses.

Maybe there were circumstances beyond my knowledge leading Eric to conclude he was justified in making the termination decision unilaterally, disregarding the new procedure. This didn't seem likely, but I'm determined to remain in inquiry and hold the space for having possibly missed something.

Situational: Looking back, it was possible he'd been in touch with Regional and they granted him some sort of exemption, or perhaps he had found a loophole in the policy. If either of these occurred, he chose not to fill me in. That might be why Regional never contacted me about my role in the situation.

Even with many years of hindsight and acquisition of better tools and practices, developing a good intent motive for this exchange was still a challenge. I have often noticed, though, the harder the motive is to construct, the more impactful and liberating the resulting shift in my perspective (and energy) regarding the situation.

Good Intent: Maybe Eric was taking a stand for our area's sovereignty. What I considered as unilateral decision-making could have been viewed by him as a stand for empowerment and self-determination for those of us who remembered the old days at the company. He might have been willing to go to the wall for us.

Was this too much of a stretch to consider? I still have a pragmatic tendency to quickly dismiss potential alternatives. Yet I have learned that unlikely hypotheses, even those that seem next to impossible, serve to stretch my thinking. I often remind myself that the desired outcome in considering alternatives is not to determine the best answer or solve the mystery but to create the space and willingness to be wrong. I don't know what I don't know.

### Step 3. Reframe the negative hypothesis.

Constructing my reframed hypothesis was a learning process. It took several iterations, along with some guidance and feedback, to arrive at an ideal approach.

First Attempt at Reframing: "I thought maybe you were just doing what you wanted, how you wanted . . ."

In this initial attempt, my negative assumptions were still present and would likely have been counterproductive. It would only have made Eric mad.

Second Attempt at Reframing: Maybe he did in fact follow protocol and went to Regional himself as a favor to me, to spare me the arduous task of building and defending our case for termination.

Hmm. This stretches credibility and doesn't really test my negative assumption. To truly reframe the negative hypothesis, I needed to voice it in a way that would be palatable to Eric yet also getting to the core of the negative assumption I was testing.

Third Attempt at Reframing: Maybe he was taking a stand on behalf of us all.

With this, I was acknowledging that while Eric was deliberately breaking protocol and putting us both at risk, it might have seemed justifiable from his vantage point. If I were to have approached him from this genuinely inquisitive space, it would likely have resulted in productive dialogue. Perhaps I would have obtained the information I felt was missing.

### Step 4. Putting it all together

I might have made this statement to Eric: "I'm curious about how you arrived at your decision and was hoping you could help me understand. First, I thought maybe Regional had granted you some kind of exception making it okay for you to fire Michael. Then I thought maybe you'd found a loophole so you could get around the new regulations. Finally, I thought maybe you were just taking a stand against what you thought was unworkable red tape and were willing to go to bat for it even if you and I paid a price. Is there something else I'm missing?"

Would that have worked? Maybe.

## Learning Is Valuable Whenever It Occurs

The key is whether I was willing to open my mind to the possibility of a good intent or situational hypothesis driving Eric's behavior. If I couldn't, my inauthenticity would have made the whole exercise backfire.

Maybe he really was just carelessly violating protocol, regardless of consequences to himself or me. Maybe there was an even more beneficent explanation than I could imagine. Regardless, I do believe I missed an opportunity to expand my understanding and possibly strengthen our working relationship.

Equipped with the wisdom and tools presently at my disposal, I certainly could have navigated the situation with less wasted cognitive and emotional energy. My confidence in the effectiveness of the Three Hypotheses Method to shift my perspective on emotionally provocative scenarios has increased significantly since that interaction with my old boss. I am now more aware of situations where I can leverage these tools and be more adept in their application. Rather than avoiding conflict, I now find myself welcoming these emotionally rich encounters as opportunities for education and exploration.

## Avoid the Co-creation of Negative Interactions (Reflections on Eli's Story)

• • •

Eli's story is an illustration of how things are often much clearer in the rearview mirror! As he looks back on a previous interaction with his boss, Eric, and analyzes how he could or should have handled it, he describes some of the inner turmoil and self-questioning experienced at the time of the incident. That he still remembers the interaction after six years suggests it carried a hefty emotional charge.

Eli clearly missed an opportunity to clear his emotions, test his assumptions, and provide feedback to his supervisor. Instead, he thinks suppression of his emotions around this and other situations may have contributed to his burnout—leading to a voluntary transfer to another department within the company.

He admits to having been emotionally triggered by the interaction with Eric but even in retrospect doesn't fully recognize how helpful it might have been to clear those emotions before attempting to deal with the cognitive task of testing assumptions. In fact, it might be useful to him, even after all this time, to think back to the situation and see what emotions arise. There may still be remnants of unresolved emotions he could benefit from clearing—either through journaling or some other emotional-clearing technique.

Despite his dissatisfaction with how he handled the situation, Eli did take personal responsibility for his part in it: "It was not the changes per se causing the stress but how I chose to respond to them." He is describing an important underpinning of the notion of conscious use of self, specifically acceptance of the ways in which we often co-create negative experiences and interactions, leading to stress and less-than-full effectiveness as leaders. Many of us walk around frustrated, blaming bad bosses rather than identifying opportunities to seek communication and feedback we could benefit from.

Eli does a good job of giving a step-by-step description of generating multiple hypotheses to explain why his boss might have taken the action he did: the original negative hypothesis, a good-intent hypothesis giving Eric the benefit of the doubt, and a situational hypothesis considering possible extenuating circumstances.

Using these, Eli reframed his original hypothesis as a statement to his former supervisor that might have led to a more productive discussion, as well as increased understanding and learning. Eli recognized he would have had to enter into the question and approach the hypothesis testing from a position of genuine curiosity.

As he demonstrates, even in hindsight, this is not always an easy task. Holding on to what we believe is much easier than testing our assumptions, especially when those assumptions are steeped in negative emotions.

Eli's story demonstrates the benefit of revisiting situations that trigger us. He clearly learned from analyzing this workplace experience. He now welcomes what he considers "emotionally rich encounters" as opportunities for learning and growth.

• • •

## Conscious Change Principles and Skills in This Chapter

■ *Test Negative Assumptions*
- Move from the answer into the question
- Consciously test your negative assumptions

■ *Clear Emotions*
- Avoid emotional suppression
- Clear your negative emotions

■ *Build Effective Relationships*
- Learn how to give, receive, and seek feedback

- *Conscious Use of Self*
  - Accept responsibility for your own contributions

# About Eli

Eli Davis received a Master of Social Work from the University of Houston Graduate College of Social Work. After a circuitous career track through a few different helping professions, he found his passion in social justice advocacy and policy work. An avid lover of animals, nature, science, and the human experience, he can often be found wandering the woods with his latest four-legged rescue.

He first learned the Conscious Change skills in a course taught by Dr. Latting in the Graduate College of Social Work at the University of Houston, then later worked with her as a graduate assistant.

CHAPTER 6.

# Dashed Hopes and Expectations

*By Tracy Forman*

Photo © Tracy Forman

Two months after receiving my Master of Social Work, I was offered an employment opportunity with a rapidly growing inpatient behavioral health facility. One of the facility leaders, Ms. Anderson [a pseudonym], with whom I had worked in another professional setting, extended the invitation.

"I am familiar with your work ethic and style and believe you would align and assist with my ultimate goal of building a great team," she said. "You will be the fourth social worker to join the team if you accept my offer."

"Thank you so much," I replied. "Could I have a few days to consider this offer?"

"Of course."

I spent the next few days weighing competing opportunities, as well as my financial obligations, and decided to accept the offer.

## All That Glitters . . .

The salary was appealing, and I liked the mission and vision of the facility. Moreover, the company's leadership seemed committed to creating a flagship behavioral health facility, one that could serve as a statewide model. Being an integral part of this team seemed to present a unique and perfectly tailored opportunity for me to help turn this vision into a reality. For a new licensed master of social work (LMSW), the experience seemed to provide an opportunity to become more knowledgeable in the field of behavioral health and make significant differences in the lives of those I served.

Ms. Anderson, also fairly new to the organization, was upbeat as she gave me an initial tour of the facility.

She did admit, "The décor of the facility *is* a bit unsavory and drab, but I'm optimistic about the future. It's on its way up!"

This reaffirmed my excitement. "I'm pleased to be part of this effort."

I felt we were on the same page, working toward the same goals and committed to making a difference. After completing the necessary paperwork and prescreening activities, taking the required trainings, and attending a full day of orientation, I was still enthusiastic. I couldn't wait to begin.

A week later, during my first day of work, I was abruptly reminded that everything that glitters is not gold. I learned there would be only three social workers instead of four as I had thought. The individual with whom I was to have shared the unit and caseload had been suddenly dismissed. My caseload would now be between twenty-two and twenty-seven patients. This number of patients might have been normal for a social worker in Child Protective Services but represented a daunting task in behavioral health. My responsibilities included completing psychosocial assessments and coordinating discharge plans for each of these patients, as well as facilitating groups and attending Treatment Team meetings. The patients' stays averaged one to three days, creating narrow timeframes for such a high volume of casework.

I also quickly learned there was no shortage of organizational problems. Specifically, the culture of the organization seemed toxic. In addition to general disarray at all levels of the organization, there were problems with nepotism, ineffective communication, patient complaints, HIPAA violations, premature employee terminations, and employee resignations. My initial vision of the facility becoming a flagship was beginning to fade.

# Taking Responsibility to Initiate Change

I thought long and hard about what I could do to facilitate cohesion within the facility without appearing pretentious or being perceived as a troublemaker. I began to journal my thoughts, clearing any type of emotional connection I had to the issues at hand. Strong emotional reactions to my discoveries were easy, even reasonable. I was disappointed, angry, and exhausted from the workload. However, I had grown to understand that negativity doesn't solve anything. I needed to recognize and acknowledge my legitimate emotions but take steps to intervene at a higher cognitive level. I also believed that to be an effective leader and communicator, to help bring about change, I had to get others to buy in. I could not accomplish this by spreading negative energy.

As part of my journaling process, I listed each discipline within the facility and, to the best of my knowledge, their tasks. At the center of all these tasks were the patients. This made me think of a puzzle. I made a crude drawing of a jigsaw puzzle, showing patients as the center puzzle piece, with the various disciplines surrounding it. Next, rather than focusing on deficiencies or opportunities for improvements, I outlined the strengths I observed in each department and how those benefited patient care. After pulling all my thoughts together, I arranged a meeting to share them with Ms. Anderson.

There was excitement in my voice as I explained, "My logic is simple: if everyone, in every department, were valued as an essential piece of the puzzle then patient care would inevitably be great. Excellent patient care would lead to enacting our larger, collective vision of flagship status."

To my surprise, after asking a few questions, Ms. Anderson seemed to be on board, saying, "Hmm. This makes sense. Would you put together a formal and detailed writeup and send it to me via email?"

"I would be glad to!" I replied. And I eagerly did so.

A few days later, she sent me her version of what I had provided. Instead of using my original and deliberately themed title of "You're an Essential Piece of the Puzzle," she entitled her writeup, "Piecing It Together."

I felt insulted and angry at how she seemed to have distorted my message. My title was intentionally focused on conveying a belief that if everyone felt essential, the company stood to get the best from each employee. Her title deflected that focus. I felt misunderstood. To me, the notion of piecing something together had ragged, negative undertones.

So back to my journal I went. This time around, not only did I need to clear more negative emotions; I also needed to question my assumption that Ms. Anderson was out to drive me crazy with that awful title. So I generated other hypotheses for why she reframed my original message. I knew she was in no way malicious and would never have done anything intentionally to upset the situation. After all, her goal was also to assist this facility in becoming a flagship.

I wrote: "Maybe changing the title from 'You're an Essential Piece of the Puzzle' to 'Piecing It Together' was just a matter of semantics for Ms. Anderson.

"Maybe Ms. Anderson imagined the beauty of how quilts are pieced together. Thus, she used 'Piecing It Together' metaphorically to describe the potential beauty of cohesiveness among the disciplines within the facility.

"Maybe Ms. Anderson used the word 'piecing' in its most literal sense, meaning to assemble something from individual parts. In this regard, the word 'piecing' could be thought of as each discipline coming together, to strengthen the mission and vision of the facility."

As I wrote and pondered alternative explanations for her actions, I intentionally treated each as a serious possibility, thus making my original assumption more tentative. It was important to focus on what I knew, not what I might be making up about the situation.

After I wrote until I was on the verge of carpal tunnel, I concluded that I could not afford to allow my emotions or subsequent feelings and thoughts to overly influence me. As Dr. Latting's work had taught me, I had to interrupt or intervene in old habits of processing thoughts and emotions. Only then could I effectively help the company fulfill its goal of rendering the best possible care to patients.

After reconciling my thoughts, clearing my emotions, and testing my assumptions, I was able to discuss the issue further with Ms. Anderson. My goal was to birth a mutual understanding and reignite commitment to the vision.

Fortunately, we were able to get to a point of common understanding. Unfortunately, the campaign never came to fruition—the operative goal of the hospital shifted to simply keeping the beds filled.

## Capturing the Learning Despite Disappointment

The company continues to be successful, but the important puzzle pieces of the employees and patients have been forgotten, as was the mission that inspired me.

Nevertheless, by learning to clear my emotions, I also learned to choose my battles and focus my energy where I can exert the most positive influence. In doing so, I stress less and am more present for myself, my family, and my patients. I no longer hold on to negative thoughts or feelings because I now understand they are like visitors who come and go.

## Emotions as Visitors That Come and Go
## (Reflections on Tracy's Story)

• • •

Being able to identify negative emotions is an important first step in learning to regulate them. When Tracy discovered things were not as they first seemed within the behavioral health facility, she identified her feelings as "disappointed, angry." Similarly, when she saw the altered version of her proposal to her supervisor, she felt misunderstood—"insulted and angry" at what she perceived as a distortion of her original meaning. In both cases, she recognized the importance of clearing these negative emotions if she wished to be effective in negotiating change. Although she could have used other methods to do the emotional clearing, Tracy chose journaling.

Tracy's ability to clear her emotions around her early disappointment and anger helped broaden her perspective and led to her coming up with a proposal for centering patient care as a pathway to achieving the vision of flagship status. If instead she had simply walked around feeling mad and betrayed, she would not have had the cognitive bandwidth to take this broader view.

To deal with the second round of negative emotions, Tracy used a version of uncensored journaling: "I wrote until I was on the verge of carpal tunnel." Uncensored journaling works best when writing continues until you experience an aha moment or feel a sense of relief from the negative emotion. It's not clear whether she continued to write until she hit a release point—it's easy to short-circuit the process. But the journaling did seem to help her move past her initial negative emotions and allowed her to have what she described as a productive discussion with Ms. Anderson. Her ability to view her emotions as "visitors that come and go" bodes well for her ability to avoid being emotionally hijacked in the future.

As part of her journaling process, Tracy interrogated her initial beliefs about why Ms. Anderson reformulated her concept of "You're an Essential Piece of the Puzzle" to "Piecing It Together." In her words, she reconsidered her assumption that "Ms. Anderson was out to drive me crazy with that awful title." She looked at several alternative explanations for her supervisor's action. In so doing, she moved out of the answer into the question, intentionally tested her negative assumptions, and focused on Ms. Anderson's strengths.

She was also able to begin to see that legitimate differences might be attached to the meaning of words and phrases. Treating each of her alternative hypotheses as a serious possibility helped make her original assumption more tentative. This cognitive reframing, in turn, helped her clear her emotions.

Tracy recognized the importance of others "buying in" for effective change to occur. Aware that negative energy might hamper the change process, she was intentionally mindful of her emotions and attitudes. She was using herself consciously by recognizing her power and using it responsibly. She knew the ways in which she showed up would impact her ability to enroll others in change.

• • •

## Conscious Change Principles and Skills in This Chapter

- *Test Negative Assumptions*
  - Move from the answer into the question
  - Look for multiple points of view
  - Consciously test your negative assumptions

- *Clear Emotions*
  - Avoid emotional suppression
  - Clear your negative emotions

- *Conscious Use of Self*
  - Focus on others' strengths
  - Recognize your power and use it responsibly

■ *Initiate Change*
- Gain support for the change one person (or small group) at a time

## About Tracy

Tracy Forman, LCSW, received a Master of Social Work from the University of Houston's Graduate College of Social Work (GCSW). For over fifteen years, she has worked in the field of social services and behavioral health, subsequently finding her passion working in forensics and inpatient behavioral health, as well as in her private practice. Tracy enjoys spending time traveling with her family and shopping.

Her introduction to Conscious Change came by way of Dr. Latting's leadership, administration, and advocacy course at the University of Houston's GCSW. Upon learning these skills, Tracy began to put them into practice by making a commitment to test assumptions in both her professional and private lives.

## CHAPTER 7.

# Can Anyone Be a Social Worker? The Challenge of Correcting Misinformation

*By Alicia Beatrice*

Photo © J. Golden Photography

When I first became a social worker, I decided to seek experience working with as many different populations as possible. Since then, I had worked as a case manager and clinician with individuals who were homeless, disabled, dealing with chronic and acute mental illness, or had substance-abuse issues. Clients included families, children, men, women, people of different faiths, individuals identifying as LGBTQ, and those of different races and ethnicities. I was pleased to have a new opportunity to continue my work in an agency focused on serving various populations.

## The New Supervisor—Sigh!

A few months after I took the position, there was a change in leadership.

*Here we go again,* I thought. *Why do I always seem to land in agencies in the middle of mergers, reorganizations, policy changes, or new program developments?*

"Do we know anything about the new supervisor?" I asked one of my coworkers.

"Not really. Upper management will be interviewing the candidates and making the final decision. I haven't heard any details."

I told myself not to worry too much. *Maybe it'll be a good thing. I'll get to observe the transition and learn early on whether this agency is going to be a good fit for me. I get along well with the rest of the staff; why wouldn't it be the same with the new boss? But maybe I'll plan an exit strategy, just in case.*

When the announcement was made, an individual I will call Kim was selected. Since she had extensive experience working in similar agencies, I was eager to hear about her background and how she could help us. When Kim met with our staff the first time, she introduced herself and outlined her education and work experience.

"I've performed all of your roles, except that of nurse," she said, then proceeded to list the various titles she'd held over the years.

As soon as she mentioned the role of social worker, I was curious to inquire about her credentials and hopeful that there would now be another social worker on the team. At the first opportunity, I asked her, "Can you tell me your qualifications to be a social worker?"

She replied, "My education. As I said, I have a PhD."

With effort, I hid my distaste. Kim's tone sounded more than a little arrogant. *I won't ask any more questions right now. But I do wonder if she's another one of those people who call themselves a social worker because she's "helping" someone. I find that so annoying.*

In Texas, professional social workers must have a degree in social work and be licensed by the state. They practice in a variety of settings and are professionals who pursue the betterment of the lives of individuals, families, groups, communities, and societies. Social workers receive specialized training in health, mental health, diversity, and social issues so they can practice effectively with vulnerable individuals. The licensing process is extensive and requires demonstrated competence in the field.

I often found myself advocating for my profession. This had been a "cause" for me for some time, one I felt passionately about. I had worked long and hard to become a social worker—it takes almost as long to become a clinical social worker as it does to become a medical doctor.

Normally, I would debate with anyone who called themselves a social worker without the proper credentials, explaining what social workers do, their educational requirements, and what it takes to become one. I often succeeded in enlightening individuals about the profession. But in this case, I decided it was too early to have a disagreement with my new supervisor.

A few weeks after that initial meeting, the issue of who was or was not a social worker came up again.

During a staff meeting, Kim said, "If anyone needs to take time off, I can help out," adding, "I can fill in for anyone except the nurse."

My annoyance and frustration began to surface again: *She thinks she can do everyone else's job but needs to do her own.* I could feel myself getting hot and emotionally distancing myself from the group. *I don't want to play these games anymore.*

I decided to consult my former clinical social work supervisor, Sue [a pseudonym]. As an outsider, I figured she might help me get levelheaded.

"Kim told me she can fill in if we need to take time off. She said she can do everyone's role except the nurse. Why can everyone be a social worker, but no one can be the nurse?"

Sue asked, "Does she have a social work degree or license?"

"I know she has a PhD." I made a face, recalling the snooty way Kim informed us of that. "But I don't know what it's in. And I don't think she has a license."

Sue checked the online verification site of social work license holders in Texas: "She doesn't have a license. It's illegal for her to perform any social work duties or call herself a social worker without a license. I'll have to report her if you tell me she's doing a social worker's job."

## Shifting Myself for a Better Outcome

I didn't want Kim to be reported, nor did I want to compromise my responsibility to the National Association of Social Workers Code of Ethics and Texas Social Work Board of Examiners Code of Conduct. This dilemma added to my emotional turmoil.

The only way I could think to get some perspective on all this was to take some time off from work to separate myself from it. I prayed, cried, and slept. And I spent some time doing uncensored journaling, writing:

> *If Kim thinks she can do my job, doesn't that devalue what I bring to the organization and its clients? If she, a non-social worker, can do my job, is my position even necessary to the organization?*
>
> *How was she able to get by with performing social work duties without a license at another agency?*
>
> *I hate this! I don't need this crap; I can find another job.*
>
> *Values, morals, privilege, that's what this is. She's privileged. Lived in a bubble all her life and thinks she can do whatever she wants.*

I wrote along those lines until I felt calm enough to conclude: *No one can be a social worker unless they meet the requirements. The social work role is not only valuable but legally necessary to organizations with some types of government funding.*

I then switched gears and, instead of complaining, began journaling things I was grateful for.

> *I have the job I wanted.*
>
> *I have a flexible schedule, where I don't have to sit in traffic and can spend more time with my family.*
>
> *I have a supervisor who is willing to help her team any way she can.*
>
> *I have a social work license and a career that has given me the reward of helping better lives and the community.*

I also reflected on the initial interaction between Kim and me. Had she been offended by my asking about her credentials to do social work? Just as I heard arrogance in the tone of her response, could she have heard the same in *my* tone?

I knew Kim had extensive experience and had supervised a team before. Could the issue of her facing legal consequences be avoided by talking to her about the legal boundaries of social work? Or maybe I could give a presentation to the staff about the role of social workers, as well as their qualifications?

## Speaking Up for My Profession and for Myself

When the opportunity arose for me to communicate with Kim one-on-one via email about the legal requirements to be a social worker, I felt calmer. But in the interim, I'd learned our agency was taking on clients related to staff members.

Concerned, I emailed Kim:

> *I have learned that our agency has taken on clients who are relatives of some of the staff members. Providing counseling to relatives of my colleagues is problematic. I cannot be the social worker to a staff member or a relative of a staff member because it creates a dual relationship, against my license code of ethics.*

She replied,

> *Where does it say that about dual relationships of a social worker? Can you send me that document?*

I wrote,

> *Social workers must be licensed by the state and adhere to a set of professional standards.*

I attached a copy of the section of the Administrative Code covering dual relationships before I hit Send.

Kim responded,

> *It still seems unclear to me.*

I suggested,

> *Why don't we meet to talk about it?*

She did not respond about meeting but acknowledged during a staff meeting later the same week that social workers were licensed by the state, and no one could be a social worker unless they had a license.

I asked for a brief, impromptu timeslot during the same staff meeting to discuss my job description with the rest of the staff, thinking I could help them better understand the value the social work role brought to the team. I read them my job description and discussed some of its elements in detail.

I also introduced the problem of dual relationships. To provide effective counseling to clients, it is often necessary to involve their family members. And since these family members were also colleagues of mine, it presented boundary issues or conflicts of interest violating the codes of my profession. It made me sad that I could not be of support to them in my role as social worker if their family members needed agency services, but I was bound to the codes through my licensure.

Several colleagues said they would let me know when our clients could benefit from meeting with me. That made me feel good.

After the meeting, I sought out a coworker and asked her for feedback. She said she was not aware that staff family members as agency clients represented a dual relationship for me. So it was not just Kim who was unaware of my concerns.

I felt vindicated for speaking up.

## Educate without Alienating: Speaking Up Effectively (Reflections on Alicia's Story)

• • •

To Alicia, hearing "I can be the social worker" from her new supervisor, Kim, was an emotional trigger. This represented an ongoing issue for her. An uninformed outsider might assume Kim was simply unaware of the formal licensure required of social workers. Within a hierarchical health organization, however, where professional role boundaries are upheld to protect patients, Alicia expected her supervisor to know this. Instead, Kim seemed aware of the role distinction of nurse but not of social worker.

When her new supervisor did not acknowledge the unique advanced training and skills of social workers, Alicia began to wonder if Kim felt she was easily replaceable. This led her to feeling undervalued. These emotions clearly influenced Alicia's perceptions of Kim. Unless Alicia questioned her emotional response and assumptions, the potential for disruption, suspicion, and distrust between them was inevitable.

Fortunately, Alicia made good use of journaling in clearing her negative emotions and in identifying and amplifying her positive emotions. Uncensored journaling allowed her to dig below the surface of her reaction and look for effective ways of dealing with the troublesome issue. Working through her emotional response was a crucial first step. It gave her new options for dealing with her dilemma—that's when she first had the idea of making a presentation to the staff about the role of social workers.

Alicia consciously used herself in some ways. How to maintain her integrity as a social worker seemed to be the driving question for her throughout. And after journaling, she accepted responsibility for her own possible contribution by questioning whether her own arrogance might have been a contributing factor in her brief initial interaction with Kim.

Alicia also recognized her power in the situation. At no time did she throw up her hands and decide that since Kim had more formal power, there was nothing she, Alicia, could do. Instead, she sought expert advice outside the organization by consulting with her former clinical social work supervisor.

When Kim failed to follow up on Alicia's suggestion of meeting to discuss the issue of dual relationships, Alicia could easily have interpreted the topic as something Kim didn't want to talk about, an undiscussable. But it was important to Alicia, and she chose to address it directly in the staff meeting. In doing so, she demonstrated a growth mindset; that is, she believed her colleagues were capable of change.

It was to Alicia's credit that she looked past the single individual, Kim, and saw an opportunity to initiate change throughout the organization. Her earlier emotional processing work was her commitment to personal change. But she also wanted her colleagues on board. She decided to try to get them there by sharing more details about her profession, the constraints placed on her by professional standards, and ways she could (and could not) be of service to colleagues and clients.

As Alicia discovered from feedback after her presentation to the staff, Kim was not the only one unaware of the services she provided or potential conflicts of interest. There was a larger void of information about her role as a clinical social worker.

By providing more information about that role and clearing up misconceptions about dual relationships, she increased the likelihood of her peers' referral of clients to her when appropriate. She effected change in the organization that would outlast her tenure there.

. . .

# Conscious Change Principles and Skills in This Chapter

■ *Clear Emotions*
- Avoid emotional suppression
- Clear your negative emotions
- Build your positive emotions

■ *Conscious Use of Self*
- Accept responsibility for your own contributions
- Maintain integrity
- Adopt a growth mindset
- Recognize your power and use it responsibly

■ *Initiate Change*
- Commit to personal change
- Emphasize changing systems, not just individuals
- Surface undiscussables
- Gain support of one person (or small group) at a time

# About Alicia

Alicia Beatrice received a Master of Social Work from the University of Houston Graduate College of Social Work. After an adventurous career track through several different helping professions, she continues to find purpose in her work as a therapist and entrepreneurial pursuits supporting Black and Brown women entrepreneurs. In her spare time, she enjoys movies, music, and spending time with her two sons.

She first learned the Conscious Change skills in a course taught by Dr. Latting in the Graduate College of Social Work at the University of Houston, then worked with her while completing her graduate internship.

## CHAPTER 8.

# Clearing Emotions
# Can Be a Daunting Task

## By Carole Marmell

Photo © Karen Bernstein

I didn't murder anyone last night. I do admit to having murderous fantasies, though. More realistically (given that I'm a wouldn't-hurt-a-flea, can't-stand-the-sight-of-blood person), I had fantasies of a devastating laser-focused attack email that would draw blood. I've always taken pride in my rapier skills with words.

But I didn't do it. This is why.

## The Group Rules. Who Rules the Group?

I head up a group of Democratic women in a very red county who meet monthly. In my role as chair, I keep a tight rein on the membership list to avoid internet trolls, who are active and numerous. For that reason I never give out the location of our meetings ahead of time, and our Facebook group is private.

One month, one of the members—I'll call her Harriet—decided we could benefit from an increase in membership. While I admit this is always a great idea, she also decided, without my input, to invite several new people to our next meeting and, in doing so, gave them the details of when and where we were convening. Giving out our location without vetting is risky.

The result—good and bad—was a doubling of the planned attendance. Good, because it was great to have so many like-minded women coming together. Bad, because we weren't prepared for such an increase in attendance and the new members hadn't been screened.

The situation left me fit to be tied. My initial impulse was to unleash a scathing email to Harriet, but I stopped myself.

*Maybe sending an email while I'm so angry is unwise,* I told myself.

I heard Jean Latting's voice in my head: *What results will you get if you send her that email? What results do you want to get?*

*Well, my outbursts in the past have often caused grief,* I admitted to the Jean in my head, *which usually accelerates the conflict. I think I've finally realized how catering to my emotions without considering other perspectives is a fast track to further conflict. Since this is a completely volunteer organization and the cause is so important, I'd like to avoid that if I can.*

*What might you do instead?* my imaginary Jean asked.

*In my work as content editor for Leading Consciously, I've seen you repeatedly describe the skills of clearing emotions and testing assumptions in the blogs and other materials,* I replied. *I understand the skills intellectually but have always been skeptical of my ability to actually use them. Maybe I'll try some of them to do some emotional clearing . . . even though it seems daunting.*

## Clearing the Anger

And it *was* daunting. I felt entirely justified in my outrage and wanted to sound off. It was easy to believe in the virtue of my anger. In truth, I was attached to my emotions and my sense of righteousness. I also knew from my social work training that trying to simply replace strong negative emotions with calm ones often leaves an emotional hole.

Clearing my anger was more difficult than I expected, however . . . like being told not to scratch a mosquito bite. I wanted to respond *right now!* I wanted my resentment to dissipate *immediately.*

Instead, I remembered what I had read and been told: I waited. Something would come to me if I held off. I decided to concentrate not on Harriet's personality—which grated on me—but instead on what she was trying to do.

I was quite sure that she didn't say to herself, *Oh, I think I'll be annoying and violate Carole's norms.* More likely she was thinking, *What can I do to boost membership?*

Engaging in a little introspection, I asked myself, *Why are my rules inviolable? Have I ever shared them? If we are big 'D' Democrats in a small 'd' democracy, where do I get the authority to demand total obedience?*

This led me to think about what I wanted to achieve personally and through the group, rather than continuing to center attention on my grievance. I recognized that I needed to shift from "What do I want to do in the heat of the moment?" to "What is it I wish to accomplish?" It took a while, but contemplating that last question yielded several answers:

- I wish to not look like a jerk.
- I wish to not sever my connections.
- I wish to be able to work peacefully with everyone.
- I wish for this to not happen again.
- I wish to hear the other side.

In looking at this list, it became clear that I needed to accept the situation gracefully and let go of my outrage before responding to Harriet. And accepting the situation, thinking about it from a different perspective, *did* help me clear my anger. I knew that remaining furious would not serve me well.

## A New Understanding

With this new understanding, I wrote Harriet a calm and reasonable email:

> *I appreciate your enthusiasm for increasing our membership and attendance at the next meeting. I do wish you would have consulted with me before issuing the invitations, however. My major concern*

*is the need to keep a tight leash on membership, attendance, and information about our meetings. So far, we have avoided protests or other public displays in reaction to our political beliefs in a county where the majority doesn't share our views. I'd like that to continue. A secondary concern is the stress caused by the ballooning size of the guest list and having to scramble to accommodate additional people at the last minute.*

Harriet responded to my second concern,

*What can I do to help handle the larger attendance?*

I wrote back,

*I appreciate your offer of assistance, but I think the hostess and I now have it under control. We'll be sure to let you know if we need anything.*

I also made a mental note to myself to start an online discussion with the membership about what might be a good process and a good set of rules for inviting new members going forward.

In retrospect, I realized I had unknowingly followed the ABCDE model developed by Martin Seligman:[1]

**A:** Adversity (the triggering situation). The triggering situation in this instance was Harriet's decision to invite people to the next meeting of our group without checking with me.

**B:** Beliefs (one's interpretation of someone's actions). My initial take on her motives was that she was acting irresponsibly and not following my unspoken chain of command.

**C:** Consequences (resulting behavior). I became angry and upset about the possible infiltration of our group.

**D:** Disputation (arguing). In examining my reaction further, though, I realized I was acting out of false assumptions about my role and responsibilities. Were there more small 'd' democratic ways of managing the group? I also considered a benevolent explanation for Harriet's behavior—she was simply being enthusiastic about increasing our membership. And to be fair, there were no formal guidelines about inviting new members.

**E:** Energizing (the effect of redirecting one's thoughts). Seriously questioning all the assumptions that fed into my initial, strong emotional reaction allowed me to rethink the situation and react to it from a place of calm.

My understanding of what Seligman is advising (I'm not an expert here) is that we falsely think consequences flow from the *facts of* a situation, when often the outcomes are a result of our *beliefs about* a situation—which may or may not be accurate. Rather than arguing about the situation, thinking it through from alternate perspectives might allow us to discover the core of the problem and to consider other points of view. This, in turn, allows us to redirect our thoughts in a more positive direction. As a result, we are energized and centered.

I certainly found this to be the case: when my anger dissipated, the world felt a little emptier, a little less exciting, but very self-affirming. I can still learn new skills. I can still handle situations properly. I can find another way. I slept well that night.

### It Worked! Clarifying Desired Results Rather than Giving in to Immediate Emotional Response (Reflections on Carole's Story)

• • •

Carole's story is a cautionary tale of the vast difference between merely understanding the Conscious Change skills and doing the more difficult work of using them. In her role as content editor for Leading Consciously, one of her tasks is editing the biweekly blogs published by Leading Consciously. Part of that work includes identifying the Conscious Change principles and skills illustrated by each blog post or interview. So Carole had a working intellectual familiarity with the skills needed, but she admitted that she found it difficult to put them into actual practice.

When one of the members of her Democratic women's group, Harriet, invited new members without first seeking approval, Carole had an immediate and strong emotional reaction, primarily of anger. Recognizing her strong desire to act out of her emotions, she decided to instead slow down and reflect on the situation rather than giving in to her initial impulse to send Harriet a scathing email.

Carole knew from past experience that catering to her emotions without considering alternatives was a "fast track to further conflict." So despite seeing the task as "daunting," she looked for ways to clear her negative emotions.

She started by looking for alternative explanations for Harriet's actions—a move from being in the answer to being in the question. Rather than sticking with her original conclusion that Harriet was acting irresponsibly, Carole was willing to consider multiple points of view. She entertained the possibility that Harriet's actions might have stemmed from enthusiasm about increasing the organization's membership.

Equally as important, Carole was also introspective about the source of her initial reaction to Harriet's actions. Shifting from thinking "What do I want to do?" to "What do I wish to accomplish?" led to a major reframing of the situation. It allowed her to recognize how she had, perhaps unknowingly, contributed to the situation by not articulating her expectations regarding adding members. Her list of desired results also reminded her to identify with her democratic small 'd' values rather than with her emotions.

And, to give her even more credit, she immediately saw that she should raise the issue with the membership at some future point . . . a systems view rather than assuming it was simply an interpersonal conflict between herself and Harriet. This is an excellent example of recognizing her power and consciously choosing to use it responsibly. Clearing her emotions before sending an email to Harriet allowed her to maintain her integrity as leader of this group.

In retrospect, Carole realized she had used a version of the Seligman method of disputation (ABCDE) to clear her negative emotions. She literally tested her assumptions by articulating them and then arguing against them. The Seligman method is an especially effective emotional clearing tool for people oriented more toward thinking than feeling.

There was a "happy ending" to Carole's story, too, in the way she gave herself credit for having done the right thing and acknowledged her ability to learn new skills.

• • •

## Conscious Change Principles and Skills in This Chapter

- *Test Negative Assumptions*
  - Move from the answer into the question
  - Look for multiple points of view
  - Consciously test your negative assumptions

- *Clear Emotions*
  - Identify with your values, not your emotions
  - Clear your negative emotions
  - Build your positive emotions

- *Conscious Use of Self*
  - Accept responsibility for your own contributions
  - Maintain integrity
  - Seek to understand others' perspectives
  - Recognize your power and use it responsibly
  - Build resilience through self-affirmation

- *Initiate Change*
  - Emphasize changing systems, not just individuals

## About Carole

Carole Marmell received her BA from Tufts University and MSW from the Graduate School of Social Work at the University of Houston. She worked as a social worker in various medical settings until finding her passion in hospice care. After retirement, she returned to her previous career as a proofreader and copy editor for her most inspiring social work professor, Jean Latting. In her leisure time, she corrects typos on the internet.

## CHAPTER 9.

# What You See Depends
# on the Lens You Use

## *By Steven Hayes*

Photo © Steven Hayes

I worked in a large freestanding full-service HIV clinic in Houston as a medical case manager, assigned to work with young adults, ages seventeen to twenty-four. Unlike many HIV clinics, this one had medical doctors on staff, so clients could view the clinic as their medical home. The clinic offered comprehensive health care, including psychiatric services. Almost anything an HIV patient might need medically was present in the building.

My role was to connect patients with services and resources. In the process, however, I ended up doing far more counseling than anything else. There were lots of relationship issues and disclosure of HIV issues. The young people were trying to figure themselves out. Disenfranchised individuals have poor adherence to HIV medication schedules and appointments and a low rate of returning to therapy.

## Meet Them Where They Are . . . Slang and All

I believe, in every sense of the word, in meeting clients where they are; in my practice this meant cultural competency in the use of language. It was normal for me to have pretty graphic conversations with patients, particularly regarding their bodies and sex.

One of my clients was having a difficult time, in every way possible: housing, employment, relationships. He would end up coming to see me, as many of them would, just to talk—sometimes two or three times a week. It was almost as if the clinic were a second home, a setting in which they could feel comfortable.

One of the main reasons for nonadherence to HIV treatment protocol was fear of judgment—worry that someone was going to see them, someone was going to judge them, consider them "nasty" (pick your word). But none of the patients felt judged by me.

So the fact that I was able to get them to come in for appointments, take their meds regularly, keep coming in for group therapy, or just come in to hang out was a measure of success. Now some might have seen my interactions with these young adults as questionable—my conversations with them were more open and franker than many in the building were used to. I might, for example, tell one of the young men to "sit down!" Observers would be shocked since these were young adults, not children, but our relationships were such that I could be a bit more abrupt and confrontational with them than most.

A client to whom I've given the name David came to see me and reported, "I'm dripping."

"Again?" I asked. "What have you been doing?"

"Nothing."

"How is it that you think you can keep coming here saying you're not being sexually active and then complain of sexually transmitted diseases?"

"Well, I don't know."

"Look," I responded, "you're being a ho. I need you to stop being a ho. Can we just talk about that?"

He laughed. I laughed. And then we got into a conversation as to why he was being as sexually promiscuous as he was. I had learned from previous conversations that no one had ever educated him on sex, at all. This was not uncommon. People were having sex indiscriminately and didn't know why.

They didn't know how, nor did they know who. So many of the conversations I had were often quite graphic and, by some definitions, vulgar—but using polite words like *penis* and *anus* didn't cut it much of the time. I kept my language as appropriate as I could, but it was always borderline. I knew that. I owned it and had no problem defending it since my numbers were so good.

When I first started, there were five appointment slots daily. And they were lucky if one person showed up. By the time I left there were eighteen slots, and we were often overbooked to eighteen. Adherence to medication and show rates for appointments had been 30 percent before I arrived at the clinic. My rates were 80 percent. People were coming and they were taking their medication. Part of it was just the entertainment value of coming and having these odd conversations with me. But I knew it was my relationship with the patients that created the success.

I knew because I had been doing this for nearly thirty years. I was on the first mobile testing unit ever in the country. The Minority AIDS Project in Los Angeles started mobile testing with sex workers in the park. I was doing this when I was nineteen years old, long before I thought about it as a profession.

## Balancing Professionalism with Genuine Engagement

One thing I think is important as a professional is to remember those things that lead to success and kind of codify what might otherwise be considered unprofessional, figuring out a way to actually serve the population in a way they're going to receive it, and still be able to keep your job and not mess with the reputation of the organization you're working for. All of this has to be balanced. And it's a really hard thing to do. Really hard.

David came in on Friday, telling me his symptoms were back again.

"Are you still dealing with the same individuals?"

"Well, yeah."

"So, you introduced someone new to the pool?"

"Well, yeah, I had to."

"No, David, you did not *have* to. Why did you do it?"

So we had a conversation and, really, he didn't have to. It was just his unthinking routine—he was going to wake up, turn on his phone, check the various phone apps for where one can find sex, and then sex was going to happen. It was just the norm. His mind and body were operating in a "cog" system, on autopilot, and this is just what he did without thought of person or anything.

## A Nurse with an Attitude—or Was It?

Fridays were notoriously slow days at the clinic. It was around one o'clock, the clinic was quiet, and I needed to see if I could get him in to see a nurse practitioner to get the needed treatment. As we walked through the building to the medical care unit, there was really nobody there. We continued our conversation, using some colorful language—nothing really horrible, and not loud or rambunctious, but for us, a normal conversation about his behavior. A nurse I will call Jenny was at the nurse's station.

I approached the nurse's station and said, "David really needs to see the nurse practitioner this afternoon. Can he be seen right away?"

"Yes," she replied. "I'm sure they can see him. Just give me a minute."

While we waited, David and I continued our conversation, peppered as before with graphic language. After a few minutes, Jenny interrupted us and said loudly and sternly, "You two are being quite inappropriate! I've just never heard anybody talk like that before. Ever!"

What I wanted to say in response, but didn't, was, "Well, I don't know who you know, but that's how they all talk. And why are you yelling at me in front of people? Why are you yelling at me at all? Much less in front of people?"

I didn't like being corrected publicly, in front of the patient. And I really didn't think it was her place to say anything. That's where my head was. But I bit my tongue and got his appointment. I went back to my office and David went on about his business.

There's a backdrop here. There is generally some animosity between social workers and nursing staff, a sort of tension existing in virtually all hospital settings. So this was not the first time a nurse had said something to me that didn't quite rub me the right way.

I complained to my supervisor about this latest incident, "Could you please do something about Jenny's attitude? I can't keep serving the patients while fighting what feels like a battle against the nurses."

"Well, you're the social worker and therapist," my supervisor replied, as she had before. "You're supposed to know how to talk to people and make things work. You go figure it out."

And I thought to myself, *Well, hell, they're on the clock and they're professionals too. What kind of training do they have that they don't know you shouldn't chastise a coworker in front of others? That is so offensive to me.*

Out loud, I said, "I ain't got nothing to say to that woman. And you better tell her not to say nothing to me. And that's how we're handling it because I'm not her therapist. I'm the case manager, not her supervisor, so it will not fall on me to do any corrective action with this woman."

Over the next several weeks, I simply avoided Jenny when I could. My office was on the second floor and she always worked on the fourth floor, so there was really no reason for us to interact unless I initiated it. I went to other nurses when I needed to get something done.

## Openness and Sharing Lead to New Understanding

Then one day, I saw her right by my office. I don't know why she happened to be there, but she was.

I called her over, saying, "Come holler at me right quick."

"Yes, brother. Yes. What do you need?" she responded loudly.

In my head, I'm saying, *What do you mean 'brother'? If I was your brother, you wouldn't have treated me like you did.*

Instead, I said, "I'm gonna need you to fix your tone. Why do you yell? Do you know how aggravating that is? Do you know how many times I've heard people complain about you? And I didn't say nothing about it, but now you done did it to me. So, I got something to say about it and what you not going to do any more is yell at me. At a minimum, your tone need to be changed."

She looked at me and simply said, "I'm Nigerian. That's how we talk."

That stopped me dead in my tracks. I had not previously considered that her tone might have been an "ethnic yell," if that's what we want to call it. I had to ask myself, *Is hers a normal yell, or just not normal to me?*

"Okay," I said to her, "but what do you think? Maybe you could be a little less yelling?"

"Brother, I would never say anything to offend you. I know how much you love these kids. You do your job and you do so much good. But do you have to use the language, though?"

"Actually, yes, I do. By using their language, I become them. But I'm also aware that I am becoming them, so I'm able to keep the proper boundaries. I really am purposeful in how I interact with the young people. It's not that I'm just some idiot walking around with random words coming out of my mouth, unaware of what the words mean or how they might be perceived. Can you understand that?"

"I do understand what you're saying, but I don't like the crude language. I never have and I never will. We just don't talk like that. I'm old," she said, pointing to her sure-enough gray hair. "Could you maybe just do it in your office instead?"

I realized that after coming at her as hard as I had, she had still heard and understood me. And the way I came at her probably didn't surprise her. She'd seen me be assertive, even blunt, on a regular basis. She had to have. But now she had demonstrated a certain amount of acceptance of me, which made me able to hear her. I realized that both of us had felt disrespected in the situation.

After this, our relationship improved. Every now and then I would tease her, threaten to say something that might be offensive to her. She'd roll her eyes in response and keep going with what she was doing. Not long after that she left the HIV clinic. She just disappeared one day. I didn't know what happened to her.

Sometime later, I too left the clinic and took a position as a therapist in a psychiatric hospital. Here, all the nurses are Nigerian, every one of them. And when I work with patients, they often complain to me about them. So I tell them about me and the Nigerian nurse at the HIV clinic.

"You have to listen to the words they're saying and decide if the words match up with their tone. If they don't, there might be something else going on. You've got to cut them some slack."

Then one day, walking down the hall, whom did I run into but Jenny! We were both surprised and greeted each other with a big hug. She had been working in this hospital since she left the clinic. And it turns out, she often tells the story about our interaction too, sometimes in my presence.

"I remember when Steven brought this young man to the nursing station to make an appointment, he was carrying on a real conversation with him, looking out for him. He loved his patients. He took care of them better than anybody else had ever taken care of them. But he can also be rather raw at times."

That's it. She tells only that part of the story, with no mention of our later interaction. What she remembered is that I was speaking to the patient, and it made her feel a certain way. I was the one emotionally invested in the interaction, not she. She also sees it through a nursing lens—when she remembers the story, it is about the patient. I see it through a social work lens—when I remember the story, it is about our relationship.

## Surfacing Differences Can Strengthen Relationships (Reflections on Steven's Story)

• • •

Steven's attitudes and actions toward his clients clearly illustrate his conscious use of self. In his own words, the key was "figuring out a way to actually serve the population in a way they're going to receive it, and still be able to keep your job and not mess with the reputation of the organization you're working for."

Steven drew on past experience for knowledge about his clients (their assumptions, feelings, and differences) and how they were likely to perceive him and the clinic. This awareness shaped the nature of his interactions with them, made him deliberate in his choice of words and behaviors.

He had learned the importance of seeing things through the eyes of these young HIV clients—he put himself in their shoes and related to them accordingly. He phrased this as "using their language, I become them." Yet he was also able to hold a type of dual consciousness by "becoming them" while maintaining "proper boundaries." Steven also engaged in inquiry effectively—he asked a lot of questions and was unaccepting of the clients' initial attempts to avoid answering them.

By understanding these young people's experiences, motivations, and fear of judgment, Steven was able to positively influence their behaviors—get them to keep their appointments at the clinic, stay on their HIV medication schedules, and participate in therapy. He clearly believed they were capable of change and seemed determined to help them do so.

Steven's story also illustrates giving and receiving feedback—it was not always done artfully, but it worked. The nurse, Jenny, engaged in what felt to Steven like a putdown in front of a client. Steven "bit [his] tongue" in the moment but later tried to get his supervisor to intervene. When she brushed him off, Steven didn't give up. Instead, he took advantage of a later opportunity to initiate discussion with the nurse—"Come holler at me," he said.

When he gave Jenny feedback about the impact of her behavior on him, she responded, "I'm Nigerian. That's how we talk." He was immediately willing to reconsider his interpretation of what had happened. So, while the feedback wasn't by the book, it had a successful outcome. Both listened to one another, which went a long way toward improving their relationship. He discovered Jenny wasn't judging him as harshly as he had thought—she appreciated his rapport with patients, just disliked the language he used with them.

Steven also quickly accepted the idea that Jenny's level and tone of voice might represent a cultural difference. He was willing to acknowledge that the language he used bothered her without feeling compelled to change what was working with the clients. They implicitly agreed to disagree about this—it even became a joke between them. And they grew closer as a result. If people can joke about cultural differences, it's a pretty good sign they have resolved them.

In his advice to patients complaining about Nigerian nurses in the psychiatric hospital, Steven is really cautioning them about their stereotypes and bias, as well as revealing how his own previous ones had distorted communication between him and Jenny.

Steven further understood that differences in the professional cultures of nursing and social work influenced their separate reactions to the interaction: "She also sees it through a nursing lens—when she remembers the story, it is about the patient. I see it through a social work lens—when I remember the story, it is about our relationship." So there were multiple differences operating simultaneously, a not-uncommon situation. What *is* uncommon is how they were able to surface their differences and appreciate where the other was coming from in a way that strengthened their relationship.

• • •

# Conscious Change Principles and Skills in This Chapter

- ***Test Negative Assumptions***
  - Move from the answer into the question
  - Look for multiple points of view
  - Check to see if you are making cultural assumptions

- ***Build Effective Relationships***
  - Engage in powerful listening
  - Develop skills in inquiry and openness
  - Learn how to give, receive, and seek feedback
  - Distinguish intent from impact

- ***Bridge Differences***
  - Check for stereotyping tendencies, unconscious bias, and lack of awareness in your behavior, especially as a dominant-group member

- ***Conscious Use of Self***
  - Accept responsibility for your own contributions
  - Seek to understand others' perspectives
  - Adopt a growth mindset
  - Recognize your power and use it responsibly

- ***Initiate Change***
  - Surface undiscussables

# About Steven

As a sociologist, Steven has taught a variety of classes, including Social Problems, American Pop Culture, LGBT Perspectives, Minority Relations, and a variety of social work classes as a visiting professor at Lincoln University in Missouri. As a licensed master social worker, he has acted in the role of therapist, medical case manager, and supervisor of community health workers. Steven has assisted incarcerated individuals who have spent as many as twenty-five years behind the walls to successfully reenter society. He has helped navigate patients to healthier living and through insurance and other barriers that can hinder progress in health and life.

Steven's research interests include best practices in psychotherapy, Black masculinities and shifting roles in African American families, love styles, and learning strategies. Steven uses motivational interviewing and a strengths-based approach to cognitive behavioral therapy. In addition to client and student success, Steven includes the search for joy, peace, and clarity as part of his mission.

## CHAPTER 10.

# I Need to Understand
# Where She's Coming From

*By Ashley Ochoa*

Photo © Laurice Larsen

I was preparing for maternity leave from a small company for which I had worked since it opened. I reported to the executive director of the organization (whom I will designate as Phil) and was the person responsible for much of the institutional history, organization, and leadership communication. My leave would last almost a full quarter, hopefully longer, so I could be with my baby. Since my staff were already at full capacity, Phil agreed to hire someone to fill in for me while I was gone. He even generously hired the new employee two months before I was scheduled to leave so I would have ample time to train them.

## Even a Great Hire Can Be Stressful

Human Resources (HR) helped me find and hire the perfect person. I really couldn't have asked for a better individual to fill in for me—and maybe even replace me permanently if I decided to leave full-time employment for my family. The new employee, called Marcy in this story, also had a background in accounting, an area that needed additional support. She was hired with the expectation of working with me 80 percent of the time and 20 percent with another supervisor.

A note here on the chain of command since it can be confusing: I reported to Phil, the executive director, so Marcy would be under his supervision for 80 percent of her time. Marcy would also report to Cecil [fictitious name], who did double duty as both the HR manager and accounting manager, for the other 20 percent of her time. Cecil also reported to Phil.

I did not have a good relationship with Cecil. She didn't seem to like me, no matter what I did or how hard I tried to cooperate with her. Her dual supervisory responsibility for accounting and HR made everything more difficult. But Marcy had worked with Cecil before, at a previous company, and they were already friends. I felt like a new kid on my own block.

Training Marcy was somewhat stressful. Because of the dual-reporting relationship in such a small organization, I was required to interact with Cecil more than usual. I felt as if I were walking on eggshells with her. Marcy picked up on the tension, even though I made it a point to avoid criticizing Cecil—not just because they were friends, but because Cecil was a member of the management team and Marcy's other supervisor. I felt it important for them to have their own good working relationship moving forward.

## Dealing with the Unexpected

About a month before my maternity leave was scheduled to begin, Cecil unexpectedly turned in her two weeks' notice. What had been a steady-paced training process became a frenzied battle of fluctuating and competing priorities for Marcy's time.

The Monday afternoon of Cecil's last week, Marcy came into my office and timidly asked, "Can we talk for a few minutes?"

"Sure," I said, putting aside what I was working on and gesturing for her to sit down.

"I have some questions about what my job will be when Cecil leaves. And questions about whether these different responsibilities will mean an increase in pay."

"As far as I know, your job responsibilities won't be changing," I responded, a little surprised by her question. "But I can discuss this with Phil. Maybe there's something I don't know."

For the rest of that week, when I had time, I continued to have brief conversations with Phil, Marcy, and Cecil, trying to get us all on the same page regarding what Marcy's job and pay were going to be moving forward. Finally, late Friday afternoon, Marcy, Phil, and I met and talked it out—Cecil didn't attend this meeting because it was her last day on the job. I felt all the questions had been verbally cleared up but still sensed that Marcy seemed confused and uncertain. Unfortunately, she left immediately after the meeting, so I didn't get a chance to process with her.

## Trust Your Instincts and Be Conscious, and Clarity Will Be Revealed

Marcy's seeming uneasiness weighed so heavily on my mind, I did something out of the norm—I called her on my way home. It was 7:00 or 8:00 p.m., already well into a weekend evening. I almost talked myself out of it several times.

My internal conversation went like this: *I mean, really, we've been talking about these issues nearly every day for the entire week, yet it still doesn't feel resolved. What is one nervous phone call from me, on her personal time, going to accomplish?*

*Maybe I should wait until I see her again on Monday,* I continued in my self-talk. *But somehow, I feel that in waiting, I'll miss this window of opportunity. I need to try to figure out what she found so unclear—while it's fresh on both our minds. I really feel like something more is going on here. I need to understand where she's coming from.*

So I made the phone call.

I didn't really know what to say when I called, so I just started with something general: "Hey, Marcy. I'm sorry to bother you at home, but I wanted to call and follow up after our meeting. It felt like some things were still unclear or unresolved."

"I don't mind. In fact, I appreciate your call." Marcy didn't hesitate, getting right to the point. "I just don't understand why I'm not getting an increase in pay when I'll be doing your work full-time when you leave and the accounting work too."

I was surprised because we had never discussed this arrangement. "But you won't be doing my work full-time when I go on leave. You'll be spending 80 percent of your time on what I trained you for and the other 20 percent of your time on accounting work."

"That's not what Cecil told me when I was hired," she said. "And then when I ran into her just before our meeting this afternoon, she gave me new information different from that."

"Really? What did Cecil tell you?"

"When I was first interviewed for the job, she said I would be working on the 80/20 time split until you went on maternity leave. Then after you left, I would be 100 percent filling in for you, and she would take over the accounting responsibilities again. So after Cecil resigned but you kept talking about the split of responsibilities in the same way, I was confused. Today, she said that since no one was replacing her, it looked like I'd have to continue doing the accounting stuff in addition to doing all your work."

Eureka! I finally understood the disconnect. Marcy had been misinformed about her job since the initial interview. Phil and I had the same expectations for the new employee, but Cecil had conveyed a different impression to Marcy. This misunderstanding caused an upset that might have lost us a valuable employee and irretrievable months of training time.

At this point, all I could do was tell Marcy that what she'd been told by Cecil had never been the plan and apologize for the misinformation leading to some pretty gut-clenching conversations.

"I'm so sorry you were misinformed by Cecil," I told Marcy. "And I'm sorry I didn't take the time to have a longer and more in-depth conversation with you about this when you first came to me earlier in the week. Instead, you endured some uncomfortable conversations because I didn't fully understand what had happened."

"I didn't want to bring it up anymore during the meetings this week because I was afraid of what people would think of me," she confided. "And I'm really nervous that Phil or some of the other managers already think I don't want to do this job, or that I can't do it. I *can* do it and I'm willing to do it, but it just didn't seem fair, given the circumstances."

I was quick to reassure her. "Marcy, no one questioned your capability to do the work. We wouldn't have hired you otherwise. Yes, some things changed along the way, but the plan for what you'll be doing is the same as it was in the beginning. And you've shown time and again that you're willing to do the work. Based on what you just told me, I have a much better understanding of your concerns. I'll call Phil right now to explain everything. It's too important to leave until Monday. When I do, I'll remind him how committed and willing you are."

The call ended with both of us on the same page. I felt relieved, as if we'd achieved a major accomplishment—because we had.

I was so glad I'd spent time trying to form a meaningful relationship with Marcy throughout the months of training . . . and pleased that we had built enough trust between us to make it possible for her to come to me and initiate this rather difficult conversation. I was glad, too, that I'd stayed attuned to her uneasiness and taken the risk of calling her at home. It took the Friday-night phone call to break through to a new level of confidence and understanding.

## *If It's Bothering You, Do Something: Another Way to Use Power Responsibly (Reflections on Ashley's Story)*

• • •

Training her maternity leave replacement was stressful for Ashley because the new hire, Marcy, would be reporting to two supervisors—the executive director of the organization as well as the accounting manager. Despite having a troublesome relationship with Cecil, the accounting manager (and the hiring manager), Ashley chose to operate out of her values rather than her emotions and was careful to monitor what she said about Cecil. She didn't want to stand in the way of Marcy developing healthy relationships with both supervisors.

Ashley was clear from the beginning that Marcy would be splitting her time between two responsibilities—80 percent doing what Ashley normally did and 20 percent carrying out accounting tasks. Marcy, on the other hand, seemed a bit confused and misinformed about this. Ashley tried to address Marcy's confusion while remaining curious about its source—a good illustration of staying in the question rather than the answer.

When Cecil unexpectedly resigned, Marcy went to Ashley to try to get clarity. Ashley immediately set aside the work she was doing to give full attention to Marcy, an attribute of powerful listening skills. During this meeting, Marcy broached the uncomfortable topic, despite her worry that bringing it up might reflect negatively on her competence. Ashley also deserves credit for establishing the kind of environment that allowed Marcy to take this risk.

It is interesting to compare Marcy's two statements of the problem:

> "I have some questions about what my job will be when Cecil leaves. And questions about whether these different responsibilities will mean an increase in pay." (This was when she was in Ashley's office.)

Compare this to: "I just don't understand why I'm not getting an increase in pay when I'll be doing your work full-time when you leave and the accounting work too." (This was when Ashley called her at home.)

The second statement was clearly more precise and transparent. Could this clarity have been obtained during the first meeting if Ashley had asked more questions, tried harder to coax Marcy into saying more clearly what she meant? Ashley seemed to think so—she apologized to Marcy later for not taking the time during their earlier meeting to explore her confusion in more depth. This was understandable, perhaps, due to the pressures of time and a myriad of things to handle before she left, but Ashley was missing that key piece of information, which led to more time spent in multiple frustrating meetings.

Ashley made good use of the Conscious Use of Self principle. It kept nagging at her that there was something she was missing, something she needed to understand. She continued searching for her own contribution to the confusion, instead of placing all blame for the uncertainty on Marcy.

She found it difficult to put herself in Marcy's shoes but tried—and stayed attuned to her own uneasiness: "I need to understand where she's coming from." Later, Ashley empathized with Marcy's having had to endure "uncomfortable conversations."

Ashley was able to get past her misgivings and place the phone call to Marcy. Simply identifying and voicing her present emotional state likely helped her clear it.

This was also an example of Ashley understanding her power in the situation and using it responsibly. Marcy, as a nondominant in that setting, would not have felt comfortable calling Ashley after hours. In fact, until that phone call, Marcy was not able or willing to state clearly what was bothering her. She was afraid she would be unfairly judged as complaining or incompetent. Ashley's unusual phone call to Marcy after hours demonstrated that she (Ashley) cared, opening the door Marcy needed to feel safe enough to admit what had really been troubling her.

The phone conversation was quite revelatory, laying bare the key to Marcy's confusion. She had been misinformed about expectations from the beginning. We remain clueless regarding Cecil's motives. She may have meant no harm or been under a false impression herself—but the miscommunication had a definite negative impact.

Instead of lowering her opinion of Marcy because of her confusion and lack of clarity in expressing her concerns, Ashley focused on the strengths Marcy brought to the organization. She also provided strength-focused feedback directly to Marcy, noting her willingness and ability to do the work during the training period. Ashley's offer to call Phil about Marcy's responsibilities, instead of expecting Marcy to do it herself or waiting until after the weekend, was an example of support for a nondominant-group member (in this case, hierarchically).

This story vividly demonstrates how the smallest misunderstanding can create havoc in relationships and highlights how helpful the Conscious Change principles and skills can be in unearthing barriers to effective communication.

• • •

## Conscious Change Principles and Skills in This Chapter

- *Test Negative Assumptions*
  - Move from the answer to the question

- *Clear Emotions*
  - Identify with your values, not your emotions
  - Clear your negative emotions

- *Build Effective Relationships*
  - Engage in powerful listening
  - Develop skills in inquiry and openness

- Learn how to give, receive, and seek feedback
- Distinguish intent from impact
- Apologize effectively

■ *Bridge Differences*
- As a dominant-group member, provide support to nondominant-group members

■ *Conscious Use of Self*
- Accept responsibility for your own contributions
- Seek to understand others' perspectives
- Focus on others' strengths
- Recognize your power and use it responsibly

■ *Initiate Change*
- Surface undiscussables

## About Ashley

Ashley Ochoa is a licensed master of social work in Houston, Texas. She earned her BSW from Brigham Young University–Idaho in 2009 and MSW from the University of Houston Graduate College of Social Work (GCSW) in 2011. At the GCSW, Ashley took Dr. Latting's leadership course and was introduced to the Conscious Change skills. The skills became a natural part of her work that evolved into management opportunities.

Ashley's work has primarily been with policies and organizations in the field of recovery from alcohol and other drugs. She was also a policy analyst with law enforcement and the Texas legislative session in 2011. In 2018, Ashley started teaching policy courses as an adjunct with the University of Houston GCSW and found a special place in her heart for teaching students on their social work journey. Ashley has served as a practicum instructor for over twenty-five interns. The Conscious Change skills have positively impacted Ashley's professional and personal relationships, and she seeks to strengthen them in herself and those around her.

## CHAPTER 11.

# De-escalate Tense and
# Dangerous Situations

*By Larry Hill*
*(with Eli Davis)*

Photo © University of Houston

I'm Eli Davis, and some time ago, I served a
graduate internship with Jean Latting. One day,
she told me she was working on a second book featuring stories by her
former students and clients. She asked, "Would you be willing to interview
one of them for the book?" Of course, I said yes.

"Where should I start?" Larry asked as we sat down for the interview.

"How about you walk me through one of the encounters where you
had a gun pointed at you?" I asked.

"This leads into the principles described in *Reframing Change*
perfectly," he replied. "I should clarify, however, that in my case the
officer's hand was on the gun, but the gun was not drawn. There are a lot
of times when guns *are* drawn. Those are the stories that receive attention
in the press. Mine didn't play out that way, though it could have."

Drawing her gun was the officer's implied next step. But Larry had
an opportunity to influence the situation and disarm her, metaphorically.

He explained, "There are some very specific steps I take when
encountering the police. But before I tell you about these, I want to give
you some context."

## Play It Cool and Try to Bridge Differences

Larry went on to describe his predominantly White, suburban neighborhood in Northwest Houston. It wasn't far from the spot where, just a few months earlier, an officer had been gunned down. Having moved there with his family early in the neighborhood's development, Larry had watched the community grow around him. As the area grew, he noticed a dramatic shift in the dynamics of neighborhood interactions. More to the point, perceptions of him as a young, dark-skinned Black male changed.

"I went from being inside the community to being on the fringe." He then recalled one of his first encounters with police in the neighborhood: "I was teaching at the University of Houston at the time. Ironically, I was preparing for a class entitled Overrepresentation of African American Males in the Criminal Justice System in Texas. I was sitting under a tree at a nearby lake, reading a book on arguments against the death penalty, when I heard a vehicle approaching.

"I looked up to see the local constable getting out of her vehicle and approaching. *Here we go again*, I thought to myself. *I've been through this before. What do I need to do to survive this situation?*"

He was all too aware that the Black Lives Matter movement and the Blue Lives Matter response were fresh in people's minds. This added intensity to an already-tense scenario. In a split second, the most basic question popped into his head: "Why?"

Larry is brilliant. He already knew the answer based on his academic expertise (he had taught a course in the Graduate School of Social Work using *Reframing Change* as the text), social justice orientation, his personal experiences while growing up, and the experiences of his family and friends.

"She may have thought I looked out of place. But the officer was doing her job by confirming that I posed no threat to anyone."

He spoke in a flat, pragmatic tone as he continued to walk me through his internal process: "My next move was to notice the details of how she was approaching me. I saw her hand ready on her weapon as she walked silently in my direction."

"So, what did you do?" I asked eagerly, even though I already knew the general outcome.

"I knew I had to engage first. That's my win. So I offered her a polite greeting, while reminding myself, *Don't stand up. Don't reach for your bag.*"

As the conversation began to unfold, the officer maintained a hand on her weapon. As Larry suspected, she had received several reports of a suspicious person in the neighborhood and was following up.

"My role was to play out this conversation as long as possible ... play it calm, play it cool, and try to bridge some of the differences.

"I recognized a disparity of power and authority, and my goal was to respectfully show I also had status worthy of respect, that I could engage at a level familiar and comfortable to her. I referred to my status as a research professor with a PhD and an expert in the criminal justice system. I was signaling to her that we could have an intelligent conversation, right the imbalance between us.

"As we kept talking, I noticed our conversation shifted toward more amicable career talk. Her energy began to shift, and eventually, so did her hand."

He understood that the officer was dominant in this situation, and he was nondominant. Her job was to protect the neighborhood. She had been alerted by residents to what they deemed "suspicious activity" and was fulfilling her role as a police officer to investigate. This answered his immediate why him/why now question.

I was riveted by Larry's story. Having been raised in a typical White middle-class neighborhood, I wanted to know what led Larry to make the choices he did. Specifically, I wondered why he didn't just ask her what it was about him or his behavior that warranted calling the authorities. As Larry explained to me, it wasn't the time to inquire about this, let alone a time to teach or argue. Those were privileges enjoyed by some that could cost *him* his life.

"My goal in that moment was to get home safely to my family," he stated bluntly. "I understood she had assumptions she was testing out, and I had a few of my own."

"Was there anything that would have/could have altered the situation?" I persisted. "Anything that could have been done differently, so as to create a safe space to question the officer's actions or facilitate a teachable moment?"

"No," he emphatically replied.

The undeniable conviction of his response startled me. It occurred to me that my questions likely stemmed from my own position as a White male (dominant in this society), but I was angry for him. I wanted action.

## The Risk/Reward Equation Was Clear

To illustrate why my propensity for action was far from appropriate, Larry shared another example of an encounter with the police, an eerily similar situation.

"I was at this same lake one evening a few months ago, hanging out with a well-meaning Latino friend. The same scenario occurred. But this time, as the officer approached, I could feel my friend growing upset and frustrated. As the patrol car slowed down and pulled over, my friend became noticeably huffy. As he grew more agitated and jittery, I let him know before the officer got out of the vehicle that I was handling this, and he was not to say anything."

Initially, the interaction was nonconfrontational. The officer requested they relocate, even though Larry and his friend were well within their rights to be there. Larry agreed but sensed his friend growing increasingly and dangerously aggravated by the infringement on their rights and freedom.

"I could see he was struggling," Larry said. "I put my hand on his shoulder to remind him I had this and needed him to follow my lead."

Larry knew he didn't have the luxury of pausing to fully explain the complexity of their situation. He needed his friend not to fight back, not at this perilous moment. His friend's buy-in was essential to getting through the present precarious exchange. They could discuss, debrief, and brainstorm change strategies later, once they were safe.

"My task wasn't to educate the officer. My task was to get home. The risk/reward equation was clear to me. I didn't want to risk being another victim of police violence, becoming more fuel for the Black Lives Matter movement. This wasn't the place for resistance, or as I call it, 'fire.'"

# The Time and Place for Change

Larry succinctly explained how police officers in this much-too-common situation were manifesting the racism of the larger community. That was where he strategically directed his resistance.

In his view, "The action needed is for truly impactful, sustainable change on a deeply embedded systemic level. The problem of racism and racial profiling penetrates far deeper than the individual encounters or the individuals directly involved."

I began to understand how and why Larry was so adept in applying the Conscious Change principles and skills. He had been practicing them his entire life. Navigating these kinds of situations is akin to survival for him. Unfortunately, he has frequent opportunities to practice—encounters ripe with division and discrimination happen daily.

## Shape the Outcome of Interactions
## (Reflections on Larry's Story)

• • •

The stories Larry tells are complex but also all too common in today's culture. As a Black man encountering a White police officer, there are undoubtedly assumptions on both sides. But Larry clearly knew that attempts to test his assumptions in these settings might well be interpreted as direct challenges to the officers' authority—and endanger his life.

Larry was acutely aware of the unequal power and status between himself (as nondominant) and the police officers (as dominant). He knew the officers might hold stereotypes of Black men and were likely to be unaware of their own unconscious biases.

As the initial interaction demonstrates, the first thing Larry did was to get his emotional attachment to the situation out of the way. He cleared his negative emotions by reframing his thoughts about why the officer was approaching him: "The officer was doing her job by confirming that I posed no threat to anyone." Because of this, he was able to maintain the presence of mind to notice all details of the officer's verbal and nonverbal messages. And he was clear about his priorities: to de-escalate the situation and return safely to his family.

His strategy was to encourage the officer to question her assumptions about who he was and the legitimacy of his presence in the area. He did this by engaging in conversation and skillfully revealing information about himself as a way of encouraging her attribution of some power and status to him— letting her know he was a university professor, an academic with knowledge and expertise in criminal justice. He was trying to create a situation where the two of them were more equal. His attempts at doing so were evidence of his confidence in his ability to influence the officer's viewpoint, even though she was clearly in a dominant position.

To do this effectively, Larry needed to understand the officer's perspective, to place himself in her shoes. Understanding how others perceive or react to you is a prerequisite to Conscious Use of Self. He may not have liked or agreed with the officer's perspective, but he knew how it worked.

There was also evidence of his having a growth mindset. He was confident that the officer's initial view of the situation was not cast in stone. He believed her capable of changing her view . . . that he could shape the outcome of the interaction.

Larry spoke up responsibly and maintained his integrity while doing so. He demonstrated the value of articulating his position in a way that was respectful yet spoke to his truth. But he also recognized when it was *not* appropriate to engage in inquiry. He was aware that questioning why a resident considered his presence "suspicious activity" might be viewed as a challenge to the officer. That, he could not afford, not with her hand on her gun.

In the second interaction, Larry was again intentional in his choice of actions and behaviors. This time his consciousness was directed not only to the officer but also to his friend. Had he let his own or his friend's emotions get in the way, the likely outcome would have been significantly different.

Whether the situation was fair or not, Larry clearly understood that his own behavior could directly affect the direction and outcome of the interaction. In both incidents, he was able to anticipate how the officers would react and alter his actions (toward them as well as his friend) to create positive outcomes.

Finally, Larry was clear that systemic racism lies at the heart of the problem with police encounters with Black men. He was (and is) more concerned about addressing systemic racism than endangering his life by confronting unfairness in individual encounters.

• • •

# Conscious Change Principles and Skills in This Chapter

- *Test Negative Assumptions*
  - Move from the answer into the question

- *Clear Emotions*
  - Identify with your values, not your emotions
  - Clear your negative emotions

- *Build Effective Relationships*
  - Develop skills in inquiry and openness

- *Bridge Differences*
  - Address underlying systemic biases
  - Learn to recognize dominant/nondominant dynamics
  - As a nondominant, resist any tendency toward internalized oppression or viewing dominants as beyond your ability to influence
  - As a nondominant, recognize dominants' potential unawareness about the impact of their behavior

- *Conscious Use of Self*
  - Accept responsibility for your own contributions
  - Maintain integrity
  - Seek to understand others' perspectives
  - Adopt a growth mindset

- *Initiate Change*
  - Emphasize changing systems, not just individuals

# About Larry

Dr. Larry Hill received a PhD in social work from the University of Houston Graduate College of Social Work. His mom and dad worked for thirty years in the space industry on world-renowned projects like NASA's Space Shuttle Main Engines, International Space Station, J-2X Rocket Engine, and various satellites. Like them, his passion is to help teams with great humanitarian missions to exceed their goals.

After receiving his PhD, he developed expertise focused on high-impact solution-making for university administrators and large nonprofit agencies. Now, Dr. Hill has twenty years' experience leading community engagement and social impact projects and ten-plus years' experience working on funded research studies (federal, state, and corporate); he has also supported philanthropic efforts in Cambodia for the past twenty years. Dr. Hill is described by his friends as a faithful, God-fearing man who values family, integrity, and authenticity. Larry serves alongside his wonderful wife, Keathya Hill, and three daughters, Abigail, Ercel, and Lydia.

Dr. Hill was introduced to the Conscious Change model as he conducted early analysis of the surveys and assessments Dr. Latting conducted with the American Leadership Forum in Houston. Since then, he has taught graduate-level leadership courses with the *Reframing Change* book and currently facilitates group sessions with Leading Consciously.

## CHAPTER 12.

# Change in a Bureaucratic Organization Can Be a Slog

## By Chamara Harris, LCSW-S, LPC-S, CCM

Photo © Chamara Harris

I spent five years working in a large medical center as a social worker, in their homeless veterans' program. The program used a "housing-first model": get veterans housed and stable first, then assess their psychosocial needs, which often included substance abuse, money-management issues, and mental health concerns.

My primary role as a social worker was case management but also included some one-on-one therapeutic intervention and facilitation of small psychoeducational groups focused on stress management, substance abuse, money management, and other daily living skills—issues that make veterans especially vulnerable to homelessness.

Four of the five members of my team were social workers. Two other individuals worked with multiple teams and had only partial assignment to ours—a peer specialist (who was also a previously homeless veteran) and a housing specialist. Both were licensed chemical dependency counselors. Sometimes I co-led small groups with peer specialists.

An individual I will call William was our team lead and served as the main point person for our supervisor. If we needed to be represented at meetings, he would attend. If there was information distributed from above, he would update us on it. And when we had new veteran clients, he would manage and assign them.

William tended to be blunt in his manner. While he had a positive relationship with some of the veterans, he didn't have good rapport with most, especially those with whom he had significant interactions, such as monitoring adherence with program requirements and holding them accountable for noncompliance. They complained all the time about his attitude, his responses to them, his lack of respect . . . things of that nature.

He didn't have the best relationship with the team, either. There were, I believe, some diversity issues. He was Caucasian, but everyone else on the team was either Hispanic or African American. He often used the phrase "you people," which upset quite a few African Americans. His leadership style led to a great deal of friction.

## An Unnerving Situation

Our team's offices were initially within the main complex of the medical center, but we were moved to a subleased satellite office. The new facility was small, with a single entry and exit point and no emergency alert system or on-site police, as had been the case at our previous site. These were all safety concerns for me, particularly since we often dealt with veterans with aggressive tendencies and behaviors, who made threats against the staff.

One day, there were two coworkers in the office with me—I'll choose to call them Harrison and Alyssa—when a veteran came in looking for William, his speech peppered with explicit language.

"Where's that *#!%&!-ing William," he yelled.

"He's not here right now," I responded. "Can one of us help you?"

"I came here looking for William. I've got a *#!%&!-ing score to settle with him!" he said loudly, knocking things off some of the desks in his agitation. "I'm going to kill the *#!%&!"

The veteran was clearly high on some unknown substance and tripping out. I tried to calm him down by talking to him and letting him know we were hearing his concerns.

We were all frightened by the veteran's unleashed anger but tried to stay calm and de-escalate the situation. We were acutely aware, however, of being closed in, with the enraged veteran standing in front of the only exit. There was no escape option within our office suite, either—the doors had no locks.

In the middle of the veteran's rant, William showed up. That only made the situation worse!

"There you are, you *#!%&!" the veteran shouted. "You're finally going to get what you deserve!"

William's reaction was equally loud and combative. After a few moments of explosive back-and-forth, we asked him to leave. "William, just go ahead and leave. You're only making things worse!"

Somewhere in the middle of all this, I used my cell phone to call security: "We've got a serious situation here. We need immediate assistance."

Security officers arrived after what seemed like forever but was probably less than five minutes. In another ten or fifteen minutes, the local police arrived. Not surprisingly, the situation left all of us unnerved.

This was not the only incident of this type, just the most extreme. Our clients frequently came in upset: they had been evicted; they felt hopeless; they were suicidal. And some of them had guns. At times, other veterans as well as the staff were at risk.

## A Voice for Change

Following this particularly dangerous incident, I spoke to my immediate supervisor, asking for changes to be implemented. He was young and had only been in his position for a year. I believe this was his first management or supervisory position.

His reaction was, "Well, this is just what we have. There's nothing I can do. You simply have to accept it."

I was unwilling to "accept it," so I went to his supervisor. She said, "You don't want to challenge the system, Chamara. There's nothing you can do. Hopefully, it will change soon. I understand your concerns, but there's no way they're going to provide security at the subleased offices. Nor is it likely they will implement any kind of emergency call system in the building. You are, of course, welcome to go to the union to express your concerns and see if you get anywhere with that."

Dissatisfied with that response, I presented the issue to the next level of supervision, making suggestions for what could be done, or at least what could be considered. I was met with the same lack of concern and dismissiveness: "Don't rock the boat. It's a temporary situation. There's nothing we can do."

What made these reactions even more difficult to accept was that I knew two of these supervisors personally, having worked with them in the field prior to their being promoted. They knew I had valid concerns but felt compelled to try to dissuade me, making me feel as if my efforts for change would not be heard, much less prioritized.

Yet despite feeling isolated, I was determined to do everything I could to bring about change, to be the "voice of change" for others. So I emailed the director, four levels above me. Yet again, the response I received was less than supportive. This was frustrating but not entirely surprising. I knew the organization well enough to know that accepting things as they were, whether safe or not, was standard behavior. Past management practices had given very low priority to safety concerns.

## Finding an Ally and a Way to Be Heard

My other options exhausted, I finally went to our union and filed a grievance. Although union membership was optional, I had chosen to become a member. You usually didn't know whether your colleagues were union members or not unless you saw them at union social functions or if they mentioned it. Union membership was not a normal topic of conversation.

The problem with going to the union was the possibility of being labeled a troublemaker. I was willing to take the risk because this was, in my mind, such a serious safety concern. It had been genuinely frightening when the veteran threatened to kill William. Even though the veteran's anger and outrage were directed at William, the rest of us worried about becoming collateral damage. After that incident, just going in to work became stressful.

Before going to the union, I reached out to some of my coworkers to enlist their support. My conversation with Harrison, who had actually witnessed the encounter, went like this:

"Harrison, I know you're a union member and have sometimes been an advocate for change."

"Yes," he replied. "I was involved in helping bring about a change a few years ago."

"You remember how scared we were when that veteran threatened to kill William? I really feel like I need to try to get our office situation changed so we can feel safer. Would you be willing to join me in trying to get the organization to address our safety concerns?"

"I really don't see that it's worth raising a big stink," he replied. "I suspect our physical location is only temporary, that things will change soon on their own. On the other hand, you know that once the powers-that-be make decisions, that's it. It's almost impossible to get them to change their minds. Go ahead and file a union complaint if you feel like it. It's important, but if it were me, I'd just let it go. Hopefully, we won't be here that long."

"I don't share your optimism," I said. "You know the organization is trying to form a long-term partnership with the entity who owns the building we're in. It looks to me like they're thinking about us being here for a while."

There was one other team member who was supportive, even though they were not present during the altercation. They were, however, unwilling to openly associate with a formal demand for change. I was pretty much on my own.

I could empathize with my colleagues' concerns. Unlike myself, many of them saw their employment with the organization as long-term—as the place from where they would eventually retire. Thus, they felt getting involved with the union or taking complaints up the chain of command might jeopardize their ability to move up or around within the system. And it does. It really does.

In contrast, I knew I would not be spending my entire career within this organization. I've also always been willing to lead change for the better, to try to make a difference.

In my complaint to the union, I described the incident in which the veteran was particularly aggressive, both physically and verbally. I mentioned the lack of an emergency call system and the absence of security in our building. I pointed out that because we were housed off-site, we were not afforded the same protection as the rest of the employees, and it could take thirty minutes or more for the police to respond, depending on their judgment or perception of what was transpiring.

Taking the matter to the union didn't make me feel secure. In fact, I felt even more unprotected than before. The union did not have a good reputation. Many fellow employees told me they felt the union "just took monthly dues and did nothing for the employees." My observation was that the union representative would act as if they were 100 percent behind you, but when they got in front of management, they presented things differently.

Union officials did eventually call a meeting of all the staff to listen to their concerns about safety, lack of adequate space, and other issues. Based on this, they agreed to do what they could to get us back in the main complex or in a safer building as soon as possible. They went to the director and held several meetings, during which they expressed concerns and explored avenues for improvement. Throughout this process, however, it was necessary for me to hold the union representatives accountable. I became quite familiar with the Union Manual Guide and reviewed it thoroughly to acquaint myself with their role and responsibilities.

I also sought outside counsel in the event adverse actions were taken against me. Going against a resistant government agency on my own, despite the validity of my safety concerns, was extremely difficult and stressful. Despite all the resistance, I continued to press forward because I knew the safety concerns were real and resolving them would be for the good of all, including the veterans served.

## Waiting for Change and the Ultimate Cost

One of the main things that helped me get through the experience was my regular practice of positive self-affirmation:

*I choose to be optimistic. I choose to be the difference. I am an unstoppable force of nature.*

These are the affirmations I used then and continue to use today.

I have always tried not to take job-related stress home with me. This did present a challenge, because I used my time away from work to research compliance, work safety measures, and the union's role. However, I purposely did not let it consume all my off-work time and attention. Relaxing and enjoying my family helped, as did increasing my physical activity.

The first sign of change was the assignment of the aggressive veteran to another, more intensive case-management team. Leadership also implemented a plan to have this individual seen only on the hospital grounds, escorted by security guards. He could no longer visit the satellite office. Some weeks later, my team was transitioned back to the main complex.

My immediate supervisors didn't resist once the union got involved and changes began to occur. In fact, my supervisor was the first to alert me that folks at the upper levels were beginning to listen to my concerns and were considering moving us back to the main campus. That made me feel somewhat vindicated. William, the team lead, said he was okay with it; he was glad we were moving back to the main complex. The next two levels of management were not too friendly, however. I felt I was somewhat a target of their disdain.

Not long after that, William passed away, and the team lead position became open. I, along with one other person, applied for the position. I was not selected, despite having seventeen years of supervisory experience. The person chosen had three or four years of social work experience but none in supervision. I concluded that speaking up and advocating for change had indeed been held against me.

Soon after not getting the promotion, I transitioned to a position working with homeless students and families in the local school district. Six months later, I left the organization.

Someone asked me, "Was it worth it, and would you do it all over again?"

My answer was, "Absolutely, I would!"

And I felt good when, in parting, Harrison commented, "Continue to be the difference."

# Persistence Pays Off
## (Reflections on Chamara's Story)

• • •

Chamara was trying to bring about change within a large and unwieldy bureaucratic organization. She and her team members had been concerned about safety for some time, due to a combination of the sometimes-volatile nature of their clients and the increased vulnerability brought about by a change in their office location. Then a particularly explosive incident made it a more salient issue.

Chamara deserves credit, for she wasn't seeking change just to achieve her own personal safety. Instead, she was committed to achieving it for the entire team. Systems-level change was what she sought, recognizing individual-level change as insufficient to achieve the desired level of safety.

She had a specified outcome in mind—increased safety—but didn't seem locked into a specific path to obtaining it. She mentioned "making suggestions for what could be done, or at least what could be considered." She was clearly open to alternatives, whether it be changes in processes for handling unstable veterans, changes in the current facility to enhance its safety, or a move back to a more secure location.

Chamara systematically (and stubbornly) went up the ladder from one manager to the next with her request for change. She started with her immediate supervisor and worked her way up the chain of command. From these conversations, she learned there was more energy for maintenance of the status quo than for change. Little incentive existed for lower levels of management to join her in calling for change. It was easier to wait passively for change to occur on its own.

She also reached out to fellow team members, especially those who had been in the office with her the day of the encounter with the aggressive veteran, identifying them as most likely to be supportive. Though some of her colleagues voiced support privately, they were unwilling to put action behind their sentiments. No one really encouraged her to actively pursue change. This is not uncommon.

Chamara didn't hold her colleagues' unwillingness to join her advocacy of change against them. Instead, she empathized with their concerns, knowing they had more invested in their long-term relationship with the organization than she did—in terms of both career advancement and retirement. She was, however, frustrated by the lack of support, especially from several she knew personally, having developed a relationship with them earlier in the field prior to their promotions.

Several individuals—a fellow team member as well as one of the supervisors—suggested she go to the union for support. Those suggestions may have helped her gather courage to take that step, knowing it might serve as a strike against her, career-wise. Because of the seriousness of the issue, she was willing to take the risk of being labeled a troublemaker for going to the union. It was a moral issue for her, a matter of integrity to ensure the safety of herself and her team.

She exhibited patience and did not give up when her efforts to obtain change met with discouragement or outright refusals. She persevered in the face of adversity, taking a longer view. She felt she could afford to take the risk, since her self-esteem and ultimate career success were not tied to this single organization.

She did not, however, simply submit a complaint and then trust the union to handle it. Instead, she used her own power in a responsible way by doing her homework, monitoring the union's activities, and holding them accountable.

She mentioned a supervisor who gave her an alert when upper management was beginning to listen to her—after she had taken her complaint to the union. Undoubtedly, that news provided encouragement, even vindication, counting as a small win in her efforts to bring about change. Aspiring change agents should note, however, that she received little support until after signs of change had begun to occur. People who are initially reluctant tend to join the bandwagon once they realize it won't topple over. Maintaining radical patience often involves feeling alone and unsupported for a prolonged period. Chamara eventually obtained the support of the union, and changes were made.

The effort involved in initiating and following through on this change effort did, however, take an emotional toll on Chamara. No doubt, she felt under great strain as she sought change. The emotions she mentioned were frustration and fear. Her fear was strong enough to prompt her to seek private counsel, just in case of reprisal. Nevertheless, she chose to give precedence to her values over her emotions.

By intentionally valuing family time more and increasing her physical activity, she avoided suppressing her emotions. Those outlets helped her both clear her negative emotions and amplify positive ones. The primary mechanism she used to maintain her resilience while under so much pressure was her regular practice of self-affirmation. This was and continues to be effective for her.

One is left with the impression that this situation was not a one-off but that Chamara will be a committed and effective change agent in her future organizations.

• • •

## Conscious Change Principles and Skills in This Chapter

■ *Clear Emotions*
- Identify with your values, not your emotions
- Avoid emotional suppression
- Clear your negative emotions
- Build your positive emotions

■ *Conscious Use of Self*
- Maintain integrity
- Seek to understand others' perspectives

- Recognize your power and use it responsibly
- Build resilience through self-affirmation

- ***Initiate Change***
  - Emphasize changing systems, not just individuals
  - Gain support one person (or small group) at a time
  - Set directions, not fixed outcomes
  - Learn from resistance
  - Cultivate radical patience through the time lag of change
  - Acknowledge small wins

## About Chamara

Chamara Harris, LCSW-S, LPC-S, CCM received a Master of Social Work from the University of Houston Graduate College of Social Work and a Master of Education: Counseling. Chamara works with individuals, groups, and organizations to amplify their authenticity and empower them to become better versions of themselves. Chamara is passionate about high-risk children, pregnant women, end-of-life care, veterans, and serving the geriatric populations. In her free time, she likes to experience different eateries, practice hot yoga, travel, and obsesses over all things Frenchie.

She was first exposed to the Conscious Change skills in a course taught by Dr. Latting in the Graduate College of Social Work at the University of Houston, then later applied those skills in various settings to include public, private, state, and federal agencies.

## CHAPTER 13.

# How Do I Deal with a
# Hostile Work Environment?

*By Orfelinda Coronado*

Photo © Orfelinda Coronado

One day at work, while waiting for a department meeting to get underway, I was having a conversation in Spanish with a group of Latina coworkers. Meanwhile, the assistant to the department director, Celine [a pseudonym], began distributing handouts and agendas.

From across the conference room, Celine, who was a White woman, heard us speaking Spanish and yelled, "Speak English, this is the United States!"

A non-Latina nurse practitioner spoke up immediately in our defense. "They can speak any language they want!"

I gave Celine a pointed stare before continuing to talk with my coworkers (in Spanish).

## Considering My Options in a Hostile Work Climate

For quite some time, I had been fighting the conviction that Celine's comments, as well as her nonverbal behavior, were hostile and racist. She appeared to want to dominate me and the other Latinas in the group.

Often when I walked by her desk or attempted to communicate with her, Celine would make fun of my Spanish accent. This latest incident banished all doubt of Celine's "attacks" being related to racist behavior.

*But what will happen if I call her on it?* I asked myself. *Celine and my supervisor are friends. Will my supervisor take Celine's side automatically?*

And I could hear Celine's response to being called out: "There you go again, being oversensitive. Why do you always take everything so personally?"

Such a reaction would immediately make *me* seem like the problem. I was already feeling bullied by other members of the team. An aggressive response to Celine's racism would only bring additional grief to my already-hostile environment.

Yet this was just the latest version of Celine's abuse. From the beginning of my working relationship with her, she had taken a combative tone toward the smallest request—whether it be asking for supplies, assistance, or simply asking her a work-related question. I felt certain Celine was totally inflexible and incapable of change. With this latest incident, I'd had it! It was time for me to think about leaving the agency.

When I expressed these concerns to my clinical supervisor, she said, "There seems to be an ongoing pattern of your being involved in bullying relationships. I remember you telling me about others during prior assignments. Could it be that your personality is attracting the bullying? Have you thought about obtaining a life coach?"

"I don't think it's just me," I responded. "I see others being mistreated, not just myself. It seems to be part of a larger pattern in many of the agencies I've worked in."

"Irrespective of the source, a life coach might be helpful to you. They could help you find ways to deal more effectively with what feels like a hostile work situation. Let me give you a list of coaches available in the area. Think about it."

## Challenging My Assumptions

When I reviewed the list she gave me, I immediately recognized Dr. Latting's name as a former professor in my social work graduate program.

She had taught one of the foundational courses, and I remembered her as someone I respected and trusted. The decision to contact her would end up making a major positive impact on my work environment.

My job consisted of many tasks, including visits to different locations and assisting a population with few resources and high needs. I felt overwhelmed with trying to handle responsibilities to my family and my clients plus the stress of a hostile work environment. It was within this context that my sessions with the life coach began.

After acknowledging and empathizing with my many complaints about Celine's behavior, Dr. Latting suggested, "One of the things that can be helpful in situations like this is to treat your beliefs as assumptions and begin to challenge them. Think of it as moving out of the answer and into the question. Does Celine have any positive characteristics? Is there any way you can 'catch her doing something right'?"

I had to think about that for a bit, but then remembered, "She *did* provide help locating a walker for a client with lung disease a few weeks ago."

"Is that unusual?" Dr. Latting queried.

"Well, while collaborating to meet clients' needs is something we do as a team, it's not really part of Celine's role as executive assistant," I replied. I then admitted, "I really didn't express my appreciation for her help at the time."

I made a point of doing so the next day.

After many discussions like this, I began to more closely study my coworkers' behaviors and interactions with each other and started to practice challenging my assumptions on a more regular basis.

For example, I began to notice the relentless criticism and attacks on Celine for clocking our time, checking on inventory, and other duties she carried out as part of her position. All the criticism of her enforcement of the rules seemed unwarranted. I felt there was a legitimate need to monitor employees in some of these areas.

When I looked at Celine in a different light, I saw she liked to help others, maintained good relationships with many, and appeared reliable, punctual, dedicated, and hardworking. Recognizing these and other positive qualities opened an opportunity for me to change my relationship with her. I began to have hope in Celine's ability to change her behavior toward me.

I told Dr. Latting, "I think Celine's work is taken for granted in the office. She doesn't get the recognition she deserves."

"How might you change that?" she asked.

"I'll have to think about it," I replied.

## Building a Better Relationship through Understanding and Recognition

I decided to send a written thank-you note to Celine for her assistance in locating the walker. In addition, I utilized a formal mechanism within our agency: an agency thank-you card. This consisted of a brief abstract describing what Celine had done and my recognition and appreciation for her assistance. I copied our mutual supervisor.

Celine's behavior changed after my submission of the card. She even began to occasionally offer assistance without my requesting it.

I mentioned this to Dr. Latting: "Celine's attitude toward me has really seemed to improve. Lately, she seems to have become more approachable."

"Is your relationship with her where you would like it to be?" she asked.

"Not really. I still think she's pretty set in her ways and still has a racist attitude toward me and the other Latinas."

Dr. Latting probed further. "Do you think there's hope of her changing her behavior? Do you think there's a possibility of a better relationship with her?"

"Well . . . maybe," I reluctantly conceded.

"Is there a way you could continue to question your assumptions about her?"

"She did mention to me once that she had never been recommended for a departmental award . . . maybe I can explore whether she really has done things above and beyond her role."

Our department gives special awards to people who go above and beyond their roles in serving clients, supporting peers, promoting our work, and exceeding agency expectations. Given the little bit of progress I had made so far in my opinion of Celine, Dr. Latting and I decided that I would make a conscious and sincere attempt to build a strong relationship with Celine and truly challenge my assumptions.

To determine whether Celine had indeed gone "above and beyond," I needed a better understanding of exactly what her job responsibilities encompassed. So, one afternoon, I stopped by Celine's desk and veered our conversation toward that topic. In response to my questions, she gave me a summary of her duties.

"It seems to me that, in addition to your assigned tasks, you do lots of other things that help the rest of us do our jobs better," I said. "Don't you monitor inventory, locate resources and donations, and coordinate outreach events? I don't see these listed on your official job description."

Celine looked surprised. "No, none of those are in my formal job description, but I've always done them."

"I think that doing those things, above and beyond what's in your job description, qualifies you for recognition as Team Champion," I said. "All of them really help us better meet client needs. I'm going to recommend you for that recognition."

Several days later, I submitted the request, and the next month, she was formally declared Team Champion.

After that, Celine's behavior and demeanor toward me continued to change for the better. She was less likely to make fun of my accent or scowl when I asked her a question. I also noticed how her attitude and behavior toward the department as a whole became more positive. Her verbal and nonverbal messages were more open and friendly, and our interactions more pleasant. She began to approve requests for supplies and other things required to meet clients' needs without question.

Working with Dr. Latting helped me see aspects of Celine's personality I'd previously overlooked. This gave me an opportunity to reach out and build a stronger relationship with her. Celine not only had the ability to change, but she became one of my main sources of support within the department.

To this day, Celine continues to be supportive and amicable, and I truly appreciate her work ethic, personal values, and strong personality.

## Calling In vs. Calling Out: Bridging Differences (Reflections on Orfelinda's Story)

• • •

Elements of dominant/nondominant dynamics are evident here. As with many dominant-group members—in this case, as a White person—Celine seemed to be unaware of her behavior and its impact on the Latina members of the work group. Even if Celine understood the insulting nature of telling the Latinas to speak English, she may have been unaware of the cumulative effect of such microaggressions repeated over time.

Orfelinda considered Celine's comments and behaviors racist. She suspected, however, that direct confrontation might boomerang, making it look like it was *her* problem, *her* attitude at fault, *her* behavior needing to be corrected. She further recognized that calling Celine out directly might result in denial, resistance, and confrontation . . . and little change. One can imagine her asking herself, *Do I want to be right, or do I want to be effective?* So instead of calling Celine out, Orfelinda engaged in efforts to call Celine in, trying to bridge the differences between them.

With the help of Dr. Latting as her coach, Orfelinda shifted to being in the question rather than the answer. She opened herself up to considering things from Celine's point of view. Although she doesn't use this precise language, she began to suspect that Celine herself might be feeling unappreciated in her nondominant role as an executive assistant in an agency of professionals.

An important prerequisite to improving their relationship was for Orfelinda to shift her perceptions of Celine. To do this, Dr. Latting encouraged her to question her assumptions about Celine and test them where possible. Once Orfelinda began to practice challenging her assumptions, she could see things she hadn't previously noticed—such as the constant criticism Celine experienced from others. Celine was lower in the power and status hierarchy, criticized for doing what was part of her job—enforcement of the rules.

As a Latina, Orfelinda was a nondominant-group member relative to Celine, but as a member of the professional staff, she was a dominant-group member. By looking for Celine's good qualities and her contributions to agency effectiveness, Orfelinda was able to provide support to Celine in the form of recognition and appreciation.

One way to think about the success of Orfelinda's actions is to consider Celine's emotional bank account—whether it was positive or negative with respect to their relationship.[1] The concept of an emotional bank account is like that of a checking account. More deposits (positive and supportive feedback) than withdrawals (criticisms or negative feedback) are required to maintain supportive relationships. By focusing on Celine's strengths and finding ways to recognize her contributions to the work unit, Orfelinda made significant deposits in Celine's emotional bank account, and their relationship consequently improved.

For change to occur, Orfelinda had to accept, at least conditionally, that Celine was capable of change. And Celine demonstrated this was indeed the case. Orfelinda also began to understand that she had the ability to influence Celine's behavior. She recognized her power in the situation: by treating Celine differently, she was, in turn, treated differently by Celine.

Orfelinda can be viewed as a change agent. Her change project was to alter the relationship between Celine and herself. As is so often the case, the first step in the change process was for her to look inward and begin to question what were, by that point, strongly held conclusions about Celine. She had to ask herself what was prompting Celine's negative behavior and whether she had a role to play in it.

Change didn't happen overnight; it almost never does. But there was evidence of small changes. Orfelinda first noticed a small improvement in Celine's attitude toward her after submitting the agency thank-you card containing formal recognition of Celine's contributions. That encouraged Orfelinda to do more to continue trying to influence Celine's behavior in a positive way.

An added benefit to their improved relationship is that they are now in a much better position to discuss racial or cultural issues candidly. Working to bridge differences and address behavior experienced as negative or racist is easier within favorable relationships. It is much easier to talk with someone about a difficult subject—and dealing with racist behavior is difficult—if you have a good relationship and have demonstrated genuine caring for that person. They will be able to "hear" what you have to say more easily. It's likely that any future uncomfortable conversations between Orfelinda and Celine will go differently than they might have before.

• • •

# Conscious Change Principles and Skills in This Chapter

■ *Test Negative Assumptions*
- Move from the answer into the question
- Consciously test your negative assumptions

■ *Bridge Differences*
- Learn to recognize dominant/nondominant dynamics
- Check for stereotyping tendencies, unconscious bias, and lack of awareness in your behavior, especially as a dominant-group member
- As a dominant-group member, provide support to nondominant-group members
- As a nondominant, resist any tendency toward internalized oppression or viewing dominants as beyond your ability to influence
- As a nondominant, recognize dominants' potential unawareness about the impact of their behavior
- Call others in rather than calling them out

■ *Conscious Use of Self*
  - Seek to understand others' perspectives
  - Focus on others' strengths
  - Adopt a growth mindset
  - Recognize your power and use it responsibly

■ *Initiate Change*
  - Commit to personal change
  - Surface undiscussables
  - Cultivate radical patience through the time lag of change
  - Acknowledge small wins

# About Orfelinda

Orfelinda Coronado obtained her Master of Clinical Social Work from the Graduate College of Social Work (GSCW) at the University of Houston. Mrs. Coronado found her passion in the application of clinical assessment skills in the medical case-management field, where she assists vulnerable populations. Today, Mrs. Coronado is the grandmother of four four-legged fur babies, two of which are rescues.

Mrs. Coronado first met Dr. Latting during the leadership course provided during one of the foundational semesters of the GSCW master's program.

## CHAPTER 14.

# Walking a Fine Line:
# Building Relationships in the
# Face of Skepticism and Distrust

## By Nadia Maynard

Photo © Nadia Maynard

I was employed by a national humanitarian aid organization out of their headquarters in Washington, DC, and tasked to work with a regional office in the Southwest to assess the needs of immigrants in their area who were separated from their families. My goal was to identify gaps in humanitarian aid being provided to these immigrants. This was a relatively new area for our organization. Prior to my coming on board, little attention had been given to immigrants to the United States from Central America or Mexico.

## Crossing Borders and Building Bridges

Built-in conflicts were sources of resistance to my efforts. Our newest executive director used a big-business model for her management of the organization. Under her leadership, some reductions in force and stream-lining of processes had been made—cutting back and standardizing to make operations more efficient. Previously, each regional office had its own way of doing things. My visits to regional offices as someone from headquarters were interpreted as a check on what they were doing, which created some anxiety for those working in the field.

I was committed to connecting with the nonprofit and advocacy organizations who assisted immigrants in the local and regional areas. Many were doing amazing work with migrants in the desert. But to my dismay, some of these activists were suspicious of my organization's presence, seeing us as too often showing up only during a crisis, making a big splash by flashing our emblem around, and then leaving.

Staff at regional offices could also be wary and distrustful of the political motivations of the more activist organizations I was trying to connect with. Regionals viewed their role as upholding our national organization's avowed status of political neutrality. Part of my challenge was to allay those concerns.

I often heard myself saying, "We're not asking you to do anything political. Families have been separated. This is the humanitarian consequence of immigration, not a political issue."

I also needed to interact with representatives from the US Customs and Border Protection, which operates under the US Department of Homeland Security. Not surprisingly, many of the advocacy and aid organizations working with immigrants on the frontlines had contentious relationships with Border Patrol employees. They held opposing, and seemingly irreconcilable, viewpoints on immigration issues. Conflicting goals—blocking entry vs. assisting those who had entered—almost inevitably led to their holding negative views of one another, often exaggerated and distorted.

## From Discomfort and Mistrust to Understanding and Engagement

Thus, there were multiple challenges and points of view. I had to use quite a bit of cultural humility and inquiry to assuage fears and navigate politically sticky situations. I also had to be careful not to interpret all resistance as xenophobic. Instead, it was important to be thoughtful and collaborative, and listen to all parties with empathy. I often found myself having to sit with the discomfort of internal conflicts and navigate unspoken concerns, as well as those explicitly expressed. I did believe most individuals were committed to their work and were trying to do a good job.

To learn about the needs of immigrants stemming from family separation, I needed to make local visits and build relationships with members of the nonprofits and advocacy organizations. I had to figure out what I didn't know that I didn't know. I could only do that through numerous face-to-face meetings with folks from the immigrant community and representatives of all the groups who worked with them.

The regional office was my conduit to these groups. I relied on them to set up meetings with personnel from immigrant/refugee serving agencies, local nonprofits working directly with immigrants and refugees . . . anyone doing any kind of advocacy work around immigration.

Initially, I got pushback from the regional office about meeting with advocacy groups.

"Why do you want to meet with that group?" staff members would ask. "They have a political agenda, even a *radical* political agenda."

"Because they know the root of the problems," I would respond. "They're the ones working intimately with the people, as well as on policy issues."

Advocacy group representatives were also skeptical: "Are you for real? Are you going to be working with us or not? Or are you just here to lay down your mark . . . to check a box?" Authenticity really mattered to them. They didn't want to have anything to do with pro forma action.

I knew that making an accurate assessment of the needs of immigrants separated from their families hinged on first taking time to engage in thoughtful relationship building, to create needed trust. I wanted to enlist these individuals and organizations as partners, and to understand their concerns about our presence in this work.

Susan [a pseudonym], a part-time volunteer and part-time staff member, was my key contact in the Tucson regional office. She was very progressive in her views and struggled to deal with an extremely xenophobic director. Early on, whenever I called, I reached voicemail. And when I finally did get a call back from Susan, I could hear hesitation in her voice.

Each question I had about details of the visit yielded a version of, "Are you sure you want to do that?" followed by a long pause.

I wondered, *Is her reluctance an attempt to be diplomatic and avoid stating the problems she sees with the work I'm doing?*

After a few cycles of this, I outright asked, "It seems as if you have reservations about what I'm doing. Can you tell me what this is about? I really value your opinion and want to understand."

Susan replied, "It's just that I don't really know if you're going to get what you want by coming here. But if it's what you need to do, I have no problem setting up meetings."

I communicated regularly with Susan, by both phone and email, and continued to express gratitude for her work in bringing groups together to meet with me and navigating relationships in an astute manner. Sometimes, I would just send her a quick email to say thanks or ask how she was doing.

She continued to distrust my motives, however. "Are you sure we're supposed to be doing this?" she would ask. She would even occasionally call my boss to make sure what I proposed was legitimate.

My boss would always say, "Yeah, it's okay. Nadia is doing what she's doing and it's okay."

One day Susan mentioned she was going hiking and birding over the weekend and would be seeing some of our local partners informally over lunch. On Monday morning, I asked about her weekend, and how long she had been birdwatching. I got so caught up in her enthusiastic appreciation of nature I forgot to ask how her conversations with our partners went. I called her back.

"You know, Susan, I had such a good time chatting with you that I forgot to ask how that lunch with our partners went. I think I've gotten so comfortable with you navigating and taking care of things that I forget to check in."

Susan laughed (it may have been the first time I'd ever heard her laugh). "It's okay. I was wondering if you just called to talk about birds! We had a good lunch. Everyone is set to meet with us when you arrive. They are still . . . you know . . . skeptical . . . but they want to be open to what can happen."

Later, once she became more comfortable with my motives, she would demonstrate real excitement when introducing me to the leaders of the more radical groups around town. The community of individuals involved in immigration issues in Arizona was complex and somewhat enmeshed. Individuals might be staff members of one organization while simultaneously volunteering with another. Being well-connected among the local advocacy community, Susan was excellent at getting us to the people we wanted feedback from.

She helped me set up listening sessions to hear what volunteers and staff of the community organizations had to say about their experiences and to learn about the humanitarian consequences of immigration and deportation. I needed to understand all aspects of the immigration issue as it affected families, so I could begin to identify gaps in services provided to separated families and ways to fill them. Some of these conversations could be rough, extremely emotional. Sometimes my role was simply holding space for people expressing grief from the loss of loved ones.

I remember meeting one family whose father had been deported. They had lived in the United States for a long time, but one day the father got pulled over in his car, was taken into custody, and was eventually deported. He tried several times to recross the border to return to his family. One day his remains were found on Native American tribal land, extremely dangerous terrain that could be crossed without encountering Border Patrol agents or a wall.

I met with forensic anthropologists who worked to identify human remains, or to identify the deceased from belongings found with them. I also talked with ranchers who would occasionally find bodies of migrants on their property.

I had tense conversations with people from embassies. Some of them felt reconnecting families was their job but they were not really set up to find lost family members. Nor was the Department of Homeland Security effective at keeping track of children who had been separated from their parents. Too often data became lost in their computer system.

## Relationships Lead to Solutions

Eventually, I developed sound relationships with the local groups. An example is the partnership we were able to develop over time with No Más Muertes (No More Deaths), a small, local humanitarian aid organization.

From this partnership, we learned that immigrants had no way to reach loved ones at home—an unmet need. Being out of contact with family members made them more vulnerable to extortion or trafficking.

We were able to provide them with satellite phones to be used by individuals in camps that had been set up for them in the desert. The phones allowed the immigrants to call home, usually their first phone call since crossing the border.

People at No Más Muertes initially viewed our offer with skepticism, making remarks like, "You mean this? What's the catch?"

"No, no," I replied. "There are no strings attached. Use the phones to help the immigrants stay in touch with their families. Just track the calls and let us know how many you're making every month."

Later they reported, "Having the satellite phones helps us in making our water drops, too. They help us communicate with each other."

During a time of increased border crossings by unaccompanied minors, some of the children were transferred to Arizona detention facilities. Because of the relationships that Susan and I had built with Border Patrol and the advocacy organizations in the region, we were able to get inside the detention center and provide phone calls to the children.

None of these kids had talked to their family in six weeks. For some it had been three months. The sooner the kids could be in touch with their families, the more quickly our health and human services arm could place them into a residential facility—one step closer to being placed with a family member. We were also able to leverage our privileged access to partner with other aid organizations, allowing them to volunteer services inside the detention center.

Our partnership with No Más Muertes is a good example of our trajectory in building relationships. The early listening sessions started the trust-building process and helped establish an initial alliance. Relationships were established and strengthened as time went on, resulting in our providing satellite phones to individuals in their desert camps. Finally, our partnership gave them entry into the children's detention center, where they provided, among other services, much-needed Spanish-English translation.

Our work in walking that fine line between distrustful and conflictual parties—developing positive relationships with all—paid off in this, and many other ways.

## *Using Not Just One Principle but Many
(Reflections on Nadia's Story)*

• • •

Nadia's story clearly illustrates multiple principles. She was tasked with initiating change: implementing a new initiative for her organization. She began by setting up mechanisms to systematically gather information from as many sources as possible. To do this effectively, she had to build new and effective relationships. Staying in the question was essential to her success in building trust with members of disparate groups.

For different reasons, both local activists and regional staff were suspicious of the organization's motives, and therefore Nadia's. Approaching them initially with an already-formed answer about the type of aid they "should" need would have guaranteed failure. Instead, Nadia sought to understand their varied perspectives. She genuinely felt she needed multiple points of view, since there were multiple and diverse organizations and individuals working on immigrant issues in the region.

Nadia utilized the principle and skills of Conscious Use of Self. She was deliberate in maintaining her integrity and demonstrating the caring motives of her organization. She also had genuine interest in and a firm commitment to the immigrants and their families.

Her patience with Susan made it clear that she saw her as capable of change over time. If Nadia had not believed Susan would come around, she wouldn't have stuck with her through the period of initial distrust.

Nadia placed intentional focus on Susan's strengths, as evidenced by her expressions of gratitude for Susan's work in navigating relationships with various constituencies. Nadia's focus on Susan's strengths went beyond her interactions with her colleague—it also illustrated her stated belief that "most individuals were committed to their work and were trying to do a good job."

Instead of making assumptions and acting from them, Nadia directly asked Susan, "Can you tell me what this is about? I really value your opinion and want to understand." Simple to say, but so hard for many to do.

Nadia was also challenged to test her assumptions when working with individuals who held widely different political points of view. It would have been easy to interpret resistance as xenophobia, but Nadia strove to keep an open mind and to resist making assumptions. Instead, she felt it important to listen empathetically to all parties.

While she didn't specifically mention having cleared her emotions, Nadia did acknowledge having to sit often with the "discomfort of internal conflicts" and engage in "rough, extremely emotional" conversations—evidence of acknowledging her emotions rather than suppressing them.

As a change agent, Nadia articulated a clear direction—to provide humanitarian assistance to immigrants separated from their families—yet didn't begin the project with predetermined outcomes. She saw early on that Susan was the conduit to the nonprofit and advocacy groups in the area, so she concentrated trust-building efforts with Susan first. She wasn't discouraged by Susan's resistance or that of others. Instead, she saw it as a source of learning.

Nadia recognized her conversation with Susan about birdwatching and hiking—and hearing Susan laugh for the first time—as a small win in her efforts to gain trust and elicit collaboration. Her choice to overlook Susan's having gone to her boss to question her decisions was an example of radical patience—she knew it was a slow process to change people's attitudes.

It was clear, in the end, that her use of the principles of Conscious Change paid off.

• • •

# Conscious Change Principles
# and Skills in This Chapter

- *Test Negative Assumptions*
  - Move from the answer into the question
  - Look for multiple points of view
  - Consciously test your negative assumptions

- *Clear Emotions*
  - Avoid emotional suppression

- *Build Effective Relationships*
  - Engage in powerful listening
  - Develop skills in inquiry and openness

- *Conscious Use of Self*
  - Maintain integrity
  - Seek to understand others' perspectives
  - Focus on others' strengths
  - Adopt a growth mindset

- *Initiate Change*
  - Gain support one person (or small group) at a time
  - Set direction, not fixed outcomes
  - Learn from resistance
  - Cultivate radical patience through the time lag of change
  - Acknowledge small wins

# About Nadia

Nadia Kalinchuk Maynard (she/her/ella) has worked in academic, governmental, and nongovernmental settings to support trauma-informed and healing-centered mental health services for immigrant and refugee communities. Throughout her career, she has primarily worked at the intersection of migration, gender, and youth, specifically with survivors of sexual assault, domestic violence, and human trafficking; (im)migrants; asylum seekers; and refugees. Whether developing and managing programs, providing mental health services, examining the impact of policies, or providing organizational development, technical assistance, and consultation, Nadia enjoys leading and coaching teams to support mission-driven, client-centered engagement.

Nadia blends transformative justice, disability justice, and racial justice frameworks grounded in interdependence, collaboration, mutuality, and kindness. Nadia's leadership style was formed by her work with Dr. Jean Latting during her time at the University of Houston Graduate College of Social Work, where she first learned the Conscious Change skills.

## CHAPTER 15.

# Act Out of Values Rather than Emotions

## By Ashleigh Gardner-Cormier

Photo © Michael Smith

"What's her problem?" my coworker, whom I have named Kim, asked.

"I'm not sure," I replied, shrugging my shoulders.

Our colleague, Alice, had just stormed into our shared office, barely spoken to either of us, then left quickly, slamming the door as she stormed out.

Before we had time to speculate further, Kim hurried out the door for morning rounds on the west wing. I looked at the clock. It was eight thirty, so I, too, left the office, rushing off to make my rounds on the east wing. I encountered Alice on my rounds, but she barely made eye contact or spoke to me. This was problematic, since she was my case manager and my counterpart in the cardiovascular unit of the hospital, and we relied heavily on each other.

## A Negative Snowball Is Building

Once rounds were done, I walked over to the west wing to meet with Kim and determine my workload for the day. When we finished discussing our respective patients, the conversation shifted to Alice.

"So, did you find out what's wrong with her?" Kim inquired.

"Nope, not yet."

"Do you have any idea what it could be?"

"The only thing I can come up with is that maybe she's mad about me moving Mr. Roberts in 964 to a skilled nursing facility instead of rehab, like she wanted. To a certain extent, I can understand her not being happy with the outcome since that transfer took a few days longer. But I also know that skilled nursing is the appropriate level of care for Mr. Roberts, so she needs to get over it. Anyway, she changes course on patient care all the time without informing me or the doctor until the patient is on his way out the door. She really shouldn't have a problem with me making a change this one time. At least I *did* consult the doctor."

"Well yeah, but you know how Alice is."

"Yeah, I know how she is. But I also know she needs to get over it."

With that, we went our separate ways. Later that day, I received a call from Catherine, my supervisor, telling me I was needed at a meeting with her, Alice, and our director. The meeting was scheduled to begin in less than thirty minutes.

"I don't believe this!" I muttered as I hung up the phone.

"Don't believe what?" Kim asked.

"Catherine called a meeting with her, Alice, me, and Tim [all pseudonyms] in his office at two thirty."

"For what?"

"My guess is that Alice went and complained to her about me. You know they're friends."

"Yeah, I know. I'm not sure why Alice would go to that extent over something so trivial. I mean, the goal is patient care above everything, right?"

"That's what I thought, but apparently ego stroking has been added to the list," I said.

As I sat there thinking about the ambush I suspected I was about to walk into, I felt my head start to pound. Moisture gathered on my palms. How could Alice report me for simply doing my job? I mean, at least I'd spoken with the doctor about it . . . and the patient's insurance would never have covered the rehab Alice had recommended.

Another point of frustration was that Catherine and Alice were friends and Catherine had a reputation for being petty. I knew regardless of how right I could prove myself to be, I would walk out of the meeting the loser. This was a no-win situation, and the thought of it infuriated me. Before I knew it, I had worked myself into a mental rage and had prepared vicious responses for every possible accusation.

## A Different Perspective Can Cause a Shift

Ordinarily, my anger would have ruled in this maddening situation. I would have openly expressed to Catherine and Alice, in front of Tim, that their friendship put me in a position of feeling attacked, that it was inappropriate to call me less than an hour before a meeting to tell me it was happening, and that I felt their goal was not to problem-solve but to put me in my place.

I would have further explained how unprofessional I thought Alice had been throughout my time working with her—she consistently disregarded the knowledge, experience, and opinions of everyone on the team and made decisions as if hers were the only ones that mattered.

Kim observed the external effects of my rage.

"This is so immature of Alice," she remarked. "But don't let it get you down. She's just insecure."

Something about that statement resonated with me. Suddenly, I stopped demonizing Alice and took a fair and honest look at who she was and not just her behavior. Alice was a tall, beautiful, dark-skinned woman from the Carribean who still had a heavy accent.

Beautiful and smart as she was, I had often watched as she was ignored and overlooked in social and work-related situations, either due to people's difficulty understanding her or simply because she was a Black woman.

I knew the struggle of being a Black woman in the workplace all too well from personal experience. However, I couldn't begin to know how it felt to literally not be understood when I spoke simple words. That had to be stressful. Perhaps Alice's often seemingly flippant attitude and refusal to be a team player were defense mechanisms, built-in responses to the poor treatment she had received in the workplace over the years.

As I sat in deep thought, it occurred to me that the answer to this problem might be to try to bridge our differences rather than preparing to spar with Alice and Catherine in the meeting.

When I viewed the situation from Alice's perspective, I realized that in addition to my nondominant position as an African American woman, I also belonged to a dominant group of American-born English speakers with no accent. Where I, as a member of the dominant group, saw this situation as an isolated occurrence, it's likely that to Alice, my disregard for her opinion was just one more example of why she didn't feel like a respected member of the team.

Interestingly, I'd long been aware of my membership in this group when dealing with Kim, who was from Russia and had a non-American accent as well. When she spoke, however, I always listened carefully, to keep from having to ask her to repeat things. My reaction to Alice's abrasive approach, on the other hand, might have kept me from realizing this was true with her as well.

Also, I had been so caught up in my anger toward her for involving a member of a dominant group in our situation (in the form of Catherine, a White woman and my boss), I hadn't seen how my own dominant-group membership (whether acknowledged or not) might be viewed by her as a threat. I decided to approach the situation in a way that would empower Alice while also ensuring my own voice was heard.

"It's good to see everyone today, though I wish we were here under different circumstances," Tim said once we were all settled in his office, game faces firmly in place.

Breaking protocol, I smiled pleasantly. Alice seemed to visibly fight the urge to roll her eyes as she shifted in her chair.

"Alice, I understand you have some concerns about the way cases are being handled on your unit. Is that correct?" Tim continued.

"Yes, it is," Alice replied in an abrasive tone.

"What exactly is the problem?"

She explained how I had "gone behind her back" to transfer a patient to a different level of care than what she had initially recommended. She referred to me as obstinate, difficult to work with, and not a team player.

Her words cut like a knife. I sat in painful silence, reminding myself with every biting remark that I was not there to avenge myself. Instead, the goals were to offer a sincere apology, explain my position compassionately, respectfully express my feelings, and commit to productive collaboration moving forward.

As I'd expected, Catherine fully supported Alice. Clearly uncomfortable with where this conversation appeared to be going, with every passing second Tim's usually pale face became increasingly red.

Finally, it was my turn to speak. "First off, Alice, I want to tell you that I apologize for making you feel as if I don't respect your position as a vital part of the team, because I really do. You're an experienced case manager, and the unit wouldn't run as smoothly as it does without you. In this instance, I moved forward with a change in the level of care based on my professional opinion and because I'd consulted the patient's doctor and he agreed.

"In retrospect, I see that I went wrong by not providing you with an update on the status of the case. To be honest, I justified my actions—or inaction toward you—by telling myself that you never consult *me* when *you* make changes. But now," I continued, "I see that by reacting to what I perceived as your negative behavior, I was only amplifying the problem between us. Moving forward, I want you to know it's my intention to make sure we're always on the same page. I will be sure to effectively communicate with you every morning during rounds and throughout the day as needed. I only ask that you do the same. I think you're great at what you do and have a lot to offer the team. I want to always keep the lines of communication open so we each have access to what the other brings to the table."

As I spoke, I watched Alice's squared shoulders slowly drop. Her breathing, initially more of an audible huff, quieted, and the corners of her mouth relaxed.

"I appreciate your honesty," she said, "and you're right. I did feel excluded. Thank you for putting yourself in my shoes. I'm willing to work on my communication in the future as well."

Following our exchange, Catherine and Tim both weighed in on the outcome. We all left the meeting feeling a lot lighter than when we began, or at least I did. As an African American woman, it can be difficult, even scary at times, to express my true feelings for fear of being misunderstood or judged.

It felt good to have expressed my true feelings, to have given another member of a nondominant group the opportunity to do the same, and to have achieved a positive outcome.

## Change Your Perspective, Change the Outcome
## (Reflections on Ashleigh's Story)

• • •

Emotions were clearly running high among the staff of the cardiovascular unit of the hospital. Ashleigh knew something was up when Alice stormed into and out of their shared office without speaking. Then she was called to a meeting with Alice, her supervisor, and her supervisor's supervisor.

Sensing the meeting was going to be an "ambush," Ashleigh's emotional reaction was very strong. She was close to being emotionally hijacked, rendered unable to think clearly. However, a comment made by her coworker, Kim, about Alice jogged her out of that state and allowed her to think things through more rationally. She did some in-the-moment emotional clearing by reframing her assumptions about Alice.

As most of us might, Ashleigh initially interpreted her conflict with Alice as interpersonal, a result of Alice's attitude and behaviors. Ashleigh armed herself mentally with the ammunition she needed to place the blame there. But once she identified the conflict as the result of dominant/nondominant dynamics—that is, dynamics put in play by differential power and status attached to group membership—a more effective approach to resolving the conflict became apparent. It gave her a new lens through which to view the interactions.

Ashleigh was accustomed to thinking about dominant-group dynamics from the perspective of her nondominant-group membership. She and Alice were both Black women, thus nondominant in this (and most) work settings.

Wisely, though, Ashleigh checked to see if she was making any cultural assumptions about Alice, realizing that indeed she had. She had assumed that because she and Alice were both nondominants as African American women, they faced the same set of obstacles.

Yet Alice faced an additional barrier Ashleigh had not previously considered—her heavy accent. As a United States–born English speaker with a United States–based accent, Ashleigh held dominant-group membership relative to Alice's nondominant status. Ashleigh realized Alice might feel insecure because she was from Barbados and spoke English with an accent that was sometimes difficult for others to understand.

This realization moved Ashleigh out of the answer (certain this was an interpersonal issue), into the question (Could cultural barriers be fostering insecurity in Alice?). In so doing, Ashleigh recognized that multiple points of view might be in play.

This cognitive reframing was also effective in helping Ashleigh clear her emotions. She vividly describes what her interactions with Alice and her supervisors in the meeting might have looked like had she remained emotionally charged and acted out of her strong negative emotions instead of her values of having a strong team. Clearing emotions is often an important step before attempting to bridge differences.

Ashleigh put herself in Alice's shoes, trying to view the situation from Alice's point of view. From that position, she could begin to generate alternative explanations for Alice's reaction to her action. Perhaps Alice wasn't just being difficult, but simply reacting from a place of repeatedly having her opinions ignored. What members of dominant groups might assume to be isolated incidents may actually be experienced routinely by members of nondominant groups.

Before attending the meeting, Ashleigh vowed to respond to the accusations in a way that would empower Alice but also ensure that her own voice was heard. She realized how important it was to listen intently and demonstrate her openness to hearing what Alice, as a nondominant-group member, had to say.

Not surprisingly, though, Ashleigh's negative emotions were again triggered during the meeting. These are not easy conversations. Ashleigh admitted that speaking up was scary, but despite reflexive inner defensiveness, she remained steadfast in her commitment to improving her relationship with Alice. She consciously chose a response that might contribute to that end. Implicit in this choice was a belief that Alice would be able, and willing, to make changes as well.

In her response to Alice's charges during the meeting, Ashleigh began with an apology, followed by a statement of Alice's strengths and her value to the team. Ashleigh then moved to accepting responsibility for her own contribution to the conflict and outlined changes she would make in the future. This approach was an effective apology. Alice felt heard, visibly relaxed, and expressed willingness to do her own part to improve their communication.

It's not hard to imagine improvement in their future working relationship, even if some inevitable rough spots might occasionally be encountered.

• • •

# Conscious Change Principles and Skills in This Chapter

■ *Test Negative Assumptions*
- Move from the answer into the question
- Look for multiple points of view
- Consciously test your negative assumptions
- Check to see if you are making cultural assumptions

■ *Clear Emotions*
- Identify with your values, not your emotions
- Clear your negative emotions

■ *Build Effective Relationships*
- Engage in powerful listening
- Develop skills in inquiry and openness
- Apologize effectively

- *Bridge Differences*
  - Learn to recognize dominant/nondominant-group dynamics
  - Check for stereotyping tendencies, unconscious bias, and lack of awareness in your behavior, especially as a dominant-group member
  - Sustain chronic unease toward exclusionary behaviors
  - As a dominant-group member, provide support to nondominant-group members
  - As a nondominant, resist any tendency toward internalized oppression or viewing dominants as beyond your ability to influence

- *Conscious Use of Self*
  - Accept responsibility for your own contributions
  - Seek to understand others' perspectives
  - Focus on others' strengths
  - Adopt a growth mindset

- *Initiate Change*
  - Commit to personal change

# About Ashleigh

Ashleigh Gardner-Cormier is a licensed master social worker with over fifteen years of experience in the field. She has spent the last five years in the area of legal social work, where she works alongside attorneys to ensure that holistic services are provided to the clients they serve while simultaneously educating legal professionals on the value of collaboration between the social work and legal professions and increasing the number of social workers in the field. In her down time, Ashleigh enjoys singing (she has released two singles available on all digital platforms under the pseudonym "Ashleigh Brae") and spending time with her husband and two young children.

Ashleigh first became aware of Conscious Change skills in a course, Dynamics of Leadership, taught by Dr. Latting in the Graduate College of Social Work at the University of Houston in 2009. She values Dr. Latting's teachings a great deal and credits the skills taught in the course with helping her to obtain and maintain the position she now holds.

## CHAPTER 16.

# Compassion Wins the Day

## By Treshina Smith

Photo © Tamburo Burks

I work at a large firm, providing professional business services mostly to Fortune 500 companies. The year I joined the organization, the COVID-19 pandemic was just underway, and I participated in the company's first completely virtual program for integrating new employees into the organization.

I am in the consulting and strategy arm of the business, with its focus on providing innovative, sustainable solutions to businesses. Because the company is so large, opportunities for growth, education, and experience in different industries are vast and wide. It is easy to get lost, especially in a completely virtual environment. It's up to you to find your niche. As the saying goes, "You'll know when you've found your tribe."

The orientation program is designed to provide experience in different functional areas of the company. New employees are encouraged to move around a bit to explore. The number of moves I made on my first project, however, was unusual compared to my peers: in my first four months I worked on five different teams. My experiences with the first two team leaders were painful.

All five of these teams worked on different aspects of the same project: developing a rollout of unemployment protocols for a state agency. We designed and implemented the needed software, processes, and procedures, while also acting as staff in the state unemployment office to test them. We essentially became unemployment agents. This meant I was dealing one-on-one with individuals severely negatively impacted by the pandemic.

## Ask Questions . . . But Not Really

My initial interaction with the leader of the first team was a welcome-to-the-team and general overview.

"If you have any questions, just ask," she said.

Since I'm in the consulting development program and the team lead worked in what had been described to me as a much-sought-after part of consulting (strategy), I excitedly asked her about the possibilities. "I'd be interested in knowing more about the path you took to get to where you are."

"Well," she replied somewhat tersely, "you don't just come into strategy, you are *invited* into strategy. There's a certain process you go through. But right now, at your level, you don't need to be concerned with that. You're not doing that right now, so don't worry about it."

In my second one-on-one conversation with her, I began by asking, "What are my roles and responsibilities while on staff for this project?"

Her response was, "Just do your job."

I could hear a big period at the end of that short sentence. Regardless, I pressed on. "What exactly do you mean by 'do your job'? Do you have any details you can add to that? Are there numbers you're striving for us to reach? Is there a daily target?" I asked, filling what felt like an awkward silence.

"Don't make things harder than they need to be. Just do your job. Show up. Be where you're told to be. What else is there? What other problems do you have?" she said in a brusque manner.

"All I'm trying to do," I patiently explained, "is understand. I feel like I've somehow offended you. Your tone feels a bit aggressive and accusatory. I'm new here, and you're making me nervous. I'm desperately trying to navigate, learn my way around. I'm not understanding why you're coming at me this way."

"Whoa, whoa, whoa!" She held up a hand, palm out. "I don't know how we got here, but it's apparent to me that you need someone else over you. Because I'm not going to go there with you."

I had to struggle to keep my tone civil. "What do you mean, 'you're not going to go there'? I'm not attacking you, yet you always seem to be on the defensive. I'm just letting you know that I'm in a fearful space, because I'm feeling like I did something wrong. What exactly is going on?"

"What we're going to do," she snapped, "is cut this conversation short. And I'm going to consider other things for you. The words you're using tell me you need to be on another team."

It all happened so fast. I was asking a simple question about direction, and the next thing I knew she was telling me she was going to have me reassigned. She seemed triggered, and I definitely was. She didn't appear to want an explanation or to work through the problem. I didn't hear any attempt to gain understanding, nor did I see signs of reflection. She apparently felt threatened. Her reaction stunned me. It was quite different from how the corporate culture had been described to me. During orientation, we were told staff would be enthusiastic about helping us. And that had actually been my experience thus far.

I remember disconnecting from the virtual meeting with the team lead and crying hot tears. I was angry. I was offended. I was defensive. I kept asking myself, *What have I done? Why am I even working here? Why did I give up entrepreneurship?*

## My Reputation May Precede Me

My second assignment was on the same project, just on a different person's team. My initial interactions with the second team lead were positive. She had a gentler, more soft-spoken demeanor than the first lead. But I did notice she seemed reserved with me, a bit cold and distant, as if I were someone who was going to get her in trouble. It turned out the second team lead was friends with the first. I wondered if she had taken on her friend's antagonistic feelings and was treating me accordingly.

One day I asked a question—I can't remember the exact wording, but it felt like a normal question, such as, "Where does this go?" or "If we do this or that for the day, where are we supposed to put the file?"

Her response was immediate and sharp. "Why do you ask so many questions? Don't make waves. Just continue doing what you're doing."

I did just that, but unhappily. It must have shown, because by the end of the second week, she said, "You have great numbers. But I heard there's an opening on another team. Would you rather be on a different team?"

I was happy for the opportunity and eager to get away from the tension. But I was also apprehensive about what a second move within just a few weeks would mean for my future at the company. I didn't really understand what was happening. The uncertainty (and quarantining) brought on by the pandemic increased my feelings of vulnerability. The high number of unemployment claims from a wide range of occupations I saw daily reminded me of the precariousness of employment.

The work itself added to my heightened emotions. Screaming babies in the background and tearful mothers telling me that without immediate unemployment benefits they couldn't feed their children really got to me. It was a psychologically taxing role that sent more than a few of my colleagues into therapy. The stress was even interfering with my sleep—I had nightmares about not processing someone's application in time, with them ending up homeless with nothing to eat as a result.

As if the stress of the new job wasn't enough, I was also going through nerve-racking transitions in my personal life. I was simultaneously transitioning from being a military spouse to civilian life, and to living in Atlanta after having lived overseas for several years. Acclimating to corporate life was its own struggle since I had been an entrepreneur. On top of that, I was sued for divorce. It was, as you can imagine, an excruciatingly difficult time.

I admit I didn't deal with all of this very effectively. I tried to ignore my emotions and became even more of a workaholic. I spent many a night curled up in a ball—definitely headed toward burnout.

## Am I Stepping into the Ring Again? Leader #3

The transfer to a third team made the difference—my third team in less than six weeks with the company. This team leader appeared warm from the start. She seemed to care about each of her team members as individuals. Her attitude reflected, *How can I help you? What do you need? Here's how you're doing performance-wise—you're here now, but where do you want to be? If you're dissatisfied with your numbers, I'll find someone to help you.* This team lead also specifically encouraged me to reach out to the human resources support person assigned to me when I first joined the organization.

During an online conversation with the HR person, I described my experience with my first two assignments, without naming names. Then I asked her point blank, "Did I say something wrong? Is there something I don't understand? I thought I was asking the kinds of questions we were encouraged to ask during the onboarding process. I've always thought my ability to ask questions was one of my strengths. But in these circumstances, I felt I was being punished for doing so."

"Asking questions *is* a strength!" she insisted. "I say, 'Good for you!' You did what you're supposed to do."

I blinked back happy tears. "I can't tell you what a relief it is to hear you to say that."

"We have a saying in this company," she declared. "You have to teach people how to treat you well. You have the right to stand up for yourself, not be a doormat or have people mistreat you or talk to you a certain kind of way."

Despite this affirmation by the HR person, I still wondered whether I could be genuine with my newest team leader. During one conversation, she invited me to talk about my strengths. I decided to take a risk and be open.

"In my previous team experiences, things I thought were strengths— my ability to ask tough questions and catch mistakes—were viewed as weaknesses. I felt like I was punished for them. Now I'm afraid to ask too many questions or to be honest about what I'm feeling."

"I see your ability to ask penetrating questions as one of your strengths," she replied, emphasizing her words with a nod of encouragement. "I value that. But if you mess up—and we all do at one time or another—I'll want to know less about what you did wrong and more about how you were able to resolve the situation and move past it."

# Finally, Support and Empathy from a Team Leader

Nevertheless, the problems in my personal life began to intrude on my ability to do my work, and my performance numbers began to slip. I had come to trust this team leader and decided to divulge part of my personal situation to her.

Her reaction was, "I thought there was something going on with you. You're ordinarily such a high performer, and we appreciate what you've done. Why not step away for a few days and take some time off? That might be all you need to help you see things more clearly. We want you at your best. A few days away from the computer may help you regain perspective."

I gratefully accepted her suggestion and soon learned she was right! I badly needed to believe in myself again, to believe in my own strength and my own power. I used those days to engage in activities that never fail to renew my spirit—some yoga, quiet reading and reflection, time outside in nature. I even occasionally cranked up the music and just danced until I broke out in a sweat.

When I returned to work after a few days, the team leader said, "You know, you don't have to talk to people one-on-one every day. You can engage in other tasks some days, to relieve the stress."

I followed that advice as well, and it helped. After a few weeks, I felt much better and was once more meeting or exceeding my performance goals.

About six weeks later, the team leader said to me, "Okay, I think you're ready for the next level. Because you ask tough questions, are detail-oriented, and catch errors, I think you should move to a legislative team, one dealing with high-profile clients. I've already talked to the next person I think you should work with, and they can't wait to meet you."

The fourth team leader was also gentle with me, especially after I expressed concern about balancing a stressful personal life with taking on a new assignment. She would say things like, "You know, your numbers are great. You're performing, even though I know you're still going through some things. Good for you!"

Sometimes she would just check in with me, asking "Are you okay?" without making me feel like a charity case. Instead, she always led with statements like, "We know what you bring to the table. What can we do to help you?"

That helped me rebuild my self-confidence and mental clarity. I could now confidently say to myself, *I can do this!* So, when this team leader suggested I move to a fifth team to train incoming analysts on the team, I felt ready.

## Positive Feedback Leads to Positive Self-Care and Great Performance

Because others took the time to listen to me, I changed the way I listened. And after having those two negative experiences, I was reinforced in my belief in leading with compassion. I also recognized that becoming a workaholic, a survival reflex, was not going to resolve my issues—it was more likely to make them worse. The positive feedback and support encouraged me to take myself in hand and reengage in activities that I knew from past experience would help me get a handle on my emotions. I have now made taking time to engage in self-renewing activities, including a healthy balance of what I think of as "cocooning" and spending time with family members and friends, a nonnegotiable *must*.

I make the clearest decisions when I am in alignment with my inner core—I can only do that when I turn off the TV, shut down the internet, connect with nature by listening to the inhabitants of the pond outside my window or watching the birds, shut down all the external voices and pressures, and just tend to me. Practicing gratitude, meditation, and self-awareness helps tremendously as well.

What felt like rapid-fire experiences with the first five teams I worked on opened the way for me to continue to hit high performance numbers. Since then, there's been a bidding war for my services. It felt good to be offered roles on multiple high-visibility projects prior to rolling off my first project. Now, I'm a consistent high performer and have reignited confidence in myself. But I also like the new vulnerability I'm experiencing as I learn to set firm boundaries and practice kindness and compassion daily toward others—and myself.

My passion is teaching underrepresented, underprivileged entrepreneurs and business owners how to craft sustainable and globally competitive strategies in alignment with their desires and purpose. I don't see enough underrepresented businesses in franchise, employer, or venture-capitalist spaces. This company is providing me the opportunity to mentor these entrepreneurs through a nonprofit organization, and to work on inclusion and diversity initiatives by building recruitment bridges to Texas Southern University (my alma mater) and fellow military veterans. I want to help people lead with compassion, prepare them for the journey, and build global partnerships with those aspiring to do the same.

## The Ripple Effect of Conscious Change Principles (Reflections on Treshina's Story)

• • •

During the first conversations with her initial team leader, Treshina engaged in inquiry and was open about how she interpreted the interaction. Her input was, however, poorly received and resulted in her being moved to another team. She may have unknowingly surfaced undiscussables for this team leader.

In addition, the second team leader, being a friend of the first, may have prejudged Treshina as a potential troublemaker and showed little inclination to question her assumptions. This was unfortunate, since leaders risk losing potentially valuable contributors when they form conclusions about a new employee so quickly without testing them.

Things happened so rapidly for Treshina, she had no opportunity to test her own assumptions about either of her first two leaders. And since all the interactions were virtual and she was understandably on edge as a new employee, it may have been difficult to read nonverbal communication cues through the computer screen.

She did test her assumptions with the human resources liaison, however. The liaison did a good job of listening to her and gave her positive feedback on the legitimacy of her questions. That helped Treshina work up courage to be open with her third team leader. After doing so, she was reassured that what her first two team leaders may have seen as weaknesses, this individual considered strengths. This team leader also believed in the inevitability of mistakes and was confident in Treshina's ability to learn from them and grow.

All this helped, but the stress of the new job and being on her third team in so few weeks created a great deal of emotional uncertainty for Treshina. Meanwhile, difficult transitions in her personal life coupled with the emotion-triggering nature of dealing daily with newly unemployed individuals during the early days of the pandemic brought her close to emotional over-load. She had sleepless nights and shed many tears.

Her initial response was to suppress her emotions, mani-fested through working even harder and faster, believing that perhaps she could outrun her emotions. But, not surprisingly, her performance numbers began to slip.

Fortunately, Treshina had developed enough trust in the third team leader to share some of what was going on with her. The leader's response was to suggest a little time off to reflect—not unreasonable, given that other employees were seeking counseling as an antidote to the stress caused by acting as unemployment agents in such difficult circumstances.

Realizing she was contributing to her own difficulties, Treshina used the time off effectively. She drew on mecha-nisms she had used in the past—yoga, communing with nature, quiet reading and reflection—to clear her negative emotions, and dancing to build positive ones. Aided by slight modifica-tions in her work assignments, she began to become more confident in her own personal power and her ability to make a difference.

The fourth and fifth team leaders also appeared to demon-strate several of the Conscious Change principles and skills. Like the third team leader, they demonstrated an attitude of, "What can we do to help?" rather than seeking to place blame for any mistakes. They put themselves in Treshina's shoes, focused on her strengths, and demonstrated confidence in her ability to grow and learn. Treshina's increasing self-affirmation ("I can do this!") and alignment with her values of high per-formance also contributed to her resilience in getting through the tough times.

What's particularly interesting about Treshina's experience is the way in which it demonstrates the potential contagion of the principles for Conscious Change. Because her later team leaders listened to her, she now listens more proactively to others. Because they came from a position of compassion and care, the importance of these attributes in her own interactions was reinforced.

Treshina is now firmly committed to regularly engaging in the self-care required to maintain emotional balance. This bodes well for her future.

• • •

# Conscious Change Principles and Skills in This Chapter

- ■ *Test Negative Assumptions*
  - Move from the answer into the question
  - Consciously test your negative assumptions

- ■ *Clear Emotions*
  - Identify with your values, not your emotions
  - Avoid emotional suppression
  - Clear your negative emotions
  - Build your positive emotions

- ■ *Build Effective Relationships*
  - Engage in powerful listening
  - Develop skills in inquiry and openness
  - Learn how to give, receive, and seek feedback

- ■ *Conscious Use of Self*
  - Accept responsibility for your own contributions
  - Seek to understand others' perspectives
  - Focus on others' strengths
  - Adopt a growth mindset
  - Recognize your power and use it responsibly
  - Build resilience through self-affirmation

- ***Initiate Change***
  - Commit to personal change
  - Surface undiscussables

# About Treshina

Treshina Smith received a BA in business administration from Texas Southern University, an MS in global project management from Embry-Riddle Aeronautical University, and her license in massage therapy after serving six years in the army. She is an avid believer that compassion wins, and she has been an entrepreneur since the age of five. Traveling, connecting with people from around the world, and enjoying global cuisine are some of her favorite things to do. There is a special place in her heart for helping aspiring entrepreneurs strategize to build successful businesses and meet their life goals.

Treshina was introduced to the Conscious Change skills in a life-changing teambuilding course taught by Dr. Jean Ramsey while attending Jesse H. Jones School of Business at Texas Southern University. She was a student in her final year of undergraduate studies and found the teachings fascinating. She was immediately able to apply the methods and lessons taught to many situations, ranging from self-reflection and motherhood to teambuilding and project management.

CHAPTER 17.

# We Will Learn Today

## *By Charles D. Shaw*

Photo © Charles D. Shaw

I have come to expect difficult conversations to be tense, especially when discussing sensitive topics where one can only guess the outcome. I think of myself as both a skilled facilitator and expert in group interventions, but a meeting I had a few years ago challenged those assumptions. Given the circumstances, even *I* felt like a novice.

I was leading a team charged with rolling out an enterprise-wide and highly visible project, one touching thousands of people. It was my responsibility to define the vision, set direction, and assign work streams based on team members' individual strengths.

Through no fault of any one person, we were severely under-resourced. Individuals on the team were performing two and three different jobs at a time. It was a lean team of six carrying tremendous responsibility for flawless execution—as if we were staffed with fifty. I was the leader of the team and the only African American. The other five members were White women.

## Contents May Explode Under Pressure

Throughout the course of the project, I noticed behaviors I found passive-aggressive, even toxic—ones I characterize as unsafe for people of color. I am being thoughtful about my word choice here. As a person of color, I find some frequently displayed behaviors, accepted as "normal" in majority groups, to be hostile. I am not alone in this. I hear similar statements from people of color all around the country.

Over the course of three months, the team met six to seven times a week. Every meeting felt like an emotional battle, laced with microaggressions. I found the many thinly veiled negative undertones distracting and counterproductive. Particularly grating were implied demands couched in phrases like, "I *need* you to . . ." There were many such subtle challenges to my leadership and authority.

On this particular day, the accumulation of stress seemed comparable to a label reading "Contents may explode under pressure."

Three of us had just sat down when Helene [alias], one of the core project team members, said to me in a tone sharp enough to cut glass, "Charles, you said you were going to email Yvette and get her reaction to what we talked about yesterday. *Did you?*"

"No," I replied. "But we did meet in the conference room this morning and I asked her about it."

"And who, if anyone, was going to tell *me* about it?" Helene's hostile tone of voice implied I was intentionally withholding information from her.

"Well, we only chatted for a few minutes, and we said . . ." I launched into a summary of as much of the conversation as I could recall while thinking, *If I provide enough details, I'm sure she'll stop worrying about being left out of the loop.*

Her furrowed brows told me this was not the case. Nevertheless, I proceeded to provide an update on another aspect of the project and asked for her and Penny's thoughts. Penny [another pseudonym] was another member of the team who often partnered with Helene and mentored her.

"I'm not sure everyone is being kept as up to date as they should," Helene said, arms crossed over her chest in a display of doubt. "We can't ever succeed with this project if we don't have the information we need."

*Good grief, how long is she going to beat that dead horse?* I wondered to myself.

Penny, eager to smooth things over, jumped in, "Charles, a lot is being piled on Helene right now and I'm not sure she's getting the support she needs."

Each new statement in this steady stream of thinly veiled criticism of my leadership felt like daggers. If they had expressed concerns with an attitude of seeking to resolve them, I would have welcomed the feedback. This is not what they chose to do. Instead, they threw out statement after statement, implying I was derelict in not providing enough information and support: "Did you [email Yvette]?" "Who, if anyone, was going to tell *me* about it?" "I'm not sure everyone is being kept up to date as they should." "We can't ever succeed with this project if we don't have the information we need." "I'm not sure she's getting the support she needs."

By the time Penny joined the fray with the last statement, my blood was boiling, my heart beating fast, and my mind racing. I felt under threat. All the while, I noted the irony that I, a 6-foot, 190-pound African American man, could feel all that threatened by two small-framed White women. But there I was, because of the weight of what felt like their obvious bias disguised as reasonable observations.

Given my awareness of the constant and relentless attack on people of color in the United States, my first reaction was to respond as the Black Panther/cultural warrior, establishing boundaries, defending my family and my name, while also inflicting a blow to their egos for assuming I would tolerate their bullshit. In that moment, they were in the unfortunate position of representing hundreds of White women in my history who had not checked their own deeply embedded biases and instead were acting them out in their interactions with me.

I knew I needed to say or do something. Otherwise, I ran the risk of something being said for me and done without me. When I am experiencing intense anxiety, my ears begin to burn—my body telling me something isn't quite right, an early warning system signaling psychological or physical threat. My ears were burning then. It was a moment of intense emotion, stress, and a strong feeling of being disrespected, yet I knew I needed to come to a decision quickly.

## Authenticity and Tact Under Pressure

My mind swirled with an analysis of the position I was in. I was aware of the privilege of my position as a senior leader within the organization, my role as a coach and developer of people, and my standing as a member of a team whose members I respected. I was even quite fond of them on less stressful days. Although my body was on red alert, I still felt the need to teach, to tell the truth of what I was experiencing in this interaction.

I chose not to compromise my humanity as a Black man and instead to be a truth-telling coach and leader. I did this by drawing on my innate principles, as well as those I had learned and refined through the years: clearing negative emotions and amplifying positive emotions quickly in service of others.

I took a deep breath and steadied myself, because I knew my anger, if not channeled, could be harmful.

"Why don't we just stop right here and call a time-out?" I suggested in a voice both strong and assertive. The expressions on my two colleagues' faces told me my statement had startled them. If they didn't know I had reached my limit, they were about to, because it was time for me to express the feelings I'd been carrying around in a bubble for weeks.

"I've worked really hard to keep both of you abreast of what's happening, but the level of passive-aggressive behavior is making me uncomfortable," I said, giving myself permission to call a spade a spade and thrilled with how freeing it felt. "Frankly, I feel it's undeserved, and it's not consistent with success."

I saw a mixture of shock and fear in Helene's eyes, and that pleased me. I wanted her to absorb the truth of my feedback. I had genuine concerns about the professional development of these two White women and their capacity to receive less-than-positive feedback. I felt the only way to achieve that was for me to amplify what I wanted them to hear.

I heard my inner voice saying, *I am a Black man calling you out on your shit. You will learn today.* I wasn't looking to cause them angst, but I was determined that they "get" the impact of their actions. Despite my own internal churning, I was still opting to be a supportive leader.

"Helene, the work you're doing is great, but your lack of flexibility and inability to quickly switch direction when asked causes more confusion than it needs to. I really need you to hear that. No one is keeping information from you. People work around you because you make it difficult with the way you react. And this meeting is a prime example of that."

Helene gave me a stern look and exhaled audibly. I noticed Penny's hand shaking. She seemed to be gearing up to speak, so I waited for her to gather her words.

After a few moments of profound tension, Penny said, "Charles, I hope I wasn't coming across as passive-aggressive. That wasn't my intention at all. It's just that there have been so many changing directions on this project that it gets frustrating, and I think Helene feels the same way." She cast an expectant look at Helene, who promptly backed her up.

They made a few more statements, obviously seeking to explain their behavior as rational and justified. The meeting ended on a low note. I felt an equal mix of frustration and justification about my position and suspected they felt the same.

## Learning Is the Key

The next day, Helene approached me in the break room. "Can we talk about what happened at our meeting yesterday? I'm feeling really uncomfortable and misunderstood."

"Sure," I responded.

"As you know," Helene began, "I've just recently returned from maternity leave. I also have a toddler at home, so I'm extremely sleep-deprived and under a great deal of stress. I know this causes me to be abrupt at times."

She'd said as much yesterday. I resisted the temptation to roll my eyes and instead injected empathy into my voice. "Yes, I do know you've recently had a child, and I'm sure you're tired. I can even see how that might affect your interactions with me. But I think it's important for you to realize that you're engaging with a Black man who's had this same exact experience many times. If it only happened this one time, it wouldn't be a thing. But it doesn't only happen with you and Penny.

"It's pretty common for White people to use more aggressive language and tone with me than the situation calls for," I continued. "And since I don't see that same behavior when they're interacting with each other, I have to interpret it as them feeling they have a 'right' to treat me like I'm inferior to them."

"Oh, I never think of you as inferior," she quickly replied. "In fact, you're one of the smartest and most articulate people I know . . . although I admit I haven't interacted with a lot of Black people."

*Lord, this woman needs help*, I thought. I felt my jaws tighten but spoke calmly. "While I'm sure you didn't mean to imply as much, can you see how the statement you just made suggests that being smart and articulate isn't something you'd expect from a Black person? Those are the kinds of assumptions I live with every day. They're called 'microaggressions.'"

Helene's facial expression was almost comical; she looked like the kid caught with their hand in the proverbial cookie jar. She'd been busted, and she knew there wasn't a damned thing she could say. Her new baby, her two-year-old, her sleep deprivation, none of them were valid excuses. Maybe I should have felt sorry for her . . . but I didn't. I kept talking.

"Too often, I've seen White people position themselves as experts, and then turn around and do or say things that try to identify with me, as a signal that they understand my experience, that they're 'woke.' But it just sounds shallow to me."

"I didn't mean to come off that way," Helene said unconvincingly.

I ignored her. "If I don't speak up," I went on, "and allow White coworkers to talk to me in a manner I find unacceptable, I run the risk of diminishing myself to make them feel important. And for us to have a good working relationship, one where we feel we can trust each other, we need to be able to talk about issues like this."

"Thank you, Charles," Helene said. "I really appreciate your sharing this with me. I don't have a lot of Black friends . . ."

My inner voice chimed in again, *That much is clear.*

". . . and have no way of knowing when I'm saying or doing something offensive. And I really would like to know. Although I may seem resistant initially—probably just a knee-jerk reaction to being exposed—I really would appreciate the feedback. I want to be viewed as an ally and a really good colleague."

She actually sounded sincere, I thought. So I said, "I think it helps to accept the fact that you'll get it wrong with me sometimes . . . and that other times I'll get it wrong with you. I don't want you to feel like you have to walk on eggshells around me. I'd like us to develop a more trusting relationship where we can give each other feedback, check in with one another, to be able to say, 'Hey, here's what you said. Here's how it landed with me. I'm wondering if that was your intent.' Having an open line of communication rather than operating on assumptions and suspicions."

Helene nodded agreement. She committed to improving her awareness and asked if I would support her in building her skills in that area. Naturally, I said I would. She also said she would enlist Penny as an accountability partner on the journey. The pivot was welcome and refreshing, a breakthrough we needed as peers.

This experience made a crucial contribution to my growth as a leader. The cumulative impact of these types of interactions can be both exhausting and emotionally triggering. It was invigorating to know I could summon options for navigating these terse exchanges. Both my colleagues and I gained important learnings from this exchange and subsequent interactions. And while I can still hear that inner voice repeating, "*You* will learn today," years later it is saying, "*We* will learn today."

By the time I left that organization, we were functioning really well as coworkers. And ultimately, the project was a success.

## *Uncomfortable Conversations Can Lead to Comfortable Outcomes (Reflections on Charles's Story)*

• • •

At first glance, Charles's story seems to be about the principle for Bridging Differences, but it's about much more than that. The story also does a masterful job of showing the interconnectedness of the principles for Clearing Emotions and Conscious Use of Self, both key components in addressing the racial "elephant in the room."

Charles was acutely aware of the dominant/nondominant dynamics of unequal power and status playing out in his interactions with the other team members. As most of us do, he had a mix of roles. As team leader and a tall man, he was a member of dominant groups, but as the only Black person in a group of White women, he was fully cognizant of their possible obliviousness to how he, as a nondominant-group member, was experiencing their behavior toward him. Intended or not, some requests made of him felt like challenges to his leadership and authority.

In the first interaction, his emotions were clearly triggered. As a Black man in a leadership position for some time, he was familiar with having his emotions set off by others. He knew the danger of suppressed emotions.

Given his values and history, he was also practiced in acknowledging and processing his emotions and thus knew how to clear his strong and negative emotions in the moment: "I took a deep breath and steadied myself." This was a practice he had cultivated. He explicitly stated how, over the years, he had learned to quickly clear his negative emotions and amplify his positive emotions.

Charles consciously chose to make the interaction with Helene and Penny a teachable moment. He was aware of his power in the situation and decided to use it in a way that would strengthen the team. In doing so, he acknowledged that his strong emotional reaction to Helene's (and others') responses to him were not just about the specific situation but also a result of an accumulation of such interactions with White women over time. He didn't want to generalize the stereotype to all White women, yet he knew many White women and other dominant-group members were often totally unaware of the effect their words and tone had on nondominant-group members.

His desire to "speak his truth" demonstrated his integrity in openly dealing with what in many organizations would be undiscussable issues. As uncomfortable as it might be, he felt it his job—his responsibility, really—to teach them increased awareness. He chose to deliberately operate from an assumption that they could, and would, learn.

It was also apparent that he made a choice to call Helene and Penny into community with him rather than calling them out. He was irreversibly committed to the outcome of their improvement, not wanting to harm them or cause them angst. He knew the dominance dynamics were interfering with the development of trust among team members and keeping them from doing their best work.

When Charles referred to "frequently displayed behaviors, accepted as 'normal' in majority groups," he was describing systemic racism rather than individual racism, involving normalization and justification of dynamics routinely advantaging White people while producing adverse outcomes for people of color. He made a point to note their tone and aggression toward him as different from how they treated one another. His discussion with Helene and Penny seemed focused on the intended or unintended attitudes and behaviors of the two White women at the individual level, but it was really motivated by his experience of systemic racism. He'd had years of experiences with taken-for-granted organizational practices derogating him and others.

When he inwardly declared "you will learn today," and reflected on the women's seeming unawareness of the impact of their actions, this historical context was an important part of what he wanted them to learn: that their actions would not just be interpreted in the here and now. Rather, whether they liked it or not, their words and actions would be received by people of color within the backdrop of their historical experience.

He seemed to grasp the level of stress Helene was experiencing but also knew allowing White coworkers to talk to him in unacceptable tones would run the risk of diminishing himself to make them feel seen, heard, and respected. He resisted the slippery slope to internalized oppression.

The result Charles sought was an improved working relationship among team members. He wanted the team to create an environment where open inquiry into and transparency about dominant/nondominant dynamics existed and candid feedback was the norm. Because of his diligence and willingness to risk discomfort, by the end of his tenure with the organization, he had come much closer to achieving this goal.

• • •

# Conscious Change Principles and Skills in This Chapter

- **Clear Emotions**
  - Identify with your values, not your emotions
  - Avoid emotional suppression
  - Clear your negative emotions
  - Build your positive emotions

- **Build Effective Relationships**
  - Develop skills in inquiry and openness
  - Learn how to give, receive, and seek feedback
  - Distinguish intent from impact

- *Bridge Differences*
  - Address underlying systemic biases
  - Learn to recognize dominant/nondominant dynamics
  - Check for stereotyping tendencies, unconscious bias, and lack of awareness in your behavior, especially as a dominant-group member
  - As a nondominant, resist any tendency toward internalized oppression or viewing dominants as beyond your ability to influence
  - As a nondominant, recognize dominants' potential unawareness about the impact of their behavior
  - Call others in rather than calling them out

- *Conscious Use of Self*
  - Accept responsibility for your own contributions
  - Maintain integrity
  - Seek to understand others' perspectives
  - Adopt a growth mindset
  - Recognize your power and use it responsibly

- *Initiate Change*
  - Surface undiscussables

## About Charles

Charles D. Shaw is the head of Scaled Learning for Meta Platforms. He has held prior leadership roles with Amazon, Yum! Brands (KFC, Taco Bell, Pizza Hut), Walmart, and Spectra Energy. He specializes in advancing organizational culture, performance management, leadership and organizational development, and diversity, equity, and inclusion. Charles brings real-world application to his work. Charles began his career as a voice-over intern for learning and development initiatives at a science, technology, and engineering firm in Houston, Texas. He has also worked in a nonprofit supporting mental health and wellness professions.

He obtained his PhD in organizational psychology from the California School of Professional Psychology in San Francisco. A lover of music, art, travel, tennis, and food, Charles currently resides in Oakland, California. He is a native of Houston, Texas.

Charles became acquainted with Jean Latting while she was working with Spectra Energy's HR team and had an initial introduction to Conscious Use of Self.

## CHAPTER 18.

# Testing! Testing! Digging Deeper into Initial Resistance to Change

*By Erika Young*

Photo © PlusCorp Photography & Marketing

I was an active member in a regional chapter of a nationwide nonprofit organization. Having been involved with the organization for several years, I was currently serving on its governing board. The regional branches had relative autonomy but took guidance from national headquarters. A year or so into my board membership, the national group decided to initiate an organization-wide diversity initiative and asked the regional chapters to place increased emphasis on diversity and inclusion in their programs and structures.

Throughout my professional career, I'd been involved with employee resource groups addressing diversity, equity, and inclusion (DEI) and been passionate about advancing equity in the workplace for diverse employees, particularly at leadership levels. My parents were civil rights activists, and I had been president of my high school's Black Culture Club.

Feeling equity to be equally as important in the nonprofit sector as in industry, I encouraged the board to pursue this challenge vigorously and volunteered to participate in the new initiative. When asked to take the lead in setting up a committee to examine diversity, equity, and inclusion in our organization, I gladly accepted.

## Learning from Earlier Efforts

In taking on the assignment, my first action was to seek out another volunteer, whom I'll call Felicia. She was a Hispanic female who had headed up an earlier effort to increase services provided to the Latiné community in the region.

"Felicia, I wanted to touch base with you. A year or so ago, just as I was coming onto the board, you were heading up a committee dealing with diversity issues. A few months later you resigned, and the group was disbanded. Can you tell me what happened?"

"We were charged with identifying ways we could provide our organization's services to a more diverse group of individuals," she replied. "But I soon learned that the organization was unwilling to put their money where their mouth was."

"What do you mean?"

"Well, when we talked with a few people in the communities we serve, we discovered that to attract individuals from underserved populations, we'd have to change our delivery system. In some cases, this even involved providing new services. When I proposed those changes to the board, I was told, flat out, that there simply wasn't money available for it. It was extremely frustrating to get that reaction after having spent so much time doing the research. I also felt bad about having raised hopes in the community that wouldn't be fulfilled."

I nodded. "Yes, I can see where that would be difficult."

"I wasn't the only one frustrated. The entire committee felt burnt out, pessimistic, and suspicious that we'd been set up from the beginning."

"This time, at least, we have the support of the national organization," I pointed out. "Maybe that will help. And we've decided to focus, at least initially, on the internal makeup of our organization. Maybe if we had more supportive individuals on the board and there was more involvement of people of color in our day-to-day operations through the volunteer staff, there would be more enthusiasm for making changes. It'll take longer, but perhaps over time we can raise awareness of the need for real inclusion and equity, not just window dressing."

# Research Points the Way

Knowing some of the history of organizational efforts regarding diversity, my committee decided to conduct research on the present state of the demographic makeup of the organization before making any recommendations for what might be done to increase diversity and move toward racial equity. We looked at all aspects of our organization—the characteristics of who we served, who made up our cadre of volunteers, the makeup of chapter governance (board and committee membership), representation of members of different groups in the marketing materials, the sources of our funding, and so forth.

In reviewing the results of our initial research, I was stunned to discover that while the agency served many Black men, there were no Black men on the board or on any of its committees. Nor was there a single Black man among our volunteers. That finding took me completely by surprise. Upon seeing the data, the committee agreed this was an important lack of representation that needed to be corrected. After much discussion, we came up with proactive recommendations to add a Black man to our board, increase their representation on our board-appointed committees, and set some recruiting goals—both number and timeframes—for increasing Black male involvement in several volunteer categories.

# Garnering Support for Change

I approached Georgina [another fictitious name], Chair of Membership and Volunteers, a White woman who had held this board-appointed position for several years, with the above recommendations. Georgina and I had a good relationship. She had always sought my opinion during board meetings, and we often held similar positions on issues coming before the board. She also seemed to support the organization's new emphasis on increasing diversity. I had no hesitation in asking her opinion when I saw that many of my committee's recommendations would fall under her committee's purview.

I didn't have to do this, as her approval wasn't required, but I thought it important to obtain her buy-in. I saw her as having a dual role, since she would be at the table when recommendations were considered by the board and her committee was the one that would carry out any changes in policies and procedures.

I emailed her the recommendations my DEI committee planned to submit to the board. She suggested edits: moving the target date for the goals much further out and questioning whether we were focusing on the right categories of volunteer involvement. She agreed the data revealed a problem but seemed to be hesitant about endorsing the specific steps in addressing it. The ambiguity of her wording made it difficult for me to decide whether this was a no. If so, what was the logic behind it? Where was her reticence coming from?

I thought to myself, *I'm just going to call and have a conversation. There must be something I'm not understanding here. I think it's important we understand each other's positions fully before taking the recommendations to the board.* Even though I knew this could be an awkward conversation, I was worried that if she didn't approve of my committee's ideas and specific goals, she would veto it at the board level, so I wanted to dig deeper into what lay underneath her seeming resistance.

As our phone conversation began, I said to her, "I'm curious about why you're not more enthusiastic about our proposal. You seemed so supportive at the board meeting when I was asked to take on this initiative. Is there something about our proposal you don't understand? Is there something we're overlooking? I need to understand more about how this looks from your perspective. Can you share more of your thinking with me?"

"It seems like the major burden of implementing your recommendations will fall on me and my committee," she replied. "I just don't know if we have the capability of finding the right people."

Her response puzzled me. "But isn't that what your committee does? Find and recruit new members for the board, board committees, and the volunteer staff? You seem to have so many contacts within the community and do such a good job of finding people who support our mission."

"But this is different," she said.

"How so?" I persisted.

She took a deep breath and said hesitantly, "Here's my dilemma. I worry that if your group highlights this situation, I'll be stuck trying to find Black men with the appropriate backgrounds and skills to serve as volunteers and board members. And, quite frankly, I don't know how to find them."

"I see," I said after a moment's pause. "Well, I do appreciate your candor. It's hard to admit not knowing something, especially when it involves racial issues."

"Yes," she emphatically agreed. "I feel like I *should* know, but I don't. I don't even know where to begin such a search. It's easy enough for your committee to make the recommendation, but I'm the one who'll have to implement it."

"Perhaps the members of my committee can serve as a resource for you," I suggested. "What if I go back to the group and ask for more specific and detailed recommendations on how to go about undertaking a search . . . and add those recommendations to the goals?"

"That would be extremely helpful," she admitted. "It would give me somewhere to start."

"And maybe," I continued, "I can approach my company about providing financial support for a marketing effort. There might even be individuals within my work organization who would be qualified and interested in getting involved."

## Responding to Rather than Ignoring Feedback Creates Unexpected Benefits

We continued our conversation, talking it through a bit more and identifying actions that would make her work easier if the board approved our recommendations. I took that information back to my committee and incorporated their suggestions into the proposal.

Not long after that, I had another conversation with Felicia, the individual who had headed up the earlier diversity initiative.

"I'm sure you won't be surprised that there was some initial resistance to our Black male recruitment proposal. But you know me, Felicia. I don't view pushback as a showstopper. Once we responded to Georgina's fears about how she'd implement this and found ways to smooth her path, I ran our proposal by a few other board members. Since I'd already responded to Georgina's concerns, I was better able to respond to theirs. Some of these individuals even had their own suggestions on how to recruit more Black male involvement. When we formally submitted our recommendations to the board, they were approved."

"I'm impressed with your willingness to stick with it, talk with so many people, and make so many changes to your initial recommendations," Felicia said. "It sounds like Georgina's initial foot-dragging helped you end up with a better proposal."

"You're right, it did! It took much longer than I'd expected, but the outcomes were better," I agreed.

We went on to discuss other things the DEI committee was doing and what it was accomplishing (or not). Felicia then said, "You know what? If you've got room for me on your committee, I'd like to join you. I'm inspired . . . and optimistic that more things can be done."

"That's great to hear. We can really use your help and expertise. Plus, we really need more representation."

"I think I can help you bring in more folks who can add diversity to the group."

"Just what we need. I'm so glad you're willing to get involved again, Felicia! It makes me feel good that you want to come back. You have a lot of value to offer. We've gotten some things approved, but there's a long list of things we still need to do. We'll get them done, even though it'll take a lot longer than either you or I would like."

## Systemic Change Requires Radical Patience (Reflections on Erika's Story)

• • •

Erika was glad to take the lead in setting up a committee to examine diversity, equity, and inclusion in the nonprofit organization on whose board she served. Upon accepting the assignment, she immediately moved into an inquiry mode, contacting Felicia, who had headed up an earlier effort to encourage the organization to increase services provided to the Latiné community.

It wouldn't have been surprising if Erika had a negative reaction to what she learned from Felicia. She might have been tempted to "call out" the board for not having more fully supported the earlier recommendations made by Felicia and her committee. While she could have seen this new initiative as a "heavy lift," she set aside whatever emotional response she may have had to Felicia's experience, choosing instead to focus on her strongly held values of diversity, equity, and inclusion.

Even after hearing of Felicia's disappointment and frustration, Erika did not view the dominant culture of the organization as beyond her ability to influence. She did not assume Felicia's experience would be her experience. Instead, she approached her new task with positivity and thoroughness, assuming the board members might be more open to change this time around.

Erika did not begin her thinking about equity and inclusion issues in the organization at the individual or interpersonal levels. In contrast, from the beginning, she approached issues of equity and inclusion at the systemic level. Her committee's initial research looked at all aspects of the organization—e.g., membership, marketing, funding. The data collected were comprehensive. Her emphasis on underlying systemic issues was further supported by her early mention of increasing the involvement of people of color in the organization's day-to-day operations.

Erika encountered what felt like resistance when she shared the initial recommendations of her committee with Georgina. The two of them usually had an amicable working relationship, so Georgina's reaction puzzled her. Erika immediately followed up, wanting to learn more. Rather than accept an assumption of immovable resistance as the "answer," she went immediately into the question. She was aware that multiple perspectives were not only possible but likely.

She saw the value of testing her initial assumption—that Georgina's reaction was a firm no—and arranged a phone conversation with her. Keeping herself open to alternative interpretations, Erika again used her skill of inquiry to learn more about Georgina's perspective: "I need to understand more about how this looks from your perspective."

Erika listened closely to Georgina's explanation and continued to probe. She was also strength-focused during the conversation: "You seem to have so many contacts within the community and do such a good job of finding people who support our mission." This had to have made Georgina feel good and likely contributed to her willingness to stay with an uncomfortable conversation.

Georgina's admission—she wasn't sure her committee had the capability to find Black men with the appropriate backgrounds and skills to serve as volunteers and board members—was a signal of how difficult this conversation was for her. Despite the possibility of Georgina operating on a stereotyped belief that Black men "with appropriate backgrounds and skills" might be in short supply, Erika was supportive. Had she been less so, Georgina might have felt this was an undiscussable and never shared her underlying concerns.

Erika stayed in the conversation with Georgina until she could see where the resistance was really coming from . . . what its real source was. The result was a stronger proposal, as is so often the case when one digs into the true reasons for resistance by those who want to hold on to the status quo.

Erika was not wedded to specific outcomes. This flexibility was evident as she went back to her group to ask for more specific and detailed recommendations on how to find more Black men to involve in the organization. She also mentioned that she ran the proposal by several other board members after gaining Georgina's buy-in.

Erika saw her success with Georgina as a small win and used this as momentum to talk with other board members. She understood that sustainable change doesn't normally happen in one fell swoop but unfolds a little at a time.

She also recognized how her positive associations with other board members gave her informal power and used that power to seek feedback from them. Those positive relationships were further strengthened by her willingness to "tweak" the recommendations based on their concerns—she listened to them and valued their input. It was an effective form of calling others in rather than calling them out.

Erika had a realistic view of the change process. She knew moving the organization forward on diversity, equity, and inclusion issues was going to take longer than either she or Felicia preferred. She was, however, willing to do what was needed to make progress, albeit slowly.

In summary, this was an impressive story of bringing many of the skills to bear on a difficult problem.

• • •

# Conscious Change Principles and Skills in This Chapter

- *Test Negative Assumptions*
  - Move from the answer into the question
  - Look for multiple points of view
  - Consciously test your negative assumptions

- *Clear Emotions*
  - Identify with your values, not your emotions

- *Build Effective Relationships*
  - Engage in powerful listening
  - Develop skills in inquiry and openness
  - Learn how to give, receive, and seek feedback

- *Bridge Differences*
  - Address underlying systemic issues
  - Check for stereotyping tendencies, unconscious bias, and lack of awareness in your behavior, especially as a dominant-group member
  - As a nondominant, resist any tendency toward internalized oppression or viewing dominants as beyond your ability to influence
  - Call others in rather than calling them out

- *Conscious Use of Self*
  - Seek to understand others' perspectives
  - Focus on others' strengths
  - Adopt a growth mindset
  - Recognize your power and use it responsibly

- *Initiate Change*
  - Emphasize changing systems, not just individuals
  - Surface undiscussables
  - Gain support one person (or small group) at a time
  - Set direction, not fixed outcomes

- Learn from resistance
- Cultivate radical patience through the time lag of change
- Acknowledge small wins

## About Erika

Erika Young is senior director of origination for NextEra Energy Resources (NEER), responsible for origination of renewable power generation projects in Texas. Prior to joining NextEra in 2018, Erika spent seventeen years of her career at Enbridge's Gas Transmission group and its predecessor companies, Spectra Energy and Duke Energy. Erika also served in various roles in planning, strategy, and global sourcing and logistics. Her early career was spent at financial services firms in audit, accounting, and mergers and acquisitions.

While at Duke Energy in 2002, Erika had the opportunity to participate in diversity and inclusion training led by Dr. Jean Latting. The training centered around the Conscious Change principles and skills that Dr. Latting co-created with Dr. Jean Ramsey. Those skills enabled Erika to increase the effectiveness of her professional and personal relationships and fueled her passion to advance diversity, equity, and inclusion in the workplace.

Erika earned a bachelor's degree in accounting from Xavier University of Louisiana and an MBA from Tulane University. Originally from New Orleans, she currently resides in Houston with her husband, Brian, and two sons, Jalen (18) and Julian (15). Erika enjoys time with family and friends, going to the movies, and golf.

CHAPTER 19.

# Introducing New Ways of Thinking
# into a Risk-Averse Organization

*By Melissa Simon*

Photo © Liz Bear

How do you get employees who have been with
an organization for a very long time to think out-
side the box? To be willing to even *consider* doing things differently? That
was my major dilemma as a consultant to Elizabeth [this and all other
names are pseudonyms], the new chief executive officer of a nonprofit
organization—one that had provided intervention, counseling, and case
management services to low-income families with incarcerated loved
ones for many years. At the time of my engagement, many of the staff had
been with the organization a long time—37 percent more than ten years,
26 percent more than twenty. A number of those currently in leadership
positions began as entry-level employees.

Because Elizabeth came in on the heels of a charismatic leader, she
experienced a constant push/pull: to move the agency forward while
respecting the accomplishments of past leadership. I found the culture
of the organization to be risk-averse, one in which mistakes were usually
seen as negatives rather than as learning opportunities. Being asked to
consider innovation or out-of-the-box thinking meant exercising new
muscles for many of the staff and board members.

Too often, things were done the way they were simply because they'd always been done that way. People limited their contributions to the narrow scope to which they were assigned. I saw the potential for a more vibrant, proactive, and coherent agency culture and began seeking opportunities to capitalize on this potential richness.

The twenty-plus staff were uniformly focused on the well-being of the families they served. Program supervisors and many of the frontline staff held licenses in social services–related fields and had a wealth of knowledge about the effects of incarceration, abuse, neglect, poverty, and drug exposure on children and families.

During my first few weeks as a consultant, I spent much of my time in conversation with Elizabeth and these staff members, asking questions and listening closely to their answers. I wanted to understand the relationship dynamics, the history behind certain processes and decisions, and their expectations of leadership. My focus was on how to improve communication, especially among leadership team members. A constant refrain was encouragement to consider new ways of doing things.

## Initial Steps toward Change

As I learned more about the staff and their respective backgrounds and skills, Elizabeth shared with me that she saw a need for some personnel changes. There were mismatches in people and positions. Gerome and Evelyne, for example, had both started as entry-level employees nearly thirty years ago. Now on the leadership team, each had held numerous positions within the organization, willing to fill in where needed even if their skills were not directly applicable to the position.

Gerome was serving as director of Training, even though he'd had no previous training and development experience. He admitted that he often had to scramble to get himself up to speed in areas where staff needed continuing education. And there were some areas—counseling services, for instance—where he simply didn't have the background or expertise to search for or evaluate the needed training. What Gerome *did* have were organizational skills. He was a quick learner, able to juggle many balls simultaneously, and good at tracking outcomes. I thought to myself, *These are skills that would be extremely useful as coordinator of Family Services.*

Evelyne was the current coordinator of Family Services. A qualified therapist, she had recently acquired training and certification as a performance coach—on her own dime. In a conversation with her, I learned she was already using what she'd learned to work one-on-one with the therapists to help them improve the effectiveness of their family counseling. It seemed to me that her background in counseling and her newly acquired skills as a performance coach would bring a new perspective to the training and development needs of the staff. In our conversation, Evelyne had expressed interest in the position of director of Training if it ever became open.

Switching her role with Gerome's seemed a better use of their respective strengths and skills, and since I already knew of Evelyne's interest, I encouraged Elizabeth to approach Gerome with the idea. He wasn't particularly receptive. He thought she was criticizing his performance as training director. Plus, having been moved into different roles several times in the past few years, he was somewhat reluctant to take on yet another new position.

Elizabeth and I had a detailed conversation about how to frame this new opportunity. I advised Elizabeth to first reassure him that the contemplated move was not a criticism of his performance and stress instead how the new role played into his strengths. She could then explain why she felt it important to reorganize Family Services. I emphasized how his skills could really help shift the unit from its present reactive mode to one providing more planned intervention and skill building. This approach worked. By the end of their meeting, Gerome had agreed to assume the role of coordinator of Family Services.

## Transparency Wins

These personnel changes alone were not that unusual, but the way in which I advised Elizabeth to announce them was. Determined to be as transparent as possible, I helped her draft a lengthy email to the leadership team, telling them of the changes and why she'd made them. She asked for their feedback, wanting to get their thoughts before sharing the news with the rest of the staff. Several team members responded with helpful, constructive feedback. In the past, these changes were either not announced at all or announced with no context or explanation. In my experience, simply reporting personnel or other changes without sharing additional information invites conjecture. The organization was already rife with distrust, gossip, and rumors, and my goal was for Elizabeth to head those off by being upfront about the changes she'd made.

The timing was such that Elizabeth included the announcement of personnel changes in her first board report. In preparation for this larger submission, she asked for individual reports from each member of the leadership team. In contrast to past procedure, she added her document to theirs and distributed the collection to everyone, not just the board. Historically, board reports had been marked "confidential" and were never shared with the staff, leaving a sense of secrecy and mystery. Our goal was to increase transparency, bring greater understanding of the agency as a whole, and gain increased buy-in from the board and the leadership team.

Feeling somewhat vulnerable by the knowledge that everyone in the organization would read the new CEO's report, we'd written and rewritten it, and I suggested that Elizabeth ask a trusted colleague familiar with the organization for feedback.

This colleague's reaction was, "Wow! You're just gonna jump right in and put it all out there, aren't you?"

"Why do you say that?" Elizabeth asked.

"I'm just surprised you're talking so openly about the staff changes you've made," she replied.

"I'm not criticizing at all," her colleague clarified. "I appreciate your taking the risk. It just seems like a big break from the past practice of not talking about personnel changes openly."

"I'm thinking of the comments we got on the recent staff survey," Elizabeth explained, "about how we need to be more transparent and willing to talk openly about leadership actions. That's what I'm trying to do."

Taking a deep breath, Elizabeth submitted the entire package to the board and the leadership team . . . giving the managers permission to share it with their staff. While we felt this would reduce rumors and conjecture, she was still nervous about possible negative reactions to her new openness in sharing information.

For days, Elizabeth incessantly checked her email wondering what kind of reaction she'd get. She also talked to her husband and another colleague about it. They reassured her she was doing the right thing— what she believed in.

After receiving the report, full of details, several board members emailed or phoned to say, "Wow! This is really long." (It was sixty-four pages.)

Her reply: "I warned you when I sent it to you to put on your reading glasses and get a cup of coffee."

The staff members, for their part, were shocked to receive the document, but in a positive way. They had never been privy to the information before.

This experience encouraged Elizabeth to suggest that the board invite all full-time staff to the next board meeting—everyone, not just the managers. The board agreed, and nearly thirty people entered the virtual room. Everyone contributed, talking about their roles in the organization.

Afterward, some of the board members' responses were:

"We've never done this before."

"I didn't even know this person existed. We would just get a report and that was it."

"It was wonderful to see so many staff on the call. This was the best part of the meeting, in my opinion, and we should do this every time."

They haven't done it every time since then, but in this instance, board members seemed to appreciate the additional information the staff provided, and it made staff members feel important, that what they did mattered. The staff also liked learning about what everyone else was doing. We were surprised how little people knew about what others were engaged in. There is now regularly an open forum at the beginning of most board meetings, during which staff members may be invited to share some information, but they do not stay for the entire board meeting.

## Broad Engagement for Broad Ownership

A few months later, Elizabeth asked for my help in developing a strategic planning process. The Strategic Planning Committee was a small group— Elizabeth and a few members of the leadership team and board. Its task was not to develop the strategic plan itself (which was how it had worked in the past) but to move the planning process along.

I encouraged Elizabeth to open the deliberations by involving more of the staff. We designed and conducted another survey of the entire staff and talked to follow-up focus groups.

The chair of the Strategic Planning Committee, a longtime board member, commented on the process: "For all this time, for better or worse, the process has been upside down. We've been fed the strategy by leadership; no staff were involved. Having staff participate in both the survey and the focus groups is completely new."

"Yes," Elizabeth agreed, "and the results have been eye-opening. We've learned a lot. Now I want to continue the leadership team's involvement so they can begin to think strategically, see the bigger picture. I believe all members of the leadership team need to be at the board retreat where the strategic plan will be finalized."

He nodded supportively as she continued, "We need them to provide context, to let the board know what's already being done. They're the ones who will implement the plan, so they deserve a say in it. But it's going to be new to them. It's not something they've ever participated in before. Some people who have been here thirty years have never been asked what they think the organization's goals should be."

Later, when the Strategic Planning Committee chair explained this to the rest of the board, I heard him say, "All the managers need to be there, not just the original three we had planned to invite. Elizabeth needs them there. And we need their buy-in—by helping set our strategic goals, they will be accepting responsibility for meeting them."

With the strategic plan in place and some key staff moves, Elizabeth could now focus on another important decision: hiring a chief operating officer to share the top leadership load. She was able to find and hire Sara, who had the operations, staff coaching, and leadership experience the position required. She was also someone Elizabeth had known professionally for about ten years, had often used as a sounding board, and trusted completely.

# Responsive Change Rather than Reactive Programming

Sara and Elizabeth began their work together by examining the programs making up the organization and the structure supporting them. One of their conclusions was that programming seemed to have grown over time by responding to individual requests for help and then creating services to meet those needs. As a result, they reacted to personal and family crises but didn't always help their clients build the skills necessary to prevent future problems, address the root problems of ongoing struggles, or develop self-sufficiency. This may have made sense in the beginning, but as the organization matured, there was a need for more intentional program planning.

More forward-looking interventions might include performing regular assessments, creating a Plan of Service, or referring parents to programs that provided needed skills—such as forgiveness and reconciliation, job training, financial literacy education, or GED preparation. Some of these interventions *were* being made, but the processes were not formalized or systemic across programs.

At my urging, Elizabeth and Sara identified a core group of leaders within the organization—some directly involved in providing intervention services, others more peripherally affected by them—and asked them to join a planning group. The intent was to include a diversity of viewpoints and to be sure everyone was aware of how a change in one organizational area affected others.

They pulled in individuals from departments with no daily interaction with intervention—such as development, those responsible for telling their story to funders. Outreach needed to be involved as well, since they were the ones most likely to be aware of external resources and services that others could utilize in the intervention program.

Not everyone was enthusiastic about being part of this planning group. There was some resistance. Cross-functional meetings to discuss issues like this had been held a few years back, but with the change in leadership, the COVID lockdown, and the normal frenetic pace of a social service agency, the team was rusty. It was hard for some staff to see the value in coming together just to talk.

"Why are we wasting our time discussing these issues?" asked one director. "In my opinion, we're not having any problems. We've had them in the past, but they've been solved."

"Unfortunately," Elizabeth replied, "solutions to our problems have often been arrived at by just a few people, without input from the larger team. As a result, some crucial facts were missed, and the so-called 'solutions' weren't always effective. Decision-makers didn't always have the data needed to make fully informed decisions and recommendations."

Sara facilitated the first meeting, beginning with a request that they all take a step back to ensure that everyone was on the same page with what they were trying to achieve and what outcomes they wanted for their clients. She and Elizabeth felt they needed to go back to ground zero, interrogate what they were doing, and redefine what it was they aimed to accomplish. They wanted their new structure, staffing, and directional shift to be long-lasting.

The group began by discussing what they were currently doing. Elizabeth argued that the program had become a series of transactions, where they were responding to the immediate needs of clients without investigating what it would take for them to build long-term self-sufficiency.

"To illustrate what Elizabeth is saying," Sara said to the group, "instead of paying to restore utilities shut off due to long-term nonpayment, why not work with a family to help them plan ahead and have them call us when they first encounter financial difficulty? Could we help them determine where their shortfalls are and ask them to think about how they could make sustainable changes so they would be better able to meet their own needs?"

Elizabeth and Sara both firmly believed they needed to change from a reactive mode to a more structured and empowering one. This was not an easy sell to staff who had longstanding, personal connections with some of the families served.

Maggie was the first to speak up in defense of the status quo. "I'm afraid if we change the way we provide services, the clients won't feel taken care of. They might feel we're blaming them for being poor."

"But where do we draw the line?" asked Gerome. "We can't be all things to all people, and I'm not sure we've done a very good job of defining the boundaries."

Evelyne jumped in. "I'm wondering, too, whether we're doing the clients a disservice by making them dependent on us for help. Shouldn't we try to provide them with the tools they need to really succeed, both short- and long-term?"

"But our families *do* depend on us," Maggie said forcefully. "We can't just pull the rug out from under them!"

"Maybe it would help if we developed a purpose statement," Elizabeth suggested. "What is it we're really trying to do? What does intervention mean to us? What does success in achieving our purpose mean to families? What does it look like?"

As team members continued to toss out ideas, it became clear that before they could agree on purpose, they needed to agree on some definitions. For example, Meredith asked, "How do we decide who makes up the families we serve? Does it include extended family members?"

Tyler asked, "Should there be limits to how long we provide services to a family after their loved one is released?"

"These are all great questions," Sara said with a smile. "It's important that we wrestle with what it really means to be there for our families, while encouraging self-sufficiency."

Finally, after two and a half hours of active discussion, during which Elizabeth and Sara encouraged the participants to test their assumptions and ask questions designed to understand each other's perspectives, they agreed on a purpose statement: *Families who have experienced the trauma of incarceration can thrive when parents have the skills, support, and resources needed to navigate the complexities of daily life.*

This purpose statement appears to be simple enough. Creating it did indeed seem like an easy task when they began, but the process was not linear. There were many twists and turns, and it took a second meeting to reach agreement on all the underlying definitions.

Ultimately, however, it was a great process, one they plan to duplicate in future discussions and planning efforts. They still have a long way to go to clarify where they want to be and agree on how to get there, but the process is now in place to have the kind of open and free-flowing discussion required.

The decision to focus on skill building and not merely distribution of goods and services was a major one. Yes, people will continue to need to visit their little food pantry, parents will need assistance paying the occasional utility bill, children will need Christmas presents and back-to-school supplies. They are still going to do all that. But their primary goal in the future will be to skill build and address the underlying reasons why these supports are needed.

## Stay Tuned for More

It was exciting and humbling to help open dialogue within this organization. People are beginning to understand they really do have a voice, and it matters. To further encourage the development of the leadership team, I suggested that Elizabeth enroll all of them in Dr. Latting's online course, Changemakers, teaching the principles and skills of Conscious Change.

## Conscious Change Skills in Practice
## (Reflections on Melissa's Story)

• • •

As consultant to the new CEO, Melissa clearly sees herself as a change agent and describes ways in which she worked with Elizabeth and her staff to get them to question the status quo. In the process of doing so, she effectively used several Conscious Change skills.

As she began working with Elizabeth and the organization, Melissa stayed primarily in the question. She understood the importance of listening and made intentional use of her influence as a consultant to involve others. She was also deliberate in suggesting the inclusion of multiple voices in the planning deliberations. She saw the value of diversity—it can slow down the process but improve the outcomes.

Elizabeth, too, used some of the Conscious Change skills. She maintained her integrity by respecting the accomplishments of past leadership as she moved the agency forward. Melissa advised Elizabeth on how to consciously present Gerome with the notion of changing positions. By following her advice, Elizabeth was both strength-focused (emphasizing how his skills could really help shift the unit from its present reactivity to providing more planned intervention and skill building) and growth-oriented (having no doubt of Gerome's ability to take on the new role successfully). Melissa was not surprised when Gerome initially construed Elizabeth's suggestion for a job change as a criticism of his current job performance. She was aware of the potential for suggestions to be interpreted differently from what was intended.

Melissa urged Elizabeth to be more transparent in multiple ways. One of these was encouraging Elizabeth to provide background on why the personnel changes were taking place rather than simply announcing them. In the past, those details had not been shared with either the staff or the board members. In contrast, doing so openly was a major part of Melissa's change strategy for Elizabeth and the organization. She encouraged Elizabeth to engage in inquiry and openness, with a goal of increased dialogue throughout the organization, so employees could become more flexible, resilient, and willing to take risks.

Elizabeth's decision to break precedent by including an announcement of the staff changes in her report to the board and to share the report with all the staff caused her to feel exposed and vulnerable. Rather than simply swallowing those feelings, she sought advice from her husband and a colleague. Sharing her concerns with people close to her provided a way for her to acknowledge her emotions as a precursor to clearing them. They agreed that doing what she believed in was the right decision, providing her with needed reassurance.

In the planning group activities, Elizabeth demonstrated good understanding of the change process. She was not discouraged by the resistance she encountered. Instead, she deliberately chose to learn from it. In her efforts to move the members of the intervention services planning group from a reactive mode to one of greater proactivity, she identified sources of their resistance, e.g., their "longstanding, personal connections with some of the families served." It was also evident that Melissa knew the systemic change they desired would take a long time.

Elizabeth adopted a growth mindset with both staff and clients. With staff, she exposed them to the board report for the first time and encouraged them to look beyond providing basic services by helping clients become more self-sufficient. With clients, her focus on self-sufficiency meant she saw the potential for them to build the skills needed to prevent future problems.

When distribution of the full board report was received positively, Elizabeth used that "win" as a springboard to lobby for full staff involvement in the virtual board meeting. From there, it was an easier next step to involve all full-time staff in the strategic planning process, with emphasis on negotiating goals and outcomes, rather than legislating them. Elizabeth also demonstrated the importance of seeking support from one person, or a few people, at a time—evidenced by her early discussion with the chair of the Strategic Planning Committee about why she felt it important to involve the leadership team in the strategic decision-making process. His buy-in was another small win.

• • •

## Conscious Change Principles and Skills in This Chapter

- *Test Negative Assumptions*
  - Move from the answer into the question
  - Look for multiple points of view

- *Clear Emotions*
  - Identify with your values, not your emotions
  - Avoid emotional suppression

- *Build Effective Relationships*
  - Engage in powerful listening
  - Develop skills in inquiry and openness
  - Distinguish intent from impact

- *Conscious Use of Self*
  - Maintain integrity
  - Seek to understand others' perspectives
  - Focus on others' strengths
  - Adopt a growth mindset
  - Recognize your power and use it responsibly

- *Initiate Change*
  - Emphasize changing systems, not just individuals

- Gain support one person (or small group) at a time
- Set direction, not fixed outcomes
- Learn from resistance
- Cultivate radical patience through the time lag of change
- Acknowledge small wins

## About Melissa

Melissa Simon received a Master of Social Work from the University of Houston Graduate College of Social Work after working for several years with at-risk youth and their families involved in the criminal justice system. Her career trajectory took her into nonprofit fund-development and management, always in social-service agencies focused on at-risk populations.

She credits Dr. Latting with inspiring her passion for leadership both in courses taught at the Graduate College of Social Work and as Jean's graduate assistant. Melissa spends much of her free time with her family, including her four children and six grandchildren, and friends.

## CHAPTER 20.

# Anticipate a Certain Amount of Resistance

## By Mary H. Beck

Photo © Steven David Johnson

My mouth was dry, my mind racing: *What am I going to say? How am I going to be received? Am I capable? What do they expect? Will they be angry? Of course they'll be angry. Will they trust me? Of course not . . .*

I had been asking myself these questions and answering some of them in my head for days . . . over and over again, in an endless loop of self-doubt.

The time had come: my first meeting with the team I was going to lead was the next day, and I still had no answers.

I sat in my office, closed my eyes, took a deep breath, and decided to ask myself different questions, ones I knew the answers to: *What do I know? Who am I? What do I have to offer?*

Then I told myself something different: *Just be the best you that you can be. Be honest about your work experience, what you know, and what you believe. Most importantly, don't try to change what they're feeling or thinking. Instead, show genuine interest in understanding their experience and demonstrate respect for their knowledge and expertise.*

# Leading When No One Wants the Change

I had been working at The Council on Recovery (formerly The Council on Alcohol and Drugs Houston) for almost two years, leading a team of counselors providing services to probationary youth. As a result of drastic state funding cuts, eleven of the fourteen counselors were going to be terminated. At about the same time, a second department, one providing other resources and services to this same population, was identified as needing "new leadership."

Organizational leaders told me, "Although we don't know the extent of the problems in this department, we are aware that some staff are allowed to 'do whatever they want' . . . shopping during the workday, coming in late and leaving early, signing each other in for workshops they never attended, etc."

In addition, the group was being moved physically, from an office in Southwest Houston to the main office near downtown. This was being done mainly to save money but also because the agency lacked trust in the current departmental leadership. The plan was for the two service areas to merge. I would become director of the newly formed unit, Prevention Resources and Services.

I worried about how this new unit would receive me. In their eyes, the leader this staff had known for several years was being demoted. They would likely be hesitant to trust this organizationally mandated change. Some might even be angry, feeling they weren't trusted or were being punished for the behavior of coworkers.

I considered that they might acknowledge the inappropriate actions (or inactions) of a few people but still question the reason for the leadership change. Organizational systems can be like dysfunctional families—you protect your family at all costs, despite internal conflict. Maintaining the status quo often feels safer than change.

Reframing my thinking helped me realize that I really wanted to understand the employees' experiences and perspectives. I also wanted to explore the best use of my own motivation, feelings, and skills.

# Bringing My Authentic Self to the Role

I reflected on the principles of Conscious Change I had learned years ago in Jean Latting's graduate class. I recognized my power and wanted to use it responsibly, with the utmost integrity. I was open to uncovering staff members' perceptions of me. I also envisioned a team with a learning orientation, one focused on learning, not just performance.

Finally, I settled into an action plan and said to myself, *This is where I will start. I will learn about each team member, their skills, interests, and backgrounds. I will learn the history of prevention programming. I will study what is working and what isn't within the department.*

Viewing the situation with this lens helped me become aware of what I didn't know. As a result, I delved into the history of the department in relation to the agency and reviewed the résumés of departmental leadership and staff to learn each of their strengths.

I also made an intentional choice to try to integrate my whole self into my new role on this team—and into the larger organization. While I had been doing my job for the past two years, I realized I had not really felt like a part of the organization. I viewed it as the place where I worked, not a place in which I fully existed. I had not intentionally considered how my knowledge, values, skills, and life experiences were aligned with the mission of The Council on Recovery.

Since its founding in 1946, The Council on Recovery has been at the forefront of helping individuals and families whose lives have been affected by alcoholism, drug addiction, and co-occurring mental health disorders. The agency's prevention programs help individuals, families, and communities develop the resources needed to maintain healthy lifestyles. Through these programs, The Council on Recovery impacts a wide range of at-risk behaviors, including alcohol, tobacco, and other drug abuse; crime and delinquency; violence; vandalism; school failure; school dropouts; teenage pregnancy; mental health problems; depression; and suicide.

When I became director of the newly formed Prevention Resources and Services Department, it had over twenty employees. Most had bachelor's degrees in health education, social work, psychology, or sociology. They were divided into five distinct programs and were supervised by managers with varying levels of experience.

Many of the staff and managers had been in their positions for several years and were providing services in more than thirty schools and community centers across a thirteen-county region. The fact that they were meeting, and in some cases exceeding, contractual goals despite top management's concern about occasional laxity, told me the staff had a connection with their work and with each other. From the outside, the department appeared to be thriving. That could make my job even more difficult.

My decision to bring conscious awareness and choice to my interactions with this new team allayed these concerns. I now felt calm and confident. Anticipating the skepticism and distrust of the staff I would be supervising, I recognized the importance of being my authentic self—it was not just the *best* option, it was the *only* option.

## Engaging Rather than Forcing Change

I was tempted to try to use the power of my position to impose cooperation and productivity among the staff—after all, I was their boss! But I knew that any positive outcomes realized from an authoritarian approach would be short-lived. I also knew this leadership style was inconsistent with what I had been taught and what I observed in leaders I respected and trusted.

My goals were to build trust through open and honest communication, honor everyone's emotions, and share how I viewed my role as director. I began by meeting with the former director, whom I will call Ella, with the intent to first acknowledge my feelings and thoughts.

If I jumped right into asking Ella about the details of her work, I would miss an opportunity to connect with her. Unacknowledged feelings might also have loomed in our midst, creating distrust and negativity.

When I walked into her office, Ella seemed nervous: "What would you like to know?" she asked.

"There'll be plenty of time to learn the details of the job from you, but first, I'd like to talk about our working relationship," I responded. "This situation—my assuming the role of director and supervising you—is uncomfortable for me. Surely such significant changes all at once were a shock for you and many others."

She smiled, then admitted, "It *was* a surprise. I'm concerned about how staff members are handling the change. But I will follow your lead."

I wondered if I would be so gracious if our roles were reversed. "I'm very grateful to you," I said. After a pause, I added, "I'm going to schedule a meeting with all department staff. But before I do so, I think it would help for you and me to discuss our respective responsibilities and authority."

We agreed that Ella would continue to manage external relationships with various schools and other organizations while I focused on internal operations, including direct supervision of staff and contract management. It was helpful to have achieved this clarification before the larger staff meeting. I had learned from past mentors and other leaders how important it is to explain roles to staff in advance to avoid confusion or conflict moving forward.

Each step in this process was as intentional as it was important. My strong sense of empathy helped me in this situation, but I was careful not to make assumptions. My actions and words were intended as seeds that could grow into a culture of teamwork, accountability, respect, and trust.

Prior to the departmental staff meeting the next day, I sat down with my manager, given the name Mitch for this story, to review my plan. I trusted his insight. I always learned significantly from his advice and experience.

"My goals for this meeting are to honor the range of emotions people may be experiencing," I explained, "to express my desire to be of service to them, to ensure they have what they need to do their jobs effectively, and finally, to set expectations and goals for us to achieve collectively."

"I agree with all those points," Mitch said with an approving nod. "They show who you are and represent the culture that we, as an agency, want to establish. I also think you should add one more: To establish yourself as their leader."

"What do you mean?"

"Tell them about your work experience," he suggested, "what you've learned, and what type of leader you strive to be."

I nodded in agreement. "Good idea. They'll have more confidence in my ability to lead and may begin to understand why I was asked to serve in this role."

"Yes," Mitch agreed. "They need to see that you believe in yourself."

"You know, I've done that before," I replied after a slight pause. "When I first started working here, I said to the staff in the juvenile probation program, 'I am not a licensed chemical dependency counselor, but I was not put in this role to teach you how to be a counselor—you already know how to do that and do it well. I'm here because of what I know about building and leading teams.' They responded well to that approach."

## Change Is a Process, Not an Event

Before the meeting began, I went to the meeting space to ensure it was comfortable and that there were enough chairs for everyone. As a leader, I wanted to demonstrate genuine hospitality and servanthood from the start. As people began to enter the room, I looked them in the eye, shook hands with them, and introduced myself.

Responses were mixed. Some made eye contact, clearly stated their name, and smiled. Others looked away and spoke softly, almost mumbling. I didn't take their responses personally because I knew people's reactions are based on a multitude of factors, including culture, family dynamics, past experiences, and personality. Once everyone was seated, I went to the front and let my eyes scan the room.

"Hello, everyone," I greeted. "Thank you for coming. I'm sure it's difficult to arrange coverage for your classes. I'm Mary Beck, the new director of Prevention Resources and Services. I'm guessing it was a shock to learn that your offices were being moved and that I'd be serving as your new director. I don't assume to understand all the feelings, questions, and thoughts each of you may have as a result, but I imagine your reactions have ranged from surprise, to fear, to loss, and at times even anger. These are reasonable feelings, and I'm not here to take them away. I also want you to know that I have a lot to learn about the field of prevention and the work you do. You see, I wasn't put in this position because I'm an expert in the field. All of you are skilled at your jobs. I have other skills, knowledge, and experience to offer." I went on to share details of each, as Mitch had recommended.

I then continued, "Over the next six months I plan to work with the program managers to set and communicate goals and expectations, not only about how we will provide services but also about team values and ethics. I haven't come into this job with a predetermined set of goals and objectives. Some are set by our contracts and others can be set collectively.

"Ella will continue to serve a vital role in the department—establishing and maintaining external relationships with schools, community centers, and other organizational partners. I will assume direct supervision of staff, but she and I will work closely together. In fact, we met yesterday to discuss our roles, and I have the utmost respect for how welcoming she has been."

Some of the staff shook their heads. One person asked, "I've put in a vacation request. Do I need to resubmit the request to you?"

"For the time being, keep giving the vacation requests to Ella," I responded. "I will get them from her."

Several more questions followed along those lines. I knew the early questions from a new team are typically simple. I liken it to dipping your big toe in a pool to determine how cold the water is before diving in the deep end. As I answered each question, I made sure to thank them for asking it. In other words, *Thank you for engaging with me . . . for connecting with me, no matter how briefly.* At the end of the meeting, I explained that I would next be meeting with each program manager to learn more about the contracts and services provided.

These "baby steps" turned into building blocks, and then into a living, breathing, organizational system. Looking back, seventeen years later, I recognize that I learned several things and had existing beliefs validated during this transition. Change takes time. It is a process, not an event. Mistakes are to be expected and learned from. Having a clear vision of where you're going, staying the course, trusting the process, and staying true to specific change-management principles are vital, including overcommunication, questioning your own assumptions, and creating buy-in and ownership at all levels of the organization.

### Gain the Trust of a New Team
### (Reflections on Mary's Story)

• • •

Mary walked into what could have been a difficult situation—an intact team to which she was an outsider; a team which, outwardly at least, was performing effectively but under suspicion for "slacking off." The team's former director was being demoted and easily could have been resentful.

Mary was familiar with the concept of Conscious Use of Self as the deliberate use of mind, body, and emotions to facilitate positive interactions and influence with others. She intentionally used this principle during the early days of her transition to leader of the new team.

In preparing for her first meeting with her new staff, Mary was deliberate in getting past her initial self-doubts. She reviewed résumés of team members to identify strengths, allayed the concerns of the former director, sought and received feedback from her own manager about her planned approach, and used nonverbal means to present herself to the team in a powerful and confident manner. Her initial action plan was based on questions, not answers. She anticipated taking time to learn about each team member, their interests and backgrounds, and studying "what is working and what isn't within the department."

One of Mary's explicit goals for the initial staff meeting was to "honor the range of emotions" people were feeling about the changes. She honored her own emotions as well, cognitively reframing the situation to approach it from a clear emotional space. She interrupted what she called "an endless loop of self-doubt" by affirming herself with reminders of her strengths and what she was bringing to the new position. She anticipated that staff reaction to her would be mixed—some hesitant, some angry, some resistant to change. Doing her emotional work in advance armed her against any "hot buttons" the staff might push during initial encounters.

From the beginning, Mary set out to identify how she wanted to be perceived by her new teammates and took action to influence those perceptions. She didn't just do things the way she had always done them. Instead, she paused and considered the image she wished to portray. She also realized it was just as important to hear *from* the staff as to be heard *by* them.

One of the most impressive things about Mary's story was the way in which she endeavored, from the beginning, to put herself in the shoes of the former director, Ella, and the rest of the staff. By doing so, she communicated the value she placed on them and their contributions.

Instead of focusing on potential problem areas, she began by seeking to understand the strengths of the team members. She clearly held belief in the team's capability of change, demonstrating a growth mindset. She projected this in her meeting with Ella as well. In her interaction with Ella, Mary engaged in inquiry into Ella's experience and perceptions. The more Mary learned, the easier it was for her to perform her role effectively.

After having thought things through, but prior to her first meeting with the staff, Mary sought feedback from her manager, Mitch. This step could easily have been overlooked. Among other things, Mitch reminded her that she needed to establish herself as the unit's leader, demonstrating confidence in the skills she was bringing to them—in other words, defining for them what she saw as her unique contributions.

Holding a meeting with Ella demonstrated Mary's understanding of the importance of gaining support for change one person at a time. By openly acknowledging her thoughts and feelings in that meeting, she prevented possible distrust and negativity just below the surface from becoming an undiscussable. Mary anticipated resistance to her leadership and the change it represented. Rather than trying to avoid it, she acknowledged resistance and looked for learning opportunities from it.

Mary made it easier for the staff to believe in her integrity. By being transparent about her earlier meeting with the former director, Ella, she took a first step toward establishing trust. Her openness demonstrated the likelihood of her honoring her word to them in the future.

Mary utilized several other initiating-change skills. When she made the conscious choice to commit her whole self to her new role instead of continuing to view the organization as just a place to work, she was engaging in personal change. It was also clear from the beginning that Mary's interest was in collective change. She wanted to obtain buy-in and ownership at all levels of the organization.

Her goal was to create a "culture of teamwork, accountability, respect, and trust"—a clear goal, but one with many paths to its achievement. She saw herself as planting seeds through her actions and words. But she also knew that change is a process, during which mistakes are expected and viewed as learning opportunities.

• • •

# Conscious Change Principles
# and Skills in This Chapter

■ *Test Negative Assumptions*
- Move from the answer into the question
- Look for multiple points of view

■ *Clear Emotions*
- Avoid emotional suppression
- Clear your negative emotions

■ *Build Effective Relationships*
- Engage in powerful listening
- Develop skills in inquiry and openness
- Learn how to give, receive, and seek feedback

■ *Conscious Use of Self*
- Accept responsibility for your own contributions

- Maintain integrity
- Seek to understand others' perspectives
- Focus on others' strengths
- Adopt a growth mindset
- Recognize your power and use it responsibly
- Build resilience through self-affirmation

■ *Initiate Change*
- Commit to personal change
- Emphasize changing systems, not just individuals
- Surface undiscussables
- Gain support one person (or small group) at a time
- Set direction, not fixed outcomes
- Learn from resistance
- Cultivate radical patience through the time lag of change

## About Mary

Mary H. Beck, LMSW, CAI, is the president and CEO of The Council on Recovery, which serves more than 55,000 people annually in the Greater Houston area. A leader in addiction services for nearly twenty years, Mary is an accomplished and respected executive with a distinctive passion for supporting and uplifting the Houston community and behavioral health field. Before serving as president and CEO, she worked in various roles at The Council, including youth intervention, prevention, program development and evaluation, and clinical operations.

Mary represents the agency on the board of the Network of Behavioral Health Providers, is a member of the Texas Association of Substance Abuse Programs, and is an American Leadership Forum Senior Fellow. She is also an adjunct faculty member for the Graduate College of Social Work at the University of Houston—the same school from which she received her Master of Social Work in 1998. Prior to joining The Council, Mary served as director of the Center for Organizational Research and Effectiveness at the University of Houston, providing evaluation and consulting services to nonprofit organizations.

## CHAPTER 21.

# Goal: Create a Culturally Responsive Organization

## By Sylvia R. Epps

Photo © S.O.A. Digital Imaging, LLC

I am currently president of Decision Information Resources, Inc. (DIR), an African American–owned full-service research and evaluation firm founded nearly thirty-nine years ago by Dr. Russell Jackson. I also serve as the acting director of Research Operations, overseeing the staff responsible for large-scale data collection and national evaluation projects.

I was born in Marshall, Texas. My parents, who divorced when I was in first grade, both had blue-collar jobs for most of my childhood. I have one sibling, an older sister who also works at DIR; an eleven-year-old son; and a twenty-two-year-old niece. We didn't grow up with a lot of material comforts, but we always had what we needed.

## Increasing Racial Tensions Are Putting Us to the Test

I first learned about DIR while completing my master's degree. Initially, I was hired as a statistical consultant in 2004, retaining that position until 2007. I joined the organization full-time as a senior research associate in

2008. Fast-forward almost twenty years from my introduction to DIR, and I am now the president, as Dr. Jackson formally announced his retirement in 2023.

When I joined DIR, there were fewer than thirty full-time employees. Today, we have nearly sixty full-time employees and another sixty to seventy-five part-time staff (most in a call center)—this number varies depending on the sizes and needs of our projects. Most of our staff are in Houston, Texas, and Rockville, Maryland; however, we also have staff in Alabama, California, Illinois, Florida, New Jersey, New York, Pennsylvania, South Carolina, and Washington. A constant over my nearly two decades at DIR has been the diversity of the staff—70 percent are people of color. Given this, it is easy to assume we are a culturally sensitive and aware organization, and I firmly believe we strive to be. However, recent increasing racial tensions in the world have put us to the test.

Most of our studies involve at-risk, minority, underserved, and hard-to-reach populations, typically evaluating social policy issues related to poverty, housing, and work. We do a mix of research and evaluation for the federal government—the Departments of Education, Health and Human Services, and Labor—and with foundations, such as the Will Keith Kellogg Foundation (WKKF), the Robert Wood Johnson Foundation, and Bloomberg Philanthropies. For our foundation clients, we conduct program evaluations to measure the effectiveness of funded programs.

One day, Natalia, one of my direct reports at the time, and I were driving to Dallas to attend a meeting with the WWKF for the Truth, Racial Healing, and Transformation project. We were talking about race and racial differences in the US vs. Mexico, where she grew up. Given our work on this project, we had both been digging deeper into these kinds of discussions, and for Natalia, it had prompted her to explore her racial identity as an immigrant in the US.

"I'm curious," I asked. "How do you fill out the census?"

"Oh, I select White for race and Hispanic for ethnicity," she said.

"But you're not White," was my immediate response. Then I thought, *Wait a minute; that wasn't appropriate for me to say. She's going to be offended.*

"I'm sorry," I quickly said. "It's not for me to tell you what your racial or ethnic identity should be."

But she gave me some grace, explaining, "Actually, it's the first time I ever really thought about it. Growing up in Mexico, throughout my childhood, I was considered White because of my fairer skin tone—this came with an assumption of privilege. And I'm still considered White by most Mexican Americans with whom I interact here in the United States."

"That's interesting," I mused, recovering from my embarrassment. "I knew you identified as Mexican, but I never realized you considered yourself White."

"You know," she said thoughtfully, "I never really thought about it either until you asked me about it. I may check another box in the future."

Today, Natalia considers herself a "light-skinned Latina," perceived to have some level of privilege. I thought it was great to be able to have this conversation with her and have her react so graciously to my faux pas. It created an opportunity for a deeper discussion of how racism has evolved in the US compared to other countries. I aspire for DIR to be a safe space to have these kinds of conversations.

## If You Can Talk about Racial Tensions, You Can Talk about Anything

I know it takes deliberate work to develop skills of racially sensitive awareness and dialogue, and my goal is to lead by example and create space for others to join. So when Dr. Jean Latting began the online membership program, Pathfinders, designed to help participants effectively navigate difficult conversations about elephant-in-the-room issues like power, race, and privilege, I invited members of my team (Research Operations) to participate alongside me. Eight of us, including myself, began the journey in early 2021.

My hope is that in reading about and talking through racial and other social justice issues in Pathfinders, our shared learning experiences will help us develop an increased comfort level with difficult conversations that will spread throughout the organization. We have heard Dr. Latting say many times, "If you can talk about race and racial tensions, you can talk about anything."

What I want for us to achieve from our navigation through Pathfinders—and I see it happening—is to create a space for there to be conversations about issues previously seen as undiscussable. Instead of expecting people to find the right words and the right time to address an elephant in the room, we will start with trust between us and then help each other raise the topic and push through a discussion.

I'd like to hear us say, "Look, I don't know that I'm going to say this correctly. I'm just asking for space to talk. You have my permission to stop me if you think I'm going too far or choosing the wrong words. I need your help in navigating this." That's the kind of openness I aspire to have with everyone at DIR.

As mentioned earlier, much of the work we do in DIR focuses on communities of color. To be fully responsive in designing and carrying out the work, we must apply a culturally sensitive lens across all aspects of our projects. I'm aware more needs to be done to help our staff develop and apply this perspective effectively. Joining Pathfinders is a step toward that.

DIR is a leader in the industry, and we pride ourselves on being an organization with a diversity of cultures and experiences across our staff. We also believe part of our responsibility is to ensure the infusion of culturally responsive principles into all our projects. A key step toward that is developing sensitivity and awareness when it comes to racial issues. Because our organization is 70 percent minority, I think there's been an assumption that it is a safe space, that we've got this figured out, and that we're automatically doing culturally responsive work. But that's not true at all. We still have a lot of work to do. There are still a lot of undiscussables.

Additionally, the nature of our work requires open, honest, and respectful debate. We engage in a lot of back-and-forth brainstorming and problem-solving: *Have you thought about this? Have you thought about that?* I want the DIR space to be one where we're pushing each other as scholars and as individuals, and to do this, we must be willing to address tensions, race-related and beyond. There are still a lot of undiscussables, and not simply due to issues involving race.

# "Something's Got to Change!"
# Learning to Create a Safe Space

It's been a long road from my early days at DIR to here. When I first started at DIR, I had just finished up a postdoctoral program at Harvard. I had been a consultant with the organization for several years, and Russell created a senior position in the firm for me, likely the first hire at that level for a long time. At the time, there wasn't an executive team, just two vice presidents. My early days at DIR were also complicated by the aftermath of Hurricane Ike, which destroyed the roof of our building and forced everyone to work remotely for six months, just weeks after I started.

One of my first assignments was to support the implementation of a large-scale data collection project in New York. I was familiar with this particular client, as I'd first worked with them in 2002 when I started graduate school. For this project, I went straight into researcher mode—reviewing instruments, asking questions, suggesting changes. In retrospect, I was upsetting the applecart. I was in my comfort zone with this project, but the people at DIR didn't know me. They just knew I was asking questions and they were expected to respond. Russell was looking to me to support a process already underway with people who had no experience with me . . . and I'm sure I wasn't as polished then as I am now when it comes to asking questions and pointing out flaws.

Even though I was working with an organization familiar with me and my background, I wanted to hit the ground running in the new position. It seemed like almost overnight the company had grown and the industry had changed, but DIR remained the same, with the same staff doing their work the way they had always done it. And it was *still* working! However, the company was short-staffed, given the increase in volume, and the new contracts required additional skill sets.

This was immediately obvious to me but probably not to Pam, one of the vice presidents and the director of Survey Operations. At the time, she'd been with DIR for over fifteen years. I suspect Pam felt I was stepping into her territory, swerving into her lane, and I was not welcome. It didn't help that Russell was giving me space to direct the project. Meanwhile, the client was constantly asking, "What does Sylvia think?

What does Sylvia say about this?" In hindsight, it must have made Pam feel insecure about her contribution to the project, and I was ill-equipped to recognize and be sensitive to this. As such, she was very resistant to my ideas and frequently challenged me. Russell was aware of the tension between me and Pam, and he had made it clear that working through the challenges was important.

He said, "I need both of you. The two of you are key players in the organization. I believe you can work it out." So he hired Dr. Latting to work with the two of us. She first met with each of us individually several times, then brought us together. I remember we met in this little office behind the reception desk, a kind of hidden nook.

At the core, Pam felt me to be overly critical, challenging processes that had been effective prior to my arrival. I was simply trying to understand what had been done and offer an alternative approach. I had to be clear with her.

"I'm not trying to replace you," I assured her. "You were, after all, responsible for bringing the call center to DIR, but the industry is changing rapidly, and our contracts require more of DIR than past efforts. We had to move quickly to get this major study off the ground. These skills came naturally to me. Unfortunately, I didn't stop to think about how my approach and thus my actions might have made you feel."

After a few more meetings like this, I talked with Dr. Latting again. I remember pacing in my closet, talking to her on the phone, sobbing, and saying, "This isn't fair! I don't want to work this hard at a professional relationship. I don't work this hard in my *personal* relationships! I don't have time for this! It would be easier just to quit."

She calmly replied, "Sylvia, no matter where you go, there will always be challenges. If you don't figure this out now, the same problem will arise with someone else in the future. So it's best to address it now. Believe me, what you do and learn through this process will serve you in all areas of your life."

So I kept trying. I didn't leave DIR; instead, I dug deep to persevere!

As my conversations with Pam continued, facilitated by Dr. Latting, I began to see how I might appear to Pam—here I was, a brand-new employee compared to her almost twenty years with the firm, coming in and questioning her. She had worked her way from receptionist all the way to vice president. I could see how it would be difficult for her to just accept me and, at the same time, face that DIR's project needs were shifting beyond her experience and exposure.

The turning point came in an all-day session with Dr. Latting and the executive management team. In it, I shared how burdensome my workload was. It was hard to admit out loud, but I was overloaded, working twelve- to fourteen-hour days, seven days a week—partly because of Pam's limited staff and skill deficits. This couldn't continue.

When asked for my preferred solution, I paused, my heart beating rapidly, then said, "I think we need to give Pam other responsibilities and put someone else in charge of the survey operations."

I looked at Pam and saw her wince. Clearly this was hard for her to hear . . . but she knew it was true. I believe it took her some time to accept it internally, but fortunately for me, during the meeting she immediately agreed.

This conversation was excruciatingly difficult, but I think the reason it went as smoothly as it did was because of the work we'd been doing with Dr. Latting. The two of us now have an amazing relationship, with full transparency and deep trust. It's been that way for many years, and I share our example with folks all the time.

The process was not easy, though. Early on, I was often too emotional to even communicate. I was all sweaty palms and inward trembling, but that was my secret. No one else could tell, because outwardly I kept silent and still. I would have internal panic attacks invisible to others. Now, I'm better able to identify and process the emotions I'm experiencing. I check myself and the situation and silently ask, *Is this me? Is this them? Do I need to pause and reflect? Or should I just speak up?*

I've learned that I need to sit with statements that engender strong emotional reactions. Learning how to pause, assess what is boiling up inside me, and then come back to the conversation is a technique I'm still working on. Dr. Latting taught me that it's all right to say, "Ouch! We need to pause for a moment . . ." and to give myself permission to say, "Let me sit with that. I don't have a response right now."

# The Work Is Hard, but the Potential Payoffs Are Great

Difficult conversations are hard work, as a recent one with David, one of my direct reports, illustrates. David is also engaging in Pathfinders with me and others from the unit. He has been at DIR for nearly ten years and is a White male in his midforties. I've had an opportunity to work closer with David than with many others on my team. After hiring him, I trained him on several projects I was managing, particularly those of a major client out of New York. He has now become the main contact for that New York client.

He's been a member of Pathfinders from the beginning, heavily engaged in the activities, and open to growing and calling things out that are not working. So, during a recent performance-appraisal meeting, I shared feedback from the staff noting that he (David) was perceived as arrogant and patronizing.

I said to him, "In the name of Pathfinders, there is some feedback I've been getting about others' perceptions of you. I don't feel it would be fair to sugarcoat this, so I need to tell you that, to some, you're coming across as arrogant and patronizing. Can you think of a situation where you might have given this impression?"

The Zoom room went quiet for several long seconds, then an obviously startled David responded, "I can't imagine how that could be. This is very surprising. I'm dumbfounded!"

That reaction let me know he was totally unaware of how his interactions were being perceived by others. I said, "I know this must be difficult for you."

He immediately became remorseful: "I am so sorry people believe this about me. What can I do to fix it?" We agreed that I would facilitate a conversation between him and one of the employees with this perception, and that we might also engage Dr. Latting to work with them as well.

David nodded and said, "Yes. I'm willing to do whatever needs to be done to change this perception, because that's not the impression I want to give."

"I appreciate that, David," I replied. "I know this has been a lot for you. It's been difficult for me to have this conversation, so it must be doubly difficult for you." I decided it was appropriate to reference my journey with Pam. "I know that if I hadn't dug in and done the difficult work with Pam several years ago, I would not still be here. And, as you know, I'm in a great place now with DIR. None of that would have been possible if Russell hadn't hired Dr. Latting to work with Pam and me—I would have resigned. If the two of us hadn't been committed to doing the hard work of repairing our relationship, my career trajectory here would have been very different."

"I've heard you tell that story. And I know from Pathfinders that the work is hard, but the potential payoffs are great. So I'm willing to do whatever is necessary."

## The Hard Work Is Not Just Interpersonal, It's Also Organizational

DIR has recently been involved in evaluating a national racial-justice initiative. Fourteen communities were given funding to implement racial healing and narrative change programming to help the communities heal from serious race-based incidents. Most of these communities are navigating blatant racism that has resulted in murders and police brutality; all have suffered from systemic racism. We have been participant observers in this work since 2017, both as individuals who care deeply about the topic and as third-party evaluators.

We have been able to visit each of these communities and, in some, participate in their racial healing circles. This has given us an opportunity to see how racial tensions play out and how folks are trying to navigate through them. It's given us exposure to how these different communities are dealing with seemingly intractable racial tensions yet bringing people together to engage in racial healing. It's been really amazing!

But again, only a handful of us had this opportunity. We have many more employees who could benefit from *our* learning. I'm looking forward to being able to expose folks in other parts of the company to this kind of work.

## Culturally Responsive *External* Work Requires Culturally Responsive *Inner* Work

I chose to join Pathfinders so that I could improve my skills as a participant in, and facilitator of, conversations about race. I try to listen more than I talk. This has a lot to do with me processing my emotions but is also because I believe deep listening is required. Over the years, I have become increasingly more comfortable being vulnerable, and I believe this has a lot to do with my grit and determination to work on myself. Beyond Pathfinders, I am also seeking additional training within the industry. Toward that end, I was recently selected by the Center for Culturally Responsive Evaluation and Assessment (CREA) of the University of Illinois Urbana–Champaign as one of ten affiliate research scholars in their most recent nationwide cohort. The purpose of this is twofold: not only will it allow me to learn, grow, and engage with other scholars doing like-minded work, but it will also help shape the learning for other scholars.

In addition, I participated in a Culturally Responsive and Equitable Evaluation (CREE) Learning Series through Expanding the Bench and the Advancing Culturally-Responsive and Equitable (ACE) Evaluation Network. This training included a series of six workshops, one of which I co-led. I plan to offer a similar professional-development series for our core staff, about how to conduct culturally responsive and equitable evaluation and assessment.

That said, my commitment to culturally responsive research dates back to my graduate school training, even though at that time I was not familiar with these terms (as they related to research and evaluation). I recall being in project meetings and asked to share my opinion about how what we were learning about the impact of poverty on low-income minorities was applicable to people of color. My initial reaction was, "I don't like being singled out. My opinion isn't representative of the African American experience or that of other persons of color." In retrospect, I am thankful researchers were at least thinking about these issues, even if only informally. Still, I always caution others when seeking a global opinion from individuals.

Nearly twenty years later, there are countless examples of the absence of cultural considerations in research and evaluation, from design and planning to interpreting findings in published reports and to informing of policies. As a woman of color, a scholar, and a leader, I am deliberate about ensuring we are approaching all of DIR's projects with a racial equity lens, employing a participatory approach to evaluation projects, and creating awareness with clients and partners about incorporating contextual factors into our methodologies.

Ultimately, my goal is to lead a firm of employees doing their own personal work around racial and social justice issues while engaging in culturally responsive work at the organizational level. Culturally responsive *external* work requires building an organizational environment where culturally responsive *inner* work is being done. We've got our work cut out for us, but I know our continued participation in Pathfinders will move us in the right direction!

## *Get Comfortable Being Uncomfortable (Reflections on Sylvia's Story)*

• • •

Sylvia engaged in inquiry when she asked Natalia, of Mexican heritage, how she filled out her census form. But when Natalia said she checked the box for White, Sylvia's immediate reaction was based on a common cultural assumption in the United States that individuals from Mexico are persons of color, not White. She caught herself immediately and apologized, maintaining her integrity by acknowledging her error. Natalia, for her part, did not take offense, recognized Sylvia's intent, and in Sylvia's terms, "gave [her] some grace" (in other words, Natalia recognized Sylvia's lack of awareness).

Sylvia aspires for DIR to do truly culturally responsive work with clients and recognizes that this will require them to develop an internal sense of cultural responsiveness. It is not enough for staff to just "get along." They also need to do the deeper, more difficult work of being able to talk about race and other issues openly and allow their evolving understanding to influence the design and implementation of their research efforts. The work is systemic, and the change efforts must simultaneously occur at both the individual and systems levels because they are so intertwined.

Sylvia described how far she had come in learning to effectively manage her emotions, not an easy process for her. Her initial reaction to the constant conflict with Pam was to run away from it, an extreme form of emotional suppression. Instead, she worked with Dr. Latting and learned mechanisms for clearing her emotions. From a clearer personal space, she was able to work through the difficult interpersonal situation with Pam—and later with others.

She came to understand that she bore much of the responsibility for the negative interactions—it wasn't just Pam who needed to change. With this recognition came the decision to do what it took to work through what seemed at the time to be an insurmountable problem. She had to be willing to change herself, work through her emotions, see the situation through Pam's eyes, and build a different kind of relationship with her. Her investment of time and energy, plus her willingness to work through her emotions, paid off. The trajectory of Sylvia's relationship with Pam as well as within the organization was altered tremendously.

Sylvia held both dominant and nondominant roles in the organization as a Black woman and, at the time, chief operating officer (COO). She was sensitive to the dominance dynamics involved in both roles and how they impacted interpersonal dynamics. In so quickly questioning the appropriateness of her statement to Natalia ("You're not White"), she was checking herself for stereotypes and bias as a dominant-group member.

An important part of Sylvia's goal for her own and her team's involvement in Pathfinders is to make fewer topics undiscussable and learn to routinely offer each other the grace to mess up. Sylvia is also a stellar example of consciously using her power responsibly—everything she does appears well thought through, considering her roles as COO and president. She's aware that others can't be forced to change. Instead, she seeks to lead by example and seems optimistic that she, the other staff members, and the organization can, and will, change.

Sylvia has a clear goal for the direction of the organization—she wants it to be culturally responsive, both externally and internally—but is clear about there being no single path to get there. And she is knowledgeable about the nature of change: she first involved herself, then a small group of direct reports, in the Pathfinders program and the Kellogg work, hoping what they are learning can be spread throughout the organization. Sylvia also knows this will require a long process of change, and that they've just begun.

In deciding to share reports of his being perceived as arrogant and patronizing with David, Sylvia consciously chose her values over her emotions. She knew it would be a difficult conversation but felt it important to provide open and honest feedback. During the conversation, she listened closely to David's response and quickly picked up on his lack of awareness of his colleagues' perceptions of him. Few of us know clearly how others perceive us. In offering to facilitate a conversation between David and the other staff member, Sylvia was providing tangible support to nondominant-group members, those lower in the organizational hierarchy.

Sylvia's story is permeated with the use of the principles and skills for Conscious Change. She is making good use of these and will undoubtedly continue to utilize them to the advantage of herself and the organization she leads.

• • •

# Conscious Change Principles and Skills in This Chapter

■ *Test Negative Assumptions*
  • Look for multiple points of view
  • Check to see if you are making cultural assumptions

■ *Clear Emotions*
  • Identify with your values, not your emotions
  • Avoid emotional suppression
  • Clear your negative emotions

■ *Build Effective Relationships*
  • Engage in powerful listening
  • Develop skills in inquiry and openness
  • Learn how to give, receive, and seek feedback
  • Distinguish intent from impact
  • Apologize effectively

- **■ *Bridge Differences***
  - Address underlying systemic biases
  - Learn to recognize dominant/nondominant dynamics
  - Check for stereotyping tendencies, unconscious bias, and lack of awareness in your behavior, especially as a dominant-group member
  - As a dominant-group member, provide support to nondominants in your group
  - As a nondominant, recognize dominants' potential unawareness about the impact of their behavior

- **■ *Conscious Use of Self***
  - Accept responsibility for your own contributions
  - Maintain integrity
  - Seek to understand others' perspectives
  - Adopt a growth mindset
  - Recognize your power and use it responsibly

- **■ *Initiate Change***
  - Commit to personal change
  - Emphasize changing systems, not just individuals
  - Surface undiscussables
  - Gain support one person (or small group) at a time
  - Set direction, not fixed outcomes
  - Cultivate radical patience through the time lag of change

## About Sylvia

Sylvia R. Epps, PhD, earned her doctorate in human development and family sciences from the University of Texas at Austin and completed postdoctoral studies at Harvard University Graduate School of Education. Currently, she is president of Decision Information Resources, Inc. (DIR). DIR is an African American–owned research firm that provides contracted services to government agencies, foundations, and other research firms, including data collection; social, educational, and workforce development research and evaluation; and technical assistance.

As a woman of color, a scholar, and a leader, Epps is deliberate about ensuring that DIR approaches all projects with a racial equity lens, employing a participatory approach to evaluation projects, and creating awareness with clients and partners about incorporating contextual factors into methodologies. She loves to travel, cook, and hang out with her son.

Dr. Epps first learned the Conscious Change skills via one-on-one coaching with Dr. Latting, then through group teambuilding at her organization.

## CHAPTER 22.

# You've Read the Stories, Now What?

You're nearly at the end of this book and may be thinking, "What's next?" It's up to you to decide, but if you've read this far, you're likely intrigued by the Conscious Change skills and wondering how to put them into practice. This chapter will help you do that.

## Why We Call It "Conscious Change"

Conscious Change is not a random set of skills. When you use them, you redefine who you are in the world and how you interact with others, particularly those culturally different from you. Using the skills will lead to a deeper level of change than just altering what you do every day. As you have seen, Conscious Change is about the assumptions you make, the way you handle your emotional reactions to others, the relationships you form, and the leadership you engage in.

As you think about engaging in the personal change required to embrace Conscious Change skills, it helps to identify what you are changing *from*. The simplest explanation is that you are seeking to release firmly entrenched habits—habits that once served you but are no longer helpful for the new way you want to show up in the world. Although influenced by your genetics and environment, you also have firmly entrenched habits as part of your personality. We all do.

You may have heard someone say, "That's just who I am. I always speak my mind, no matter what. I can't change who I am and don't want to." This individual doesn't think of their actions as habits. Instead, they use their habits to define their authentic self. As a result, what they think of as authentic behavior may be reactionary and automatic rather than a true expression of their deeper yearnings for themselves. You can attain a deeper level of authenticity, one closer to your values, through repeatedly applying the Conscious Change skills.

> ### For example . . .
>
> When Carole learned that a member of her political group had invited new members without asking permission, her first inclination—out of "habit"—was to unleash a scathing email. Pausing, she remembered the Conscious Change skills and worked to accept the situation gracefully and let go of her outrage before communicating with the offender. (Chapter 8)

As we change our habits, we change our personality—who we think we are. A conscious leader might say: "I can freely speak my mind, but I choose to consider the impact of my words before saying them aloud. The real me is not someone who blurts out what I'm thinking without considering its impact. I want people to see me as someone who chooses to be considerate of others."

As you were reading the previous chapters, did you notice how each of the chapter authors had a strong sense of their agency as human beings when using the Conscious Change skills? That they felt more faithful to their ideal selves and less reactive to their environments? We call this "changing their story." The contributors engaged in Conscious Change by developing new stories about themselves. They consciously shed the old habits and ways of thinking that no longer served them and stepped into the unfamiliar territory of trying out new skills.

> **For example . . .**
>
> Orfelinda tells us her workplace felt like hostile territory; as a Latina, she experienced continual microaggressions. By experimenting with new ways of thinking and behaving, one small step at a time, she was able to drastically alter her approach to her tormenter and eventually turn the situation around. The story she told herself about the nature of her interactions with her work environment changed dramatically. (Chapter 13)

We can't claim that all of our storytellers changed permanently. As you probably know, the road back to old habits is well-worn. Yet each chapter author took this initial and most challenging step: each made a conscious and courageous decision to use a new and unfamiliar method to handle a tricky situation.[1] That crucial first step set them on the path to more lasting change. We want to help you take that first step.

## The Secret Ingredients to Conscious Change

Think of gaining competence in the Conscious Change skills as forming new mental, emotional, and behavioral responses and habits. Some of your new responses may require intense attention for quite a while; others may eventually become so automatic that they become habits. Here's how to do it:

1. Be clear about your motives and desired results
2. Willingly embark on a journey of self-change
3. Think of skill building as an exercise in forming new habits
4. Plan the coping resources you need to sustain the change
5. Set up structures to maintain your change[2]

### 1. Be Clear about Your Motives and Desired Results
First, remind yourself of the stakes. Many of the nineteen chapter authors were confronted with emotionally charged situations in which they differed

from a crucial person by race, ethnicity, or hierarchical position. Because of these differences, the other person wielded power over them and threatened the author's ability to achieve their goals. Yet despite the power imbalances, these authors used the Conscious Change skills to own their responsibility, even in potentially embarrassing or life-threatening situations. They repaired—or turned around—relationships that were in danger of dissolving or had already been broken. They reached across cultural differences to seek better understanding and collaboration. They increased their influence in vital arenas. Instead of seeing themselves as victims, they became victors, attaining remarkable benefits. As a result, they gained greater self-empowerment and expanded their sense of who they were and who they could become. You, too, can learn to navigate more effectively across differences and, at the same time, help others feel included. Here's where to begin.

#### ▶ Identify One to Three Skills You Want to Learn

First, don't try to put all of the skills to use immediately. Trying to do so almost guarantees failure. Instead, identify one to three skills of particular appeal to you. It is important not to bite off more than you can chew. It is better to make slow and steady progress than to embrace everything at once and then burn out when the change proves more than you can handle. Be selective. Choose the skills that will take you in the direction you want to grow.

Review the stories that illustrate your chosen skills. Reading about the different situations in which the authors practiced the skills will expose you to variations of how you might use them and reinforce your learning.[3]

As you review the stories, what stands out for you? Take the time to write those thoughts down. Pause now and note your reflections while they're fresh in your mind. If you made notes in the book's margins, transfer the relevant ones to a journal, notebook, or computer file. Retention doesn't come from your first reading; it comes when you reflect on what you read, connect what you already know with what you are now learning, and put it into your own words.[4]

Now write down the skills you've chosen to work on. If you only think about them without writing them down, they may become absorbed in dozens of other thoughts. The act of putting them in writing requires some time and effort ... and time and effort are the keys to sustained learning.[5]

The skills you've chosen to work on first should be those that give you the most energy. Stay away from any that feel like "shoulds," especially if you feel any internal resistance to them. In the beginning, stick with the one or two that will give you the most momentum. You can ride that energy to success.

It's important to notice any emotional resistance you feel. You can make it easier for yourself by choosing skills you are highly motivated to learn.

### ▶ Identify the Goals Most Important to You

Next, write down the stakes involved in learning these new skills. Something in your life led you to choose these particular skills as your focus. What was it? Why is it important to you?

What is your current state? Your desired state? How will those skills help you get closer to your desired status? It's important to know what you're aiming for, so you can recognize steps toward its achievement. Be prepared to be surprised, though. Your efforts may yield unanticipated rewards.

---

**For example . . .**

Mary developed her Conscious Change skills over several decades. When she took on leadership of a new team, Mary knew she would need to draw on those skills to counter her new team's distrust and resistance—she was, after all, someone coming in from the outside to turn things around. The Conscious Change skills had worked for her in the past and were now almost habits. She knew they would continue to have the desired results in this new and more challenging position. (Chapter 20)

---

### ▶ Ground Yourself in Your Integrity

Set your intention for who you want to be in the world. How do you want to be as a leader? How do you want others to see and experience you? The skills you choose to work on should lead in that direction.

All of us have experienced making—and then breaking—a promise to ourselves.[6] To avoid this, we suggest you begin by selecting any one skill that will be an easy stretch for you. Then seek opportunities to practice it. Give yourself grace if your efforts flounder, especially initially. Just keep plugging away until you have had two or three successes. Celebrate! And move on to the next skill.

## 2. Willingly Embark on a Journey of Self-Change

Things do not have to remain as they currently seem to be. You can change your story. The Conscious Change skills help you alter your story about who you are and what's happening around you. Instead of taking everything personally or helplessly floundering, you will have tools to develop agency and discover new options for dealing with difficult situations.

In a world with so much drama and so many threats, with social media amplifying our tribal instincts so we can't *see* one another, it's harder than ever to view oneself as an agent of change—an actor rather than a reactor. The Conscious Change skills encourage you to be in the moment, consider what is happening, and then consciously choose your actions.

It's easy to give in to self-pity when things don't go as you want or when people do things you feel are stupid or unfair. It's easy and somehow satisfying to blame others. Alternatively, you can step forward and use your skills to turn things right side up again.

---

For example . . .

When a key person in the organization threatened to block Erika's diversity and inclusion efforts, she successfully managed her emotions and engaged in inquiry to learn the other person's point of view. She had learned that using the Conscious Change skills was more effective than railing about the unfairness of the situation. (Chapter 18)

---

Nearly every storyteller turned potential disasters and acts of unfairness to their advantage. They converted disadvantage to advantage, pain to triumph, and suffering to advocacy and change. They got through their trial by fire using the Conscious Change skills to pull themselves through.

▶ **Accept Responsibility**

If you're like most of us, you have not always achieved the results you wanted from your interactions. Maybe someone was angry at you, or you were mad at them. Perhaps you had an exchange that put you off balance, or you were upset about how it unfolded. Maybe you think the situation wouldn't have happened if the other person had done the right thing—you only did what you did because the other person started it.

If any of this is familiar to you, it means you have somehow contributed to past unfortunate situations. Use the Conscious Change skills as a different approach in the next circumstance. Even if you believe the other person is at fault, it's up to you to take the first step. You are the one distressed about what happened. If you want a different result, you are the one to do something different to fix it. If you want to inspire a different reaction in others, you have to change yourself.

---

**For example . . .**

From Larry's perspective, it's not surprising that he might wonder if the officers had been conditioned to be suspicious of people who looked like him. Why was it up to Larry to alter his behavior when he had done nothing wrong? Shouldn't the responsibility be on law enforcement to change their community outreach so Larry and others who look like him don't have to fear them? Larry very correctly concluded it was more important to be effective than right. His ability to take the officers' perspectives may well have saved his life. (Chapter 11)

---

It's hard to own up to how we contribute to difficult situations. Most of you know someone who will do anything to avoid admitting they're wrong. If they think they have messed up in others' eyes, rather than take responsibility, they turn the tables and focus on how wrong the other person's words and actions were. They only take credit for what went right. Acknowledging their contributions to situations gone wrong is painful for them.

These individuals cannot tolerate the blow to their egos from admitting they were wrong. They equate making a single mistake to damaging their entire self-worth. Ironically, their avoidance of responsibility is apparent to all who watch them try to squirm out of admitting error. They seldom get called on it, so they think they "got over"—that their evasive maneuvers helped them escape accountability. In fact, they are unaware of how weak they look to others. As they sputter and squirm and try to explain away what happened, they miss the knowing glances other people in the room give each other.

Do you want to be that person? Or do you want to be the one who dares to admit you were wrong or that you tried, but it didn't work? Do you want to be known as courageous, or do you want to be regarded as someone who tries to weasel out of admitting your part in dismaying situations?

Admitting your contribution to a failed interaction doesn't mean accepting full responsibility. When something goes wrong, there is seldom a single cause. You are simply accepting responsibility for your part. Environmental factors and/or others' contributions may also be at play, but these don't take away from your contribution.

Owning your responsibility, however, doesn't give you a license for self-flagellation. Please don't beat yourself up over it. Instead, congratulate yourself for having enough self-awareness to recognize the error and the fortitude to learn from it.

### ▶ Experiment

Start your efforts to learn the skills with a small, low-risk target. If you want to learn to speak truth to power, for example, begin by telling the supermarket manager that you'd like the store to carry your favorite spice. Figure out what approach is right for you. If you try to use a skill that doesn't work the first time (or the second, third, or fourth), keep experimenting with it until you hit on a formula that works. Conscious leaders expect failure on the road to success. If it's worth trying, it's worth enduring a setback. You'll eventually get comfortable with the skill.

It's not uncommon to feel as if you've hit a wall. It takes a while to get a new habit to a sustainable level. When you do feel you've hit that wall, reconnect with your original purpose.

- Write down the reasons you originally wanted to learn the skills
- Go back and reread your favorite chapter or two in this book
- Review the notes you took as you were reading those chapters
- Reflect on the benefits you'd hoped to gain by learning the skills
- Search out another resource (article, book, podcast) that gets your mojo going and refreshes your eagerness to keep trying

Once you've reminded yourself why you're working so hard to acquire the skills, resume your practice.

Also, remember that you don't have to go it alone. We offer groups through Leading Consciously where you can short-circuit the go-it-alone approach.[7] A new skill is taught and practiced every two weeks. We describe this program at the end of this chapter.

### ▶ Just Do It

Many of us are familiar with Nike's "Just Do It" slogan. Simon Sinek, a well-known leadership author, explained its appeal. "It has nothing to do with winning. It has everything to do with trying and everything to do with doing. When Nike's at their best, they celebrate the ones who do, not the ones who win."[8]

Conscious Change is not for the faint of heart. It's not for those who avoid challenges or fear failure. It's for those who want to be able to stay in the game—sometimes scared, sometimes messing up, but triumphing again and again as they develop greater security in who they are, what they stand for, and what they are capable of. Conscious Change practitioners challenge themselves to continuously grow, expand themselves, and reach new heights.

### 3. Think of Skill Building as an Exercise in Forming New Habits

Upon finishing the book and deciding to adopt one or two of the Conscious Change skills, you're likely not going to be able to do so effectively right away. Prepare yourself for a more ambitious process. You have had decades to become accustomed to how you engage others in your personal and organizational lives. Old habits are hard to break, and new habits take time to acquire.

## ▶ Take Small Steps—Don't Burn Yourself Out

The secret to developing and maintaining new habits is to take small steps. Don't take the lottery approach to success, placing all your bets on making a major splash. Decide you are in this for the long haul. Day by day and week by week, make a dent in your goal of developing new habits and skills. Even a small change in your daily habits can yield compound benefits over time.[9]

Once you've begun to practice the first few skills, stay with them. Silence your inner critic and inner passivity.[10] Practice, practice, practice until you feel comfortable enough to take on another one or two skills. Choose new ones that build on what you have already more or less mastered. You will want to keep the original skills while activating the new ones. Above all, avoid feeling as though you must master *all* the skills right away or that you have to master them on the first try.

## ▶ Identify and Celebrate Small Wins along the Way

As you may already have experienced, you will continually encounter different—and complicated—situations involving individuals who differ from you in new and challenging ways. For this reason, we emphasize the *process* of change rather than its results, because you're never really done. Once you know how to approach the change process, it becomes easier. With each repeated effort, you will be able to see small wins if you look for them. Don't minimize or dismiss them because you weren't smooth in your delivery or the results were less than optimal. Celebrate *all* small wins—not just the giant leaps!

---

**For example . . .**

When Melissa suggested that Elizabeth, as a new CEO, take the unprecedented step of distributing a full board report to her leadership team, they responded positively. A more cynical person might have interpreted their response as passive-aggressive agreement and taken a wait-and-see attitude, but not Melissa. She rightly interpreted their response as a "win" and advised Elizabeth to use it as a springboard for further changes: staff involvement in a virtual board meeting and later in the strategic planning process. (Chapter 19)

Keep in mind that progress is made in small steps, and small wins sometimes disguise themselves as setbacks. There may be detours and even backsliding. Treat these temporary obstacles as opportunities for learning, not as failures. There are no failures; there are only building blocks. Every so-called failure brings a lesson, adding to your knowledge base of what does or doesn't work.

Acknowledging how your own positive actions contribute to achieving small wins is also essential. Look for how you help make small wins happen. Give yourself due credit. You may have a friend with whom you mutually share successes. If so, celebrate your success with them. If you don't have a friend or colleague who can provide affirmation, think about developing such a relationship. If people around you eschew self-congratulations, then do it privately.

As you take credit, allow yourself to feel proud. Energy generated by self-celebration provides the fuel to sustain you through the sure-to-happen disappointments along the way. Knowing you have been successful gives you the resilience to bounce back more quickly and the fortitude to persevere.

If you worry that success will go to your head, don't. The self-reflection required to implement the Conscious Change skills offsets this. Later in this chapter, we will talk about the role of humility in keeping you balanced. For now, we emphasize the importance of recognizing small wins and allowing yourself to feel good about how you contributed to them.

### ▶ Adopt Multiple Perspectives, Give Grace When Challenged

As you work to develop new habits and apply new skills, everything will not go smoothly. People will disappoint you. If whatever skill you are trying to learn involves another person, rest assured that you will be disappointed in what they do at some point. As a side note, there's a good chance you're disappointing them as well.

Let's assume you were coming along nicely in developing a new habit of giving others strength-focused feedback. Then one day, rather than accepting your feedback, the person visibly sulks, leading you to feel disappointed in either yourself, in them, or both. What do you do?

To begin, don't ignore your emotional reactions. At the first oppor-tunity, use the skill of emotional clearing to feel the full force of those emotions, then clear them. Once you gain clarity, you will be freed up to change your perspective. To make the shift, become curious about what is *really* going on. Do you have accurate assumptions about what happened or about the other person's motivations?

---

**For example...**

When Steven reflected on an uncomfortable interaction with a nurse, an unexpected new reality opened up for him. Suddenly he had new information about the nurse and her intentions. This blew his mind. He now had a different set of understandings, which allowed him to see how her perspective might be different from his. It also gave Steven further insight into the multicultural nature of his work environment. (Chapter 9)

---

One of the Conscious Change skills asks you to recognize multiple perspectives. Doing so requires stepping back and seeing your interpretation of what is happening as only one of many possibilities. In our terminology, it requires moving from the answer into the question.

A vital element of this is giving the other person "grace." Grace means you are okay with and open to hearing the other person's point of view and willing to be altered by what they say, even if only a little. It also means giving others room to make mistakes and seeing them as capable of learning and changing.

---

**For example...**

Sylvia consciously committed to increasing the cultural responsiveness of her organization, internally as well as externally. In her view, key components of this organization-wide change are making fewer topics undiscussable and learning to routinely offer one another grace to mess up. (Chapter 21)

It's easier to give grace if you maintain an assumption that if others knew better, they would do better, a paraphrased saying attributed to Maya Angelou. Think about the stories you read in the earlier chapters. In many situations, the authors could have responded with disdain toward the other persons and written them off. Instead, they were willing to give others the benefit of the doubt.

> **For example . . .**
>
> Charles made a conscious choice to confront his team members' disrespectful statements. As a Black male team leader, it might have been easier to for him to ignore what felt like passive-aggressive attacks or write off the individuals as irredeemable. He chose instead to take the risk of openly addressing the issues and was quite effective in his use of several Conscious Change skills. While they had to work through a difficult set of conversations, it paid off down the road by helping to create a productive team. (Chapter 17)

Each of the stories told in this book could have ended differently had the author not had the courage to step up and try something different. Each storyteller also had the humility to risk getting it wrong. They were unwilling to be defined by the situation. Instead, they took a chance and crafted a new ending to the story, one reflecting a higher vision of themselves and others.

### ▶ Maintain Humility, Activate Courage

As mentioned before, become an experimenter as you try these new skills. If your efforts don't work, reflect on what went wrong. Analyze what happened and discuss it with trusted friends or your support group. Doing so requires humility, the ability to openly admit that you didn't produce the results you were aiming for.[11] People who fear being wrong—or doing something wrong—can shut down potential learning opportunities. If you want to learn and grow, prepare yourself to take risks and act courageously. Then with courage, try again another time to do a better job.

Brené Brown provides an illuminating definition of courage, high-lighting the link between courage and vulnerability. To paraphrase her, courage means showing up when you can't control the outcome.[12] If there is risk and you show up, that's courage.

> **For example . . .**
>
> Ashleigh demonstrated great courage as she walked into a meeting with her accuser and their supervisors. It took even greater courage, personal insight, and a huge dose of humility for her to own up to her contribution to the friction she and her coworker were experiencing. (Chapter 15)

As our storytellers have consistently demonstrated, taking chances despite your fear gives you a greater chance of getting it right—and of acquiring a new set of tools to help you become the leader you want to be. You really can learn these skills, but it does take courage—and time.

## 4. Plan the Coping Resources You Need to Sustain the Change

Perseverance is the key to learning new habits despite setbacks. When we, Latting and Ramsey, first uncovered the skills, we each kept testing out different approaches—often under trying, sometimes heartrending circumstances. When our attempts yielded less than optimal results, we tried again in different ways. Eventually, as small successes accumulated, we were able to enact the skill (or combination of skills) with a minimum of struggle. As just one example, over time, we each found it less awkward, even comfortable, to go into inquiry. More often than not, it became more important to understand what those with whom we disagreed were really saying than to immediately dispute their statements. We had learned a new habit.

### ▶ Conquer Your Emotional Sabotage

Let's say you've passed the hurdle of committing to personal change and have resolved to put in time and effort to practice the skills you selected.

If so, what can get in the way of your following through? The answer is encapsulated in one word: emotions.

---

**For example . . .**

When a colleague interrupted Emily's work on an important and time-sensitive report, she lashed out. Emily was emotionally flooded, unable to react thoughtfully and with patience to a request she later recognized was simple and reasonable. She saw how she could have paused and asked for a short break in which to practice emotional clearing techniques before responding in such a tension-filled situation. (Chapter 3)

---

Your intense emotions can interrupt your intended responses and sabotage your best intentions in fraught situations. You want to respond thoughtfully and responsibly to a blatantly offensive comment; instead, you pop out with a counterattack in the form of an insult. You want to reach out to someone you worry is slipping away, but your shyness and fear keep your caring thoughts from forming into words. You want to speak your truth to the influential leader who doesn't get it, but to your dismay, you start stumbling over your words and end up saying something that sabotages your intended message.

In each case, your amygdala is hijacking your neocortex, keeping it from governing your thoughts.[13] What might you do to overcome this? The answer is to identify with your values, not your emotions.

In the moment, emotions may often reign over your deepest wish for yourself and your situation. When this happens, pause and take a deep breath to remind yourself of your core values and the principles you want to stand for. This can give you the nudge you need to either stay silent or take the leap, saying something like this: "I'm debating with myself whether to voice something that feels controversial or risky, and I've decided this situation calls for it . . ."

▶ **Replace Your Negative Self-Talk with Self-Affirmations**
Negative self-talk is your enemy. Discouragement is also your enemy.

Many of us undermine our best self-intentions through our inner critic and our inner passivity.[14] Our inner critic tells us we are doing it wrong, beating us up until we are demoralized. Then our inner passivity kicks in and tells us there is no use, so why bother. Sound or feel familiar?

> ### For example . . .
>
> What would have happened, do you think, if after the first two back-to-back painful interactions with team leaders, Treshina had blamed herself for the failures or decided the new job just wasn't worth it? What if she had not taken a chance on opening up with her third team leader? Even though she was under a great deal of stress, rather than giving up, she decided to take a risk. This one act dramatically changed the trajectory of her career at her new company. (Chapter 16)

Learning any new skill requires conquering both our inner critic and our inner passivity. Jean Latting has learned to counter both inner derailers by reciting her mantra, "three steps forward, two steps back." With any new endeavor, she expects to move forward three steps but back two. This helps her hold realistic expectations for her change efforts. It also helps remind her that meaningful change can be excruciatingly slow, uneven, and requires radical patience.

### ▶ Develop Radical Patience

The skills of Conscious Change appear deceptively simple. Yet as you have seen from these nineteen stories, they don't come naturally. If you go back and look at each chapter, you will see a person determined to take a risk and do something they might not typically do. Each person put themselves out there. They were willing to be wrong, unsure if their efforts would succeed. They wanted it to work out, yet they accepted that it might not. None of us learned the skills without failing sometimes.

It's easy to become discouraged as you try and fail, try again, and fail again. That is why it's paramount to put in your mind that you deserve to be good at the skills and will persist until you achieve the desired level of mastery.

Use self-affirmations to see yourself as deserving of and successful in acquiring these skills. This will help you maintain the persistence needed. Don't know where to go to find self-affirmations that will work for you? Google the phrase and try YouTube. There are many available online. Find those you like and put together your own meaningful affirmation.

Consistent, persistent, and effective use of the Conscious Change skills takes practice. Integrating them into your daily life and work requires a solid, steady drumbeat-type commitment to personal change until they become habits. As with New Year's resolutions, you may be enthusiastic about making initial changes but quickly face the difficult challenge of sustaining them over time.

When the setbacks come, remind yourself that change is nonlinear and won't be all ups. Ups *and* downs are the norm. Gird yourself for unpredictable downturns. Better yet, plan ahead for how you will make it through when the downturns come. Who will you call, and what will you read or listen to for support?

And, yes, it will take longer to master the skills than you expect. These nineteen chapters are testimony that the skills can be learned and applied, and your life will improve as a result. Reread your favorite chapter to find inspiration and hope when change seems slow or, even worse, nonexistent.

---

**For example . . .**

Chamara's persistent change efforts in a large and seemingly intractable bureaucracy is an impressive example of perseverance and its payoffs. She took her safety complaint through the successive layers of the hierarchy, sought support from her colleagues, and eventually filed a formal complaint with the union. Against the odds, through her perseverance and use of affirmations, she ultimately succeeded. (Chapter 12)

---

Go back and reread Chamara's story and others you found particularly insightful. The satisfaction achieved when you finally do master the skills—and achieve your goals through their use—is uplifting. And it *will* get easier as you become proficient in a few of the skills; they will begin to build on one another.

### 5. Set Up Structures to Maintain Your Change

If you find yourself unable to make the personal changes you wish to make, don't be too quick to conclude what the reasons for your difficulty are. Too often, when people run into the first roadblock, they blame themselves ("This just isn't going to work for me.") or others ("They're a lost cause.").[15]

Before giving up, remind yourself that you are trying to move from an entrenched set of habits to a new pattern. Your muscle memory is powerful, often operating beneath the conscious level and constantly enacting old and familiar interlaced actions and reactions. It strongly resists your desire to navigate differences more effectively and foster inclusion.

#### ▶ Set Up Cues to Help You Resist Following Your Entrenched Habits

Treating your action or reaction as an entrenched habit may also help you to identify ways to cue the desired action. Wherever possible, restructure your environment to make it easier to take action toward your desired change. When Jean Latting was still teaching, she resolved to go to the fitness center after each afternoon class. Instead, for an entire semester, as she drove home, she would decide she was just "too tired" to go to the center and drive right past. Then one day, she found herself out of breath from walking up a single flight of stairs and knew she had to get her body moving more regularly. So at the start of the next semester, she packed a canvas bag with her workout clothes, sneakers, and fitness center membership card and placed it on the passenger seat of her car. After class, the bag was there to remind her of her commitment to herself. This simple cue worked. She started going to the center regularly.

Note that she was just as tired the second semester as the first. The difference was in using a visible object to cue her new behavior. The problem, it turned out, was not that she was too tired to exercise regularly; it was that she had lost the memory of the value of regular exercise. The canvas bag on the front seat beside her activated this memory and provided the needed extra impetus.

## ▶ Find Social Support As You Practice New Skills

Change is hard. We make no claim of an easy transition from the old ways to the new. Learning new skills can be challenging and lonely. In contemplating how to begin, we strongly encourage you not to go it alone. If you do, you may end up circling through the same tired thoughts and falling back on the same habits that slow progress. Good friends and trusted colleagues can help you maintain a clearer perspective.

Three of the authors of this book belong to a dialogue group that has met, more or less monthly, for nearly three decades. (The fourth was just a child when we began meeting and now has her own social support group.) Our group is one of the places where we slow down, listen to each other's reflections, and frequently discover a new angle or direction that gives us the energy and motivation to tackle a difficult situation one more time. We share a deep respect for one another and a mutual interest in continuous learning and growth. You may already have friends or colleagues who can provide this type of support. If so, use them. If not, find them.

The Conscious Change skills are not "one and done." Once you start developing them and have some successful outcomes from using them, you will likely find yourself on a lifelong journey. For example, the authors have found that the more exposure we seek with different others, even radically different others, the more skilled we become at considering multiple perspectives. The more we challenge ourselves with dissimilar people, the greater our capacity to work with those vastly different from ourselves.

And isn't learning from different others, and utilizing this learning to help organizations make better decisions, one of the benefits of diversity? The more informed we are about people who differ from us, the more effective we are in our interactions with those more similar to us.

People aiming to do a 5K run don't train by only running 5K; they run longer races until doing a 5K is a breeze. Similarly, if you are aiming to elevate your skills, seek out opportunities to engage with those who think differently than you. Test your ability to really *get* their perspective, even when you disagree with it. Can you hold their point of view and yours at the same time? Can you entertain the paradox?

If you really want to challenge yourself, consider asking someone very different from yourself to give you feedback on how you might improve yourself or better support them. Make people willing to provide honest feedback a part of your social support network as you help one another grow.

## Resources Available to You

You have many options for learning the skills. You can:

- buy a journal and diligently reflect on your progress as you test out each skill;
- find a friend or colleague with whom to learn the skills;
- set up a book group to work through the skills together;
- engage a Leading Consciously coach; or
- join one of our Leading Consciously programs.

We at Leading Consciously offer two programs for those wishing to dive deeply into the skills: Pathfinders and Changemakers. To help you make an informed decision, we will tell you a little about each. Both are consistent with what you've been learning in this book and have several elements in common. These programs:

- are grounded in research;
- address three levels of impact: intrapersonal, interpersonal, and systems;
- consider diversity, equity, and inclusion as integral to excellent leadership rather than an add-on competence; and
- include Conscious Change skills as part of their programs.

### ■ *Pathfinders: Leadership for Inclusion and Equity*
Pathfinders is our online membership program for leaders and would-be leaders at all levels and provides quantifiable ways to:

- learn about diversity, inclusion, and equity through respectful exchanges;
- grow personally by developing self-enterprising skills; and
- become more successful by taking action.

Pathfinders provides the opportunity to lean into tough conversations, a rigorous but necessary leadership competency. Members read and discuss Leading Consciously blog posts and podcasts about provocative topics related to diversity, equity, and inclusion. Through these guided conversations, members expand their ability to critically examine contentious issues and connect them to their workplaces in safe and indirect ways.

Participants develop a shared vocabulary to surface concerns and navigate difficult conversations while building trust over time. By creating a "safe container" in which participants feel supported and challenged, the program offers space for all to grow, regardless of where they are on their journey.

## ■ *Changemakers: Leading in a Diverse and Multicultural World*

Changemakers is a ready-to-implement solution to help leaders in multicultural environments learn how to build more inclusive and equitable teams using Conscious Change principles and skills. By doing a deep dive into the skills, Changemaker participants learn how to:

- stand up to bullying behavior without appearing petty;
- respond to offensive remarks made by a colleague without damaging the relationship;
- shift to a positive outlook to combat despair;
- fully embrace successes instead of squelching good feelings about them;
- test negative assumptions about individuals they thought were deliberately trying to undermine them;
- repress the urge to argue and instead go into inquiry to understand another's thinking;
- give difficult feedback to someone without deflating them;
- garner support for new ideas from colleagues; and
- begin seeing themselves as leaders, not just doers.

## A Better You

Frankly, we are passionate about taking lessons learned from our chapter authors and bringing them to you. As you gain competence in applying the skills, your vision of what's possible will expand. You will reconceptualize your story—your place in the world—and enlarge your sense of self. You will become more agile, resilient, and better able to communicate with people different from yourself and be poised to create more empowered relationships. You will also be prepared to join with others to create more resilient, multicultural, and inclusive organizations. You will be a better you.

## Leading Consciously Resources and Services

Don't think of this as the end of a book. Think of it as the start of a new chapter on your journey toward Conscious Change. Here are some resources and services to help you continue on your path to being a stronger leader—in every phase of your life.

■ *Pathfinders: Leadership for Inclusion and Equity*
Our online, ongoing, guided membership program helps individuals and groups learn how to recognize racism, develop self-enterprising skills, and take informed action. The goal is to develop as a leader so that you can create more successful multicultural organizations. More information on Pathfinders is available at www.LeadingConsciously .com/pathfinders.

■ *Changemakers: Leading in a Diverse and Multicultural World*
This is our premium nine-month online course specifically designed for people who want to become exceptional leaders. Participants get a step-by-step manual that integrates enriching opportunities from videos and small-group discussions on real-world situations and how-to scenarios. Learn more at www.LeadingConsciously.com/changemakers.

### ■ *Consulting and Coaching Services*

In addition to our formalized programs, Leading Consciously offers customized sessions for you or your entire organization. Our goal is to help empower participants with a deeper understanding of race and other social-justice issues, so they can better understand themselves as individuals and more effectively advocate for social justice. Find out more on the Consulting & Coaching page in the Services dropdown menu at LeadingConsciously.com.

### ■ *Individual and Organizational Measurement Tools*

Assess your organization's disposition toward DEI, learn how you are perceived by others, and identify areas for improvement with our proprietary evaluations. You can find more information on the Assessment page in the What We Offer dropdown menu at LeadingConsciously.com.

### ■ *Reframing Change: How to Deal with Workplace Dynamics, Influence Others, and Bring People Together to Initiate Positive Change (2009)*

This is our first book, in which we introduce the principles of Conscious Change. You can purchase it using the link on our home page—www.LeadingConsciously.com.

### ■ *The Website: LeadingConsciously.com*

Our website offers more information on everything listed above. It also features more than a hundred blog posts and video interviews with profound insights and helpful information that can help you be a more enlightened and effective leader in your home, workplace, and community.

# Let's Connect!

Follow more of our work and other adventures on social media. And please reach out if we can be of any service. We really do believe that, together, we can change the world. Thank you.

JeanLC@LeadingConsciously.com

(713) 887-8944

**You Tube** @leadingconsciously5816

**in** linkedin.com/in/jeanlattingconsultant

**in** linkedin.com/company/leading-consciously

**Medium** jeanlatting.medium.com

**f** facebook.com/LeadingConsciouslyLLC

# Notes

## Foreword

1.  Ramsey, V. Jean, and Jean Kantambu Latting (2005). "A Typology of Intergroup Competencies." *Journal of Applied Behavioral Science* 41(3): 265–284.

## Chapter 1

1.  Ramsey, V. Jean, and Jean Kantambu Latting (2005). "A Typology of Intergroup Competencies." *Journal of Applied Behavioral Science* 41(3): 265–284.

2.  Latting, Jean Kantambu, and V. Jean Ramsey (2009). *Reframing Change: How to Deal with Workplace Dynamics, Influence Others, and Bring People Together to Initiate Positive Change.* Westport, CT: Praeger.

3.  For more information, visit our website: www.leadingconsciously.com.

4.  Goleman, Daniel, Richard Boyatzis, Annie McKee, and Sydney Finkelstein (2015). *HBR's 10 Must Reads on Emotional Intelligence.* Boston: Harvard Business Review Press.

5.  Appiah, Kwame Anthony (2020). "The Case for Capitalizing the *B* in Black." *The Atlantic,* June 19. www.theatlantic.com/ideas/archive/2020/06/time-to-capitalize-black-and-white/613159/.

6.  Latting, Jean (2023). "Who Likes the Word LatinX? Hint: Not the People You Think." *Leading Consciously Blog+Vlog.* www.leadingconsciously.com/blog/who-likes-word-latinx-hint-not-people-you-think-115.

## Chapter 2

1.  AlSheddi, Mona (2020). "Humility and Bridging Differences: A Systematic Literature Review of Humility in Relation to Diversity." *International Journal of Intercultural Relations* 79: 36–45.

2. Bushe, Gervase (2010). *Clear Leadership: Sustaining Real Collaboration and Partnership at Work*. rev. ed. Boston: Nicholas Breadley.

3. Gehlbach, Hunter, and Christine Calderon Vriesema (2019). "Meta-Bias: A Practical Theory of Motivated Thinking." *Educational Psychology Review* 31(1): 65–85.

4. https://dictionary.apa.org/either-or-fallacy

5. Olson, Michael A., Camille S. Johnson, Kevin L. Zabel, and Joy E. Phillips (2018). "Different Sides of the Same Conversation: Black and White Partners Differ in Perceptions of Interaction Content." *Journal of Applied Social Psychology* 48(8): 424–436.

6. Seligman, Martin E. P. (1991). *Learned Optimism*. New York: Alfred A. Knopf.

7. Stadler, Stefanie (2013). "Cultural Differences in the Orientation to Disagreement and Conflict." *China Media Research* 9(4): 66–75.

8. Liu, Leigh Anne, Wendi L. Adair, Dean Tjosvold, and Elena Poliakova (2018). "Understanding Intercultural Dynamics: Insights from Competition and Cooperation in Complex Contexts." *Cross Cultural Management* 25(1): 2.

9. Fitzduff, Mari (2021). "The Amygdala Hijack." In *Our Brains at War: The Neuroscience of Conflict and Peacebuilding* by Mari Fitzduff. New York: Oxford University Press.

10. Troy, Allison S., Emily C. Willroth, Amanda J. Shallcross, Nicole R. Giuliani, James J. Gross, and Iris B. Mauss (2023). "Psychological Resilience: An Affect-Regulation Framework." *Annual Review of Psychology* 74(1): 547–576.

11. Tamir, Maya, Shalom H. Schwartz, Jan Cieciuch, Michaela Riediger, Claudio Torres, Christie Scollon, Vivian Dzokoto, Xiaolu Zhou, and Allon Vishkin (2016). "Desired Emotions Across Cultures: A Value-Based Account." *Journal of Personality and Social Psychology* 111(1): 67–82.

12. Conte, Beatrice, Ulf J. J. Hahnel, and Tobias Brosch (2022). "From Values to Emotions: Cognitive Appraisal Mediates the Impact of Core Values on Emotional Experience." *Emotion*. Advance online publication. https://doi.org/10.1037/emo0001083.

13. Wang, Deming, Martin S. Hagger, and Nikos L. D. Chatzisarantis (2020). "Ironic Effects of Thought Suppression: A Meta-Analysis." *Perspectives on Psychological Science* 15(3): 778–793.

14. Hemenover, Scott H., and Colin R. Harbke (2019). "Individual Differences in Negative Affect Repair Style." *Motivation and Emotion* 43(3): 517–533.

15. David, Susan, and Christina Congleton (2013). "Emotional Agility." *Harvard Business Review* 91(11): 125.

16. Barash, Daniel (2011). "Many Emotions: Primal Therapy and Beyond." Ann Arbor, MI: ProQuest Dissertation Publishing.

17. Vieira, Kate (2019). "Writing's Potential to Heal: Women Writing from Their Bodies." *Community Literacy Journal* 13(2): 20–47.

18. Kashdan, Todd B., Lisa Feldman Barrett, and Patrick E. McKnight (2015). "Unpacking Emotion Differentiation: Transforming Unpleasant Experience by Perceiving Distinctions in Negativity." *Current Directions in Psychological Science* 24(1): 10–16.

19. Tsang, JoAnn, Sarah A. Schnitker, Robert A. Emmons, and Peter C. Hill (2022). "Feeling the Intangible: Antecedents of Gratitude Toward Intangible Benefactors." *The Journal of Positive Psychology* 17(6): 802–818.

20. Troy, Allison S., Emily C. Willroth, Amanda J. Shallcross, Nicole R. Giuliani, James J. Gross, and Iris B. Mauss (2023). "Psychological Resilience: An Affect-Regulation Framework." *Annual Review of Psychology* 74(1): 547–576.

21. Prizmić-Larsen, Zvjezdana, Ljiljana Kaliterna-Lipovčan, Randy Larsen, Tihana Brkljačić, and Andreja Brajša-Žganec (2020). "The Role of Flourishing in Relationship between Positive and Negative Life Events and Affective Well-Being." *Applied Research in Quality of Life* 15(5): 1413–1431.

22. Fredrickson, Barbara L., and Marcial F. Losada (2005). "Positive Affect and Complex Dynamics of Human Flourishing." *American Psychologist*, 60(7): 678–686.

23. Bryant, Fred B. (2021). "Current Progress and Future Directions for Theory and Research on Savoring." *Frontiers in Psychology* 12. doi. org/10.3389/fpsyg.2021.771698.

24. Mauss, Iris B., Amanda J. Shallcross, Allison S. Troy, Emilio Ferrer, Oliver P. John, Frank H. Wilhelm, and James J. Gross (2011). "Don't Hide Your Happiness! Positive Emotion Dissociation, Social Connectedness, and Psychological Functioning." *Journal of Personality and Social Psychology* 100(4): 738–748.

25. Kluger, Avraham N., and Guy Itzchakov (2022). "The Power of Listening at Work." *Annual Review of Organizational Psychology and Organizational Behavior* 9(1): 121–146.

26. Weinstein, Netta, Guy Itzchakov, and Nicole Legate (2022). "The Motivational Value of Listening During Intimate and Difficult Conversations." *Social and Personality Psychology Compass* 16(2): https:// doi.org/10.1111/spc3.12651.

27. Yeomans, Michael, Alison Wood Brooks, Karen Huang, Julia Minson, and Francesca Gino (2019). "It Helps to Ask: The Cumulative Benefits of Asking Follow-Up Questions." *Journal of Personality and Social Psychology* 117(6): 1139–1144.

28.  We are indebted to Chris Argyris and Peter Senge for their development of *inquiry* and *advocacy* as critical skills for organizational learning. We use the term "openness" instead of "advocacy" because the term "advocacy" connotes adversarial relationships in some disciplines. See Argyris, Chris (1999). *On Organizational Learning*. Malden, MA: Blackwell. Also see Senge, Peter M. (1990). *The Fifth Discipline*. New York: Currency Doubleday.

29.  Sinek, Simon (2011). *Start With Why: How Great Leaders Inspire Everyone to Take Action*. New York: Portfolio/Penguin.

30.  Gradito Dubord, Marc-Antoine, Jacques Forest, Lina Marija Balčiūnaitė, Evamaria Rauen, and Tomas Jungert (2022). "The Power of Strength-Oriented Feedback Enlightened by Self-Determination Theory: A Positive Technology-Based Intervention." *Journal of Happiness Studies* 23(6): 2827–2848.

31.  Zingoni, Matt, and Kris Byron (2017). "How Beliefs About the Self Influence Perceptions of Negative Feedback and Subsequent Effort and Learning." *Organizational Behavior and Human Decision Processes* 139: 50–62.

32.  Yeomans, Michael, Julia Minson, Hanne Collins, Frances Chen, and Francesca Gino (2020). "Conversational Receptiveness: Improving Engagement with Opposing Views." *Organizational Behavior and Human Decision Processes* 160: 131–148.

33.  Webb, Thomas L., Betty P. I. Chang, and Yael Benn (2013). "'The Ostrich Problem': Motivated Avoidance or Rejection of Information About Goal Progress." *Social and Personality Psychology Compass* 7(11): 794–807.

34.  Crommelinck, Michiel, and Frederik Anseel (2013). "Understanding and Encouraging Feedback-Seeking Behaviour: A Literature Review." *Medical Education* 47(3): 232–241.

35.  Coutifaris, Constantinos G. V., and Adam M. Grant (2021). "Taking Your Team Behind the Curtain: The Effects of Leader Feedback-Sharing and Feedback-Seeking on Team Psychological Safety." *Organization Science* 33(4): 1574–1598.

36.  Even though she didn't use the words, Peggy McIntosh popularized distinguishing impact from intent regarding gender and race in this seminal article: McIntosh, Peggy (1989). "White Privilege: Unpacking the Invisible Knapsack." *Peace and Freedom Magazine*, July/August 1989, 10–12.

37.  Gardner, Danielle M., and Ann Marie Ryan (2017). "Does Intentionality Matter? An Exploration of Discrimination with Ambiguous Intent." *Industrial and Organizational Psychology* 10(1): 77–82.

38.  Witvliet, Charlotte V. O., Lindsey Root Luna, Everett L. Worthington, and

Jo-Ann Tsang (2020). "Apology and Restitution: The Psychophysiology of Forgiveness after Accountable Relational Repair Responses." *Frontiers in Psychology* 11. https://doi.org/10.3389/fpsyg.2020.00284.

39. Butterfield, Kenneth D., Warren Cook, Natalie Liberman, and Jerry Goodstein (2023). "Self-Repair in the Workplace: A Qualitative Investigation." *Journal of Business Ethics* 182(2): 321–340.

40. Latting, Jean (2021). "Anatomy of an Apology in a Racially Charged World: What We Can Learn from Amy Porterfield." *Leading Consciously Blog + Vlog*. www.leadingconsciously.com/blog/009b-anatomy-of-an-apology-in-a-racially-charged-world-what-we-can-learn-from-amy-porterfield.

41. Catalyst (2020). *Why Diversity and Inclusion Matter (Quick Take)*. New York: Catalyst.

42. Bogilovic, Sabina, Guido Bortoluzzi, Matej Cerne, Khatereh Ghasemzadeh, and Jana Znidarsic (2020). "Diversity, Climate and Innovative Work Behavior." *European Journal of Innovation Management* 24(5): 1502–1524.

43. Payne, B. Keith, and Jason W. Hannay (2021). "Implicit Bias Reflects Systemic Racism." *Trends in Cognitive Sciences* 25(11): 927–936.

44. Jana, Tiffany (2018). *Erasing Institutional Bias: How to Create Systemic Change for Organizational Inclusion*. Oakland, CA: Berrett-Koehler.

45. Sue, Derald Wing (2021). *Microintervention Strategies: What You Can Do to Disarm and Dismantle Individual and Systemic Racism and Bias*. Hoboken, NJ: John Wiley & Sons.

46. Andersen, Margaret L., and Patricia Hill Collins (1998). *Race, Class, and Gender: An Anthology*. 3rd ed. Belmont, CA: Wadsworth.

47. hooks, bell (1989). *Talking Back: Thinking Feminist, Thinking Black*. Boston: South End Press.

48. Calvert, Linda McGee, and V. Jean Ramsey (1996). "Speaking as Female and White: A Non-dominant/Dominant Group Standpoint." *Organization* 3(4): 468–485.

49. Collins, Patricia Hill, and Sirma Bilge (2020). *Intersectionality*. 2nd ed. Hoboken, NJ: John Wiley & Sons.

50. Cox, William T. L., and Patricia G. Devine (2019). "The Prejudice Habit-Breaking Intervention: An Empowerment-Based Confrontation Approach." In *Confronting Prejudice and Discrimination*, edited by Robyn K. Mallett and Margo J. Monteith, 249–274. Cambridge, MA: Academic Press.

51. Levine, Sheen S., Charlotte Reypens, and David Stark (2021). "Racial Attention Deficit." *Science Advances* 7(38): eabg9508. doi:10.1126/sciadv.abg9508.

52. Bahns, Angela J. (2017). "Threat as Justification of Prejudice." *Group Processes & Intergroup Relations* 20(1): 52–74.

53. Latting, Jean (2020). "From Hardship to Allyship: The Value of Chronic Unease with Mark Hays, Part 2." *Leading Consciously Blog+Vlog.* www.leadingconsciously.com/blog/guide-from-hardship-to-allyship-the-value-chronic-unease-21.

54. Maoz, Ifat, and Paul Frosh (2020). "Imagine All the People: Negotiating and Mediating Moral Concern through Intergroup Encounters." *Negotiation and Conflict Management Research* 13(3): 197–210.

55. Sue, Derald Wing (2021). *Microintervention Strategies: What You Can Do to Disarm and Dismantle Individual and Systemic Racism and Bias.* Hoboken, NJ: John Wiley & Sons.

56. Johnson, Veronica E., Kevin L. Nadal, D. R. Gina Sissoko, and Rukiya King (2021). "'It's Not in Your Head': Gaslighting, 'Splaining, Victim Blaming, and Other Harmful Reactions to Microaggressions." *Perspectives on Psychological Science* 16(5): 1024–1036.

57. Williams, Tarah, Paul F. Testa, Kylee Britzman, and Matthew V. Hibbing (2021). "Messengers Matter: Why Advancing Gender Equity Requires Male Allies." *PS—Political Science & Politics* 54(3): 512–513.

58. Monteith, Margo J., Mason D. Burns, and Laura K. Hildebrand (2019). "Navigating Successful Confrontations: What Should I Say and How Should I Say It?" In *Confronting Prejudice and Discrimination*, edited by Robyn K. Mallett and Margo J. Monteith, 225–248. Cambridge, MA: Academic Press.

59. Radke, Helena R. M., Maja Kutlaca, and Julia C. Becker (2022). "Disadvantaged Group Members' Evaluations and Support for Allies: Investigating the Role of Communication Style and Group Membership." *Group Processes & Intergroup Relations* 25(6): 1437–1456.

60. Knowlton, Karren, Andrew M. Carton, and Adam M. Grant (2022). "Help (Un)wanted: Why the Most Powerful Allies Are the Most Likely to Stumble—And When They Fulfill Their Potential." *Research in Organizational Behavior* 42: 100180.

61. Chu, Charles, and Leslie Ashburn-Nardo (2022). "Black Americans' Perspectives on Ally Confrontations of Racial Prejudice." *Journal of Experimental Social Psychology* 101: 104337.

62. Chaney, Kimberly E., Diana T. Sanchez, Nicholas P. Alt, and Margaret J. Shih (2021). "The Breadth of Confrontations as a Prejudice Reduction Strategy." *Social Psychological & Personality Science* 12(3): 314–322.

63. Martinez, Larry R., Michelle R. Hebl, Nicholas A. Smith, and Isaac E. Sabat (2017). "Standing Up and Speaking Out Against Prejudice

Toward Gay Men in the Workplace." *Journal of Vocational Behavior* 103: 71–85.

64. Hildebrand, Laura K., Celine C. Jusuf, and Margo J. Monteith (2020). "Ally Confrontations as Identity-Safety Cues for Marginalized Individuals." *European Journal of Social Psychology* 50(6): 1318–1333.

65. Brassel, Sheila, Emily Shaffer, and Dnika J. Travis (2022). Emotional Tax and Work Teams: A View from 5 Countries. In *Research*. New York: Catalyst.

66. Travis, Dnika, and Jennifer Thorpe-Moscon (2018). *Day-to-Day Experiences of Emotional Tax Among Women and Men of Color in the Workplace*. New York: Catalyst.

67. Latting, Jean (2020). "From Peril to Promise: How to Promote Inclusion Through Racial Dialogue." *Leading Consciously Blog+Vlog*. www.leading consciously.com/blog/promote-equality-inclusion-from-peril-to-promise-make-racial-dialogue-work-12.

68. Byrd, Christy M. (2018). "Microaggressions Self-Defense: A Role-Playing Workshop for Responding to Microaggressions." *Social Sciences* 7(6): 96. doi.org/10.3390/socsci7060096.

69. Wessel, Jennifer L., Edward P. Lemay, and Sara E. Barth (2023). "You(r Behaviors) Are Racist: Responses to Prejudice Confrontations Depend on Confrontation Focus." *Journal of Business and Psychology* 38(1): 109–134.

70. Woods, Freya A., and Janet B. Ruscher (2021). "'Calling-Out' vs. 'Calling-In' Prejudice: Confrontation Style Affects Inferred Motive and Expected Outcomes." *British Journal of Social Psychology* 60(1): 50–73.

71. The term "conscious use of self" has been used by social workers since the early 1900s. (It is also used in organization development and other helping professions to describe deliberate and facilitative action with others.) Richmond, Mary Ellen (1917). *Social Diagnosis*. New York: Russell Sage Foundation.

72. Brown, Brené (2017). *Rising Strong: How the Ability to Reset Transforms the Way We Love, Parent, and Lead*. New York: Spiegel & Grau.

73. Moran, Brian P., and Michael Lennington (2021). *Uncommon Accountability: A Radical New Approach to Greater Success and Fulfillment*. Hoboken, NJ: John Wiley & Sons.

74. Peterson, Christopher, and Martin E. P. Seligman (2004). *Character Strengths and Virtues: A Handbook and Classification*. New York: Oxford University Press.

75. James, Alison, and David Stanley (2020). "Values-Based Leadership: A Way to Restore Integrity." *Nursing Management* 27(1): 18.

76. Nangoli, Sudi, Benon Muhumuza, Maureen Tweyongyere, Gideon Nkurunziza, Rehema Namono, Muhammed Ngoma, and Grace Nalweyiso (2020). "Perceived Leadership Integrity and Organisational Commitment." *The Journal of Management Development* 39(6): 823–834.

77. Li, Quan, Zhuolin She, and Baiyan Yang (2018). "Promoting Innovative Performance in Multidisciplinary Teams: The Roles of Paradoxical Leadership and Team Perspective Taking." *Frontiers in Psychology* 9: 1083.

78. Curry, Leslie, Thomas Calvard, Amanda Brewster, and Emily Cherlin (2021). "Building Perspective-Taking as an Organizational Capability: An Exploratory Study." *Journal of Management Inquiry* 32(1): 35–49.

79. Gradito Dubord, Marc-Antoine, Jacques Forest, Lina Marija Balčiūnaitė, Evamaria Rauen, and Tomas Jungert (2022). "The Power of Strength-Oriented Feedback Enlightened by Self-Determination Theory: A Positive Technology-Based Intervention." *Journal of Happiness Studies* 23(6): 2827–2848.

80. Shetti, Milan (2022). "Why Having a Growth Mindset Is Critical for Company Success." *CIO*, October 6.

81. Campbell, Anna (2019). "Effects of Growth and Fixed Mindset on Leaders' Behavior during Interpersonal Interactions." Ann Arbor, MI: ProQuest Dissertation Publishing.

82. Strom, Tifany (2020). "Authentic Leadership and Relational Power Increasing Employee Performance: A Systematic Review of 'Leadership and Power' as a Positive Dyadic Relationship." *Journal of Small Business Strategy* 30(3): 86–101.

83. Albalooshi, Sumaya, Mehrad Moeini Jazani, Bob M. Fennis, and Luk Warlop (2020). "Reinstating the Resourceful Self: When and How Self-Affirmations Improve Executive Performance of the Powerless." *Personality & Social Psychology Bulletin* 46(2): 189–203.

84. Koerner, Melissa M. (2014). "Courage as Identity Work: Accounts of Workplace Courage." *Academy of Management Journal* 57(1): 63–93.

85. Brehm, Sharon S., and Jack W. Brehm (1981). *Psychological Reactance: A Theory of Freedom and Control.* New York: Academic Press.

86. Cutrer, William B., Holly G. Atkinson, Erica Friedman, Nicole Deiorio, Larry D. Gruppen, Michael Dekhtyar, and Martin Pusic (2018). "Exploring the Characteristics and Context that Allow Master Adaptive Learners to Thrive." *Medical Teacher* 40(8): 791–796.

87. Gardner, Danielle M., and Jo M. Alanis (2020). "Together We Stand: Ally Training for Discrimination and Harassment Reduction." *Industrial and Organizational Psychology* 13(2): 196–199.

88. Shore, Lynn M., and Beth G. Chung (2023). "Enhancing Leader Inclusion while Preventing Social Exclusion in the Work Group." *Human Resource Management Review* 33(1): 100902.

89. Murphy, Mary C., Kathryn M. Kroeper, and Elise M. Ozier (2018). "Prejudiced Places: How Contexts Shape Inequality and How Policy Can Change Them." *Policy Insights from the Behavioral and Brain Sciences* 5(1): 66–74.

90. Latting, Jean (2023). "Are You Blaming People? Gain More Traction by Revealing the System (#45)." *Leading Consciously Blog+Vlog*. www.leading consciously.com/blog/how-change-the-belief-systems-not-the-people-45.

91. Brown, Riana M., Maureen A. Craig, and Evan P. Apfelbaum (2021). "European Americans' Intentions to Confront Racial Bias: Considering Who, What (Kind), and Why." *Journal of Experimental Social Psychology* 95: 104123.

92. Argyris, Chris (1999). *On Organizational Learning*. Malden, MA: Blackwell Publishers.

93. Schein, Edgar H. (1985). *Organizational Culture and Leadership*. San Francisco: Jossey-Bass.

94. Pascale, Richard T., and Jerry Sternin (2005). "Your Company's Secret Change Agents." *Harvard Business Review* 83(5): 72–81.

95. Woodzicka, Julie A., and Jessica J. Good (2021). "Strategic Confrontation: Examining the Utility of Low Stakes Prodding as a Strategy for Confronting Sexism." *The Journal of Social Psychology* 161(3): 316–330.

96. Bond, Meg A., and Michelle C. Haynes-Baratz (2022). "Mobilizing Bystanders to Address Microaggressions in the Workplace: The Case for a Systems-Change Approach to Getting A (Collective) GRIP." *American Journal of Community Psychology* 69(1–2): 221–238.

97. Sharot, Tali (2017). *The Influential Mind: What the Brain Reveals About Our Power to Change Others*. New York: Henry Holt and Company.

98. Weaver, Kimberlee, Stephen M. Garcia, Norbert Schwarz, and Dale T. Miller (2007). "Inferring the Popularity of an Opinion from its Familiarity: A Repetitive Voice Can Sound Like a Chorus." *Journal of Personality and Social Psychology* 92(5): 821–833.

99. Cohen, Herb (1980). *You Can Negotiate Anything*. Secaucus, NJ: L. Stuart.

100. Senge, Peter M. (1990). *The Fifth Discipline*. New York: Currency Doubleday.

101. Maurer, Rick (1996). *Beyond the Wall of Resistance: Unconventional Strategies that Build Support for Change*. Austin, TX: Bard Press.

102. Rogers, Everett M. (2003). *Diffusion of Innovation*. 5th ed. New York: The Free Press.

103. Moshontz, Hannah, and Rick H. Hoyle (2021). "Resisting, Recognizing, and Returning: A Three-Component Model and Review of Persistence in Episodic Goals." *Social and Personality Psychology Compass* 15(1): e12576.

## Chapter 8

1. Shatté, Andrew J., Karen Reivich, and Martin E. P. Seligman (2000). "Promoting Human Strengths and Corporate Competency: A Cognitive Training Model." *The Psychologist-Manager Journal* 4(2): 183–196.

## Chapter 13

1. Covey, Stephen R. (1989). *The Seven Habits of Highly Effective People.* New York: Simon and Schuster.

## Chapter 22

1. Koerner, Melissa M. (2014). "Courage as Identity Work: Accounts of Workplace Courage." *Academy of Management Journal* 57(1): 63–93.
2. The organization of this section of the chapter was adapted from Kwasnicka Dominika, Stephan U. Dombrowski, Martin White, and Falko Sniehotta (2016). "Theoretical Explanations for Maintenance of Behaviour Change: A Systematic Review of Behaviour Theories." *Health Psychology Review* 3: 277–96.
3. Carvalho, Paulo F., Elizabeth A. McLaughlin, and Kenneth R. Koedinger (2022). "Varied Practice Testing Is Associated with Better Learning Outcomes in Self-Regulated Online Learning." *Journal of Educational Psychology* 114(8): 1723–1742.
4. Brown, Peter C., Henry L. Roediger, and Mark A. McDaniel (2014). *Make It Stick: The Science of Successful Learning.* Cambridge, MA: The Belknap Press of Harvard University Press.
5. Roediger, Henry L., and Kathleen B. McDermott (2018). "Remembering What We Learn." New York: *Cerebrum*, July 1.
6. Moshontz, Hannah, and Rick H. Hoyle (2021). "Resisting, Recognizing, and Returning: A Three-component Model and Review of Persistence in Episodic Goals." *Social and Personality Psychology Compass* 15(1): e12576.
7. www.leadingconsciously.com.
8. www.youtube.com/watch?v=XDFGe4cVeGM&ab_channel=Humans ThatRun.
9. Olson, Jeff and John David Mann (2013). *The Slight Edge.* Austin, TX: Greenleaf Book Group Press.
10. Michaelson, Peter (2022). *Our Deadly Flaw: Healing the Inner Conflict that Cripples Us and Subverts Society.* Independently published.

11. AlSheddi, Mona (2020). "Humility and Bridging Differences: A Systematic Literature Review of Humility in Relation to Diversity." *International Journal of Intercultural Relations* 79: 36–45.

12. Brown, Brené (2017). *Rising Strong: How the Ability to Reset Transforms the Way We Love, Parent, and Lead.* New York: Random House.

13. Latting, Jean Kantambu, and V. Jean Ramsey (2009). *Reframing Change: How to Deal with Workplace Dynamics, Influence Others, and Bring People Together to Initiate Positive Change.* Westport, CT: Praeger.

14. Michaelson, Peter (2022). *Our Deadly Flaw: Healing the Inner Conflict that Cripples Us and Subverts Society.* Independently published.

15. Mazar, Asaf, and Wendy Wood (2022). "Illusory Feelings, Elusive Habits: People Overlook Habits in Explanations of Behavior." *Psychological Science* 33(4): 563–578.

# Index

# Acknowledgments

Creating this book has been a long but rewarding process. Throughout, we have benefitted from the efforts of many individuals. We are deeply grateful to:

- Each contributor to the book, for their commitment to learning the Conscious Change skills, courage in telling their stories, and cooperation and patience through multiple revisions of their stories. Thank you.
- Our friends and colleagues Brené Brown and Myrtle P. Bell, for taking time from their jam-packed lives to support our work by writing forewords. Thank you.
- Mary Ellen Capek and members of the Racial and Social Justice Book Group, who provided honest, illuminating, and pivotal feedback early in the process: Lea Ann Ferring, Jane Halonen, Cindy Hearne, Karen Highfill, Patricia Mishkin, and Nancy Peek. Also, thanks to Roberta Burroughs for invaluable eleventh-hour feedback. Thank you.
- Those who worked behind the scenes to help us craft a more readable and valuable book: Valentina Covarrubias, Eillen Cuartero, Ed Cyzewski, Carole Marmell, Alexis Quintal, and Bettye Griffin Underwood. Thank you.
- Diallo Kantambu, who provided support in so many forms—intellectual, technical, emotional, and more. Thank you.
- Each Leading Consciously team member who supported the work and kept the trains running while we worked on the book: Valentina Covarrubias, Eillen Cuartero, Stephanie Foy, Amy Foy

Hageman, Larry Hill, Simi Lawoyin, Carole Marmell, Alexis Quintal, and Virginia Redmond. Thank you.

- The leader-clients and students who eagerly embraced the Conscious Change work over the past decade. Only a few of them are represented in the book; many more shaped the thinking and writing about the skills. Thank you.
- Brooke Warner, for teaching us so much about publication and distribution, and Shannon Green, for so ably shepherding us through the process. Thank you.

# About the Authors

**Jean Kantambu Latting,** DrPH, LMSW-IPR, is president of Leading Consciously and professor emerita at the University of Houston. As consultant, researcher, and educator, Jean focuses on leadership in multicultural organizations. She coauthored *Reframing Change: How to Deal with Workplace Dynamics, Influence Others, and Bring People Together to Initiate Positive Change.*

Photo © Ken Jones Photography

**V. Jean Ramsey,** PhD, was a professor of management at Texas Southern University, a historically Black university, for nineteen years, retiring in 2009. She has published three previous books: *Reframing Change* (Praeger), *Teaching Diversity* (Jossey-Bass), and *Preparing Professional Women for the Future* (Graduate School of Business Administration, University of Michigan).

Photo © Crystal Tompkins Photography

**Stephanie Foy**, LMSW, is a senior partner with Leading Consciously and contributes to curriculum development and practice implementation related to the principles and skills of Conscious Change. Her master's study and current consultation practice focus on leadership, well-being, and organizational change.

Photo © Amy Foy Hageman

**Amy Foy Hageman**, MSPOD, is a junior associate with Leading Consciously. In that role, she facilitates training, creates coursework, and coaches participants through their learning goals. Amy graduated from Case Western Reserve University in 2014 with a Master of Positive Organizational Development.

Photo © Lenee Williams

# SELECTED TITLES FROM SHE WRITES PRESS

She Writes Press is an independent publishing company founded to serve women writers everywhere. Visit us at www.shewritespress.com.

*Tell Me Your Story: How Therapy Works to Awaken, Heal, and Set You Free* by Tuya Pearl. $16.95, 978-1-63152-066-2. With the perspective of both client and healer, this book moves you through the stages of therapy, connecting body, mind, and spirit with inner wisdom to reclaim and enjoy your most authentic life.

*Work Jerks: How to Cope with Difficult Bosses and Colleagues* by Louise Carnachan. $16.95, 978-1-64742-369-8. Louise Carnachan has helped thousands of people thrive at work by improving relationships with their colleagues; here, she provides concrete, actionable steps to deal with an array of problematic coworkers.

*The Book of Calm: Clarity, Compassion, and Choice in a Turbulent World* by Nancy G. Shapiro. $16.95, 978-1-63152-248-2. Using real-life stories, scientific concepts, and awareness tools, this timely, field-tested guide encourages readers to transform reaction into clarity, blame into compassion, and confusion into choice while navigating the turbulence of personal and professional shifts.

*The Way of the Mysterial Woman: Upgrading How You Live, Love, and Lead* by Suzanne Anderson, MA and Susan Cannon, PhD. $24.95, 978-1-63152-081-5. A revolutionary yet practical road map for upgrading your life, work, and relationships that reveals how your choice to transform is part of an astonishing future trend.

*These Walls Between Us: Lessons from a Friendship Across Race and Class* by Wendy C. Sanford. $16.95, 978-1-64742-167-0. In *These Walls Between Us* established feminist author Wendy Sanford, who is white, reflects on her complex lifelong friendship with Mary Norman, who is Black—her formation in a narrow world of class and race privilege, lifting up the writings and social movements that changed her views and her life, and examining a sixty-year interracial friendship that evolved in the context of white supremacy.

*Think Better. Live Better. 5 Steps to Create the Life You Deserve* by Francine Huss. $16.95, 978-1-938314-66-7. With the help of this guide, readers will learn to cultivate more creative thoughts, realign their mindset, and gain a new perspective on life.